TELL MacARTHUR
TO WAIT

by

Ralph Emerson Hibbs, M. D.

Giraffe Books
Quezon City
1996

Philippine Copyright 1996
by RALPH EMERSON HIBBS, M.D.
and GIRAFFE BOOKS
7 Visayas Avenue
1128 Quezon City
Philippines

First published 1988 by
Carlton Press, Inc.
New York, N.Y.

Philippine rights reserved.

ISBN 971-8967-30-3

Printed in the Philippines

To Jeanne--
my wife and my best friend

ACKNOWLEDGMENTS

(Personal Communications)

Amos, H.M.; Afton, Iowa
Blanchard, Rita Krabach; Lima, Ohio
Conrad, Eugene B.; Daleville, Alabama
Delich, William; Mt. Vernon, Illinois
Elward, Helen Marie Stiffer; Monroe, Michigan
Fox, Sister Anthony Mary; Historian,
Marygrove College, Detroit, Michigan
Gordon, Richard M.; Pitsford, Vermont
Galos, Bill; Mesa, Arizona
Lewis, Dr. Charles; Piedmont, California
Leu, Mrs. Carol (Mrs. Richard James Costello);
Phoenix, Oregon
Maddux, Lt. Gen. Sam; San Antonio, Texas
Mood, Margaret Guerin; St. Clair Shores, Michigan
Murphy, Justice Frank; Governor of Michigan
and Supreme Court Judge (deceased)
Musselman, Dr. M. M.; Omaha, Nebraska
Nemetz, Mrs. Margaret Ann; Birmingham, Michigan
Reddin, Mrs. M. L.; Mount Clemens, Michigan
Rees, Dr. Denton; Lake Oswego, Oregon (deceased)
Rees, Miss Judy; Lake Oswego, Oregon
Sabin, Harry G.; Lansing, Michigan
Schmoll, Margaret; Pontiac, Michigan
Schwartz, Maj. Gen. Jack; San Francisco, California
(deceased)
Schwartz, Mrs.Jack (Jessie); San Diego, California
Thornton, Mrs. F. V. J.; Anchorage, Alaska
Wilson, Dr. Warren; Pasadena, California (deceased)

4

CONTENTS

Pilar Campos

American Nurses: "Angels of Bataan"

1. OUR FIRST BATTLE

Fittingly, the 31st U.S. Infantry Regiment, a completely American unit not having seen any combat up to this time, was ordered forward on 28 December 1941, to prepare a defensive position at Dinalupihan and Layac Junction. This line, some 16 km. in advance of our main battle position on the Bataan Peninsula, was developed only as a delaying tactic to slow the Japanese invaders who had landed earlier in the month. At 2000 hours on the 5th of January 1942, the 2nd Battalion had moved into position. The word "We're on the front line. Shoot anything!" passed along the foxholes. I shuddered as the news reached the aid station.

We are really in it now, I thought.

The headquarters was positioned behind a ridge, possibly 100 meters high. Our aid station was 200 meters to the rear in a small ravine, seemingly below the line of fire. After completing further excavation on a pre-existing foxhole, I lay alongside it and trailed off to sleep, disturbed by the anticipation of our first battle.

Action along the Layac Junction line on the morning of the 6th of January began with supporting 75 mm fire. The 1st Battalion, 23rd Field Artillery, opened up first. Much to our surprise and alarm, this artillery battery had moved in during the night about 200 meters directly behind us on the next ridge. The battery was on target with its first round and switched to rapid fire. They seemed to be having a merry old time, but it didn't last very long. Within another hour and a half, by 1000 hours, larger guns, 105 and 155 mm howitzers of the Japanese, were moved up and returned the fire. These heavier and longer-range guns directed by observation planes soon began to punish our artillery batteries. The unmolested observation planes of the Japs hovered over us like vultures circling at 1000 meters, directing the artillery fire with exceeding accuracy.

Oh, no, I thought, here's the aid station right in the middle of the target area. I won't be able to hear heart murmurs with my stethoscope at sick call today. I'd have to learn to practice medicine as a front-line surgeon. We took the muzzle blast from our

7

guns, and the punishing retaliatory fire from the Japanese. By 1200 hours the Japanese had moved more artillery, including 75s, 105s and 150 mm guns, into position: The shells were soon dropping into our aid station area. The intense barrage was terrifying. It rolled towards you, over you, past you, then would turn back and then move away again. By listening to the dying whine of the shell, it was easy to tell how close the explosion would be. The longer whine and lower pitch clued proximity. I listened intently to the trajectory of the artillery shells as they came closer and closer until they were dropping immediately on top of us, kicking up dust and smoke. The ridge in front was no protection at all. The artillery fire continued. My fright precipitated an anxious communication with the Father upstairs. It is said that God makes many converts on the battlefield. "Was this the way it was supposed to end?" I can vouch for the opinion that an artillery barrage evokes an impulse to run. I had a feeling of wanting to be someplace other than where I was.

I concluded that war as presented in artillery duels depicts man's failure to govern either himself or his enemy. The format consists of lobbing explosives back and forth, evoking terrifying screams and death. Do you think God ever envisioned war as a modus operandi for solving problems, I asked myself. The wonderment of this scene belies responsibility of any deity. God must have said, "Have I made a mistake?"

It is said you never hear the one that gets you. I hoped if one had my name on it that it had the wrong address. I was convinced I would never see home again--Mom, Dad, Iowa, or my friends, Mary Fran Riley from Des Moines, Nancy Wallace from Wilmington, or Bert Clark from Billings. This was a lousy time to open the door to "Remembrance Hall." One shell burst so close it seemed as though I was being thrown out of my foxhole. Another shell reached a "B" flat before *ker-whomp.* The barrage moved up the gully.

The Filipino 88th Artillery Battery had lost three of their four 75's and half of their men. They moved the last remain-ing gun in a desperate maneuver. The observation plane banking steadily overhead soon spotted it and radioed the range. During this bombardment, Jose Calugas, the mess sergeant of Battery B, 88th Field Artillery, won the Medal of Honor. With almost the entire battery dead or wounded, he continued to fire to the end.

The agonizing barrage dragged on for hours. Finally, my foxhole gave way as I dut out a piece of hot shrapnel. "Oh, boy, I wish I had my entrenching tool now. I'd lower this hole about ten feet in a hurry," I thought. Shouts of "litter team" came down to me.

"Don't anyone move until this barrage lifts," I yelled back.

Cpl. Smith yelled, "Our corpsman has been hit."

I bellied over to his foxhole.

"I've been bit by a snake, Captain," he exclaimed, pointing towards his back. All I could see were two scratch marks. "Forget about it until the Jap artillery quits shooting at us. The Japs are more dangerous than snakes," I advised.

Our nearby Filipino battery fire became less intense, sporadic and, finally, fell silent. About 1500 hours a messenger from headquarters slid belly first up to my foxhole.

"The Jap tanks are roaming around the ridge and up the gully a few hundred meters from us, followed by Japanese foot soldiers," he panted. "The major said to stay put and keep low in your foxholes and prepare for the worst."

I wondered what he meant by "the worst." I doubted it could be worse than the barrage. The Japs had already penetrated through the 1st Battalion and were heading in our direction.

Well, at least the damnable artillery has quieted down. We'll see what we can do about the Jap soldiers. I guess we'll just have to forget about the tanks. My '38' is hardly a match, I mused. This weapon was issued the day Pearl Harbor was bombed.

Small arms fire broke out a few hundred meters away in the general direction of the front. It sounded like both our 30-06 rifles and the smaller 25-caliber Japanese rifle. After assessing my fire power, I concluded that the best position was flat on my back in my foxhole, looking up with my '38' Smith & Wesson revolver pointing skyward, clutched between both hands.

I raised my head and yelled, "Don't anyone come close to my foxhole because I'm going to shoot the first son-of-a-bitch who sticks his head over it."

This defensive pose was maintained for 15-20 minutes, and after a half a bucket of sweat, the message came down from Battalion Headquarters that the line had been re-established by the

3rd Battalion which had been in reserve. The Japanese tanks had cleared out. Our casualties had been minimal, except for my "nervous breakdown."

How did I get myself in such a mess so quickly, I questioned. Overnight, my status had changed from civilian to soldier, and in a few weeks from Stateside to the Philippines. I had lost all of my creature comforts in such a short time, and filled my nostrils with the smell of exploded gunpowder.

2. STORM CLOUDS

Armed with an M.D. degree from the University of Iowa and a first lieutenant's commission in the U.S. Army Medical Corps, I left San Francisco on 6 June 1941. Sailing on the troopship *S.S. Coolidge*, I landed in the Philippines on 20 June to join the U.S. Armed Forces in the Far East (USAFFE). The earth-shaking events that followed in the next four years were a complete surprise. The combat in Bataan and the siege of Corregidor, and the Death March, were unsurpassed in military history for bravery and horror. Approximately four years after my arrival in the Philippines, along with less than ten percent of the original garrison, I returned home, alive, but hardly the same person.

My active duty began in a mud puddle in Wilmington, N.C., which later was dubbed Camp Davis. I arrived there three days late, entertaining the idea that the late arrival might precipitate an early discharge. The adjutant allowed, "There's no problem." Soon a query from the Surgeon General arrived presenting me with a choice of overseas assignments. Mine were Hawaii, Puerto Rico, and Pananma, in that order. Sooner than return mail, I received orders to proceed to San Francisco and sail for the Philippines.

In the middle of my trip from the Carolinas to California, I stopped four days to visit my parents in Oskaloosa, Iowa. At our last meal together, Dad lowered his head in silence, then in a quavering voice whispered grace:

"Father, I know you are listening because I talked to you earlier. Protect this boy as he protects our country." After a long silence: "Give him friends as dear as the ones he leaves behind. I'll talk to you later. Goodbye."

Mother wiped tears away. I'd never seen either of my parents cry over me before. It was the first realization of how remote I was going to be.

11

The dock at Fort Mason, next to the Presidio of San Francisco, bustled with men and materiel loading on the *S.S. Coolidge*. Like me, most of the men had driven to the pier expecting to ship their cars overseas. There, two minor catastrophes befell me.

First, the transportation superintendent refused permission to export my firechief-red Ford convertible. The next day, a head protruded from the superintendent's window and a less than pleasant voice blasted me with: "Again, I'm telling you, you can't ship your car to the Philippines." Consequently, a pier-side distress sale for five $100 bills and a $300 coupon was transacted with Mickey O'Neal, a Van Ness Avenue car merchant. Ten years later I was to find Mickey and even though the coupon was lost, he honored the deal.

The second incident was the loss of six bottles of Old Grandad whiskey. Rumor had it that no liquor would be allowed in the *S.S. Coolidge*, so I secreted a cache in my golf bag. Unfortunately, it was dropped during loading and all six bottles were broken. The baggage sergeant was in a tizzy trying to find the source of the aroma until I pointed to my own bag.

Our ship docked for one night in Hawaii. We sailed west with catcalls of "sucker" coming from our troops stationed there. Two weeks later, on 20 June 1941, we were in Manila, the Pearl of the Orient0. During our voyage, Hitler had invaded Poland.

For an army officer in those days, life in the Philippines was relaxed and elegant. My assignment as Surgeon of the second battalion of the 31st U.S. Infantry Regiment gave me the responsibility for the health of roughly 700 people. It was not the greatest medical assignment since in case of war it meant front-line combat duty.

Days in garrison at Manila opened with sick call at 0630 hours. Patients came with heat rash, homesickness, clap and Queen Isabella's revenge. The clinic was in the Quartel de España of Fort Santiago, inside the walled city called Intramuros.

This old fort was constructed by the Spanish in 1565. The stone walls, 10-15 meters thick, guarded the perimeter on three sides with the lotus-strewn Pasig River on the fourth. Within the walls were dark, dingy subterranean cells. Ceilings were so low one could not stand up straight. They had been used as jails by the Spanish and were to be used again by the Japanese. Tide water filled some of the rooms nearly to the ceiling twice a day.

I was free by 1100 daily for golf at Fort McKinley or Manila's lovely Wack Wack course. Lunch might be at the Polo Club, which included Manila's social elite, both Filipino and American, and a chance for young American officers to meet gorgeous and eager señoritas. Often, by late afternoon, we were rolling dice for drinks at the Army Navy Club. About 2100 we would return there for late dinner. We patronized the Jai Alai Club occasionally for gambling and dinner.

Custom called for a *siesta* for most people, as I learned soon after arriving. On telephoning my host, Col. Sapington, at his quarters about midday, Mrs. Sapington sternly lectured me about getting in step with tropical customs, and slammed down the phone. In addition to the *siesta*, custom dictated the white double-breasted sharkskin dinner jacket.

This good life relegated jungle defensive positions to the back of our minds.

The Army Navy Club code prevented Filipinos from the membership roster. Social barriers separating American officers from native women came tumbling down as the war clouds appeared. Parties were sponsored by old-time American residents; "Sunshiners" they were called. Even the U.S. High Commissioner offered opportunities to meet the beautiful Filipina *guaparitas*. These easy days introduced me to Pilar Campos. Her father, Pedro, an international banker, was president of the Bank of the Philippine Islands.

I'll never forget our first meeting. In August 1941, just as a lovely party at the spacious mansion of an American family was winding down, I spied a beautiful native woman. She was just leaving, all by herself. I approached her, hoping she would be interested in me. She turned and smiled.

"I'm Pilar Campos," she said softly in perfect English. After brief amenities, she agreed to have dinner with me.

Pilar was then 24 years old. She was five feet four inches tall, taller than the average Filipino woman. She was pretty, her 110-pounds contoured into a slim figure capped with jet black medium-length hair. Her velvety light tan skin, the envy of Stateside girls, was inherited from her Spanish mother. Her warm face, always close to a smile, was punctuated by big brown bedroom eyes constantly searching for a friendly response. Her tapering fingers gestured an enchanting language. She had small feet and long tapering legs. Her thighs were trim as contrasted with bulky-thighed Stateside girls. When she walked, her body swayed with her hips. Charisma and confidence were self-evident. At times she would reinforce her argument, thumping on my chest with her tiny fist with the words, "Watch it, Captain." Her nickname was "Petie."

Pilar, a graduate of Marygrove College in Detroit, was society editor of the *Manila Herald*. She moved gracefully through all levels of society and business activity in Manila. Her popularity meant constantly hailing people and receiving guests at our table when we were in public places. I never knew which among the men were old boyfriends, and which were fellow journalists. She liked to date, preferably just us, avoiding large parties.

Pilar managed her life, apparently with parental approval, by American standards--much to my pleasure. Having her brother Tony accompany us on dates would have been as boring to him as to me. In her dress, she avoided the Spanish-style head piece and gowns. Her blouse and skirt accentuated a full bosom and shapely legs. Neither of us sought help in finding the moral path. We dated, drank and danced as Stateside Americans would.

Pilar spoke English, Spanish, French, German and two of the native dialects.

One Sunday morning we attended a champagne baptism, meeting Vice-President Sergio Osmeña, who later became President of the republic. I remember complaining that the women and the men were separated in different rooms. Osmeña promptly escorted me to the middle of the *señoritas'* circle. He enjoyed my embarrassment as I did his company and the *lechon*--a small roasted pig.

Another time Pilar and I went out to the Spanish Club. I shook every hand, sticking out my hand on hearing my name, but oblivious to the introduction given *en español*. We danced, and not too loosely either. Custom suggested arm-length distance, so our routine evoked some scrutiny. The matriarchs smiled and availed themselves of a second look.

I remember once, while driving across Ft. McKinley, we heard and felt the heavy blast of the parade ground cannon signalling retreat. Stepping briskly from my old Chevy, I held my salute until the bugle notes faded away. Pilar, her eyes searching my face, was crying as I returned to the car. "What loyalty," she said, her head moving solemnly. "My God, how you love your country."

In the last of November 1941, I hurried off a letter to my folks:

Dear Mom and Dad,

Things are peaceful here. Life in the Orient is easy-going with emphasis on the *mañana* and *siesta* ethic. With the tremendous military buildup here, a Jap attack seems unlikely. If I had it to do over again, I would have gone to England. There's nothing going to happen here.

Love,
Ralph

The 31st regiment went on red alert 5 December 1941. About the same time, the *Manila Times* reported "enemy airplanes were detected over Luzon for the second time this week." The start of the war was not a surprise in the Philippines; apparently, it was in Washington, D. C.

Sunday, 7 December, found Manila, the Pearl of the Orient, hot, humid and sybaritic. This evening was ushered in with the usual brilliant sunset that gave an orange hue to mammoth billowing cumulus clouds filling the skies. Representatives of Roosevelt and Tojo were having their big argument at this same time. Five of us, all military officers, were seated that night in rattan chairs around a low circular narra table in the Fiesta Pavilion of the Manila Hotel. Large-bladed ceiling fans rotated slowly overhead. In my memory bank this scene has always been associated with the Whiffenpoof boys down at Mory's. All of us wore the usual evening attire--white sharkskin double-breasted jacket, black tie, slick black slacks and black shoes. It was a light and cool combination, inherited after years of custom from the comfort-seeking "Sunshiners." We had a tradition in these islands going back almost 50 years. The similarity of the five at the table ended with

15

the dress. Each man was in Manila for a different reason--domestic, career, adventure, or possibly to escape boredom.

Included were First Lt. George Williams, a fun-loving infantry officer from Alabama; First Lt. Dwight Hunkins, a handsome West Point infantry officer; First Lt. Joe McClellan, a hell-for-leather fighter pilot from Montana; and Second Lt. Bill Tooley, a quiet signal officer from Chicago. Tooley and I were bachelors; the others were married and had children. Williams was attached to the recently expanded Philippine Army, McClellan to the Air Force, while the rest of us were part of the 31st Regiment. We would have varying experiences in the years ahead. Without reason or predictability, I was the only one to return home.

But tonight, the expression on our faces exuded confidence. Everything was under control. Our actions varied from retiring to mild bravado; our thoughts were beyond discernible worries. Each had a thirst, not uncommon in the Far East. The mood was lighthearted, the conversation relaxed and free flowing.

Scarlet bougainvillea spilled from the wide roof overhanging the Bamboo Bar where we were having drinks. The overhang, three to four meters wide, provided protection from the blowing rain during the typhoon season. This eliminated the stuffiness of glass windows; even the panels below the openings were movable to afford better ventilation. Minah birds and parakeets were in the leaves readying themselves for sleep. A willowy Filipino *mestiza* brought us another gin and tonic. A pink jasmine flower over her left ear indicated by custom that she was available. I never knew from rumor or experience the requirements for transferring the flower from the right, or "no game tonight" side, to the left, or "play ball" side. After the second drink, she consisted of pointy breasts, swaying hips, and tapering thighs glimpsed through a slit skirt draped by her waistlength black hair. Outwardly on that night, the relaxed graceful life of these beautiful islands was undisturbed.

By 2200 hours music in the Fiesta room and high-spirited laughter competed for our attention. It came from a private party of the newly arrived 27th Bombardment Group commanded by Maj. Gen. Lewis Brereton. Dwight expressed the hope they could "fly their B-17s better than they can sing." The Air Force boys were really bombarding as we left for home at midnight. The five of us, the "Whiffenpoof Boys" were never to be together again.

I awoke during the early morning hours on 8 December to discover the fly boys had apparently moved their party from the Manila Hotel to the general's suite across the garden from my apartment. Laughter, the giggling of girls, plus a few squeals and the breaking of glass echoed across the courtyard. Some time later, after a quiet phase, I became conscious of the persistent ringing of a telephone at the general's quarters.

"Hello," the voice finally growled. There was some unintelligible swearing followed by "Those sons of bitches. You've got to be kidding." Finally there was a bang as the disgusted listener hung up. Unbeknownst to me at the time, the call was the general's official notification of the attack on Pearl Harbor. Yelling voices filled the courtyard. Hurried footsteps and slamming doors echoed, then silence. I dozed off to sleep, thankful the interruptions had stopped. Little did I know that this would be the last time I would sleep in a real bed for the next over three years.

At 0630 the next morning, after a breakfast of coffee and mango served by Dominador, my number one houseboy, my old Chevy threaded its way through Pasay on the 15-minute drive to the battalion bivouac area at Nichols Field. Just ahead, a Filipino passenger in a two-wheel pony-drawn *calesa* thrust a newspaper my way. Headlines shrieked: "HAWAII BOMBED--WAR!"

A sinking nausea gripped my midsection--a feeling that was to be repeated so often during combat; a startled realization. It had started already, a sneaky way to begin a war. Somebody had just blown the whistle.

Our battalion headquarters stood on a knoll covered with cogon grass, about 1000 meters from the end of the Nichols Field runway. The Pan Am weather and communications center building was 500 meters behind us. Nichols and Neilson fields, five km. apart in the Manila suburbs, were bases for our fighter planes. The P-40s, P-35s and P-26s were flown by the 17th Pursuit Squadron. Our present mission was to guard against paratroop attack.

On arriving at headquarters there were conflicting messages of "business as usual" and "no accountability, this is war." The initial news of Pearl Harbor described a catastrophe. Later the censored version indicated "a little setback." The arms racks stood open for all troops including the medics. I secured a .38 caliber Smith and Wesson pistol which I used on several occasions. Twirling it in a John Wayne fashion, I felt braver. The supply sergeant handed out collapsible shovels, advising everyone to start digging a foxhole. My 28-man medical detachment attached Red Cross armbands to the left sleeve of their shirts. We were issued burdensome gas masks to be carried under the left arm at all times. And, finally, we traded our pith helmets for World War I level-brim metal helmets.

Those metal beanies afforded limited protection for the head, but served well as a wash basin, and for some as a pillow. After a couple of hours pressure from sleeping on the helmet, one's scalp was numb. My head seemingly changed size during sleep. Some soldiers attached nets and leaves to their helmets for camouflage. I saw one decorated with the question, "What more can a man do than lay down his life for a friend?" At the time, my wish was to treat my friends off the battlefield.

At mid-afternoon, Maj. Lloyd Moffit, our battalion commander, ordered officers call. He was a qualified and determined officer, stocky and balding, about five feet nine inches tall. The major made up for any deficiencies with grit, but may have suffered from short-stature syndrome. Our other officers included Dwight Hunkins, who commanded H company, John I. Pray of G company, Buster Conrad of F company and A. Sauer of E company. Bill Tooley, our communications officer and I rounded out the group sitting in a circle on the ground.

Moffit stood solidly in front of us, his voice steady and matter-of-fact. "Clark Field, 150 km. to the north, was bombed two hours ago," he calmly told us. "The Japs are expected any moment." He said the regiment was in the field for good, and each of us should go to Manila, secure personal belongings, tidy up personal affairs and return before the Japs arrived.

"Any questions?" the major asked. "End of meeting."

Hunkins yelled at me from his open command car. "Climb in, and let's get going." We headed for Manila.

I soon arrived at the courtyard of the strangely quiet and vacant San Carlos apartments. Dominador, my number one houseboy, was standing in the half-opened doorway.

"What is going on, sir? Tell me what to do," he said anxiously.

18

"It is war now," I replied. "The Japs made a horrible mistake in starting this. But you must stay out of it. Go to the hills! You hear me?"

"But what about the kitchen stuff, the furniture, the table service, golf clubs, liquor--" he began.

"It is all yours," I interrupted, "but get the hell out of the city. Get your wife and get out of this horrible mess."

In tears, Dominador followed me through the rooms. "What about your clothes?" he asked. "What about the table service? What about Rosita, the *lavandera*?" I was silent. I remember emptying my wallet of all my pesos.

"Divide this with Rosita," I said, "and tell her to trim her long fingernails before applying for a new laundry job." Dominador grabbed my arm, begging that he be allowed to do something."

I blustered, "God will protect you while we kick the shit out of those dirty bastards." Then I gave him the keys to my most treasured possession, the old Chevy. Climbing in with Hunkins, I waved and mumbled, "Goodbye--God bless you."

Dominador's arms stretched for mine, his face smeared with tears. I never saw him again, but the memory is forever. I'll never forget our Thanksgiving of 1941, when Capt. John K. Wallace, Capt. Jim Brennen, Tooley and I finished dinner. I went into the kitchen to find Dominador ignoring the beautiful brown turkey at his left elbow while he shoveled in *arroz y pescado* with his fingers. To each his own. For personal loyalty, Dominador had no peer. I used to wonder about this little brown-skinned man. I'm sure he would have risked his life for ours, or for his own country. I wondered if he macheted a Jap straggler along a jungle trail or if he was tortured to death by the savage enemy. Time never answered the question.

Dwight Hunkins and I quietly cruised the near-vacant streets of Manila and Pasay. Hunkins was probably my closest friend in the battalion. I guess his height was over six feet. He was slender. He had brown hair, a handsome, agreeable face and a military bearing. He possessed the internal credentials and the eye of a soldier. He was an excellent officer, but at times struggled to live up to tradition. I always felt comfortable with him.

The memories of the past six months of leisure, and times with Pilar rolled by. She had been a wonderful friend and play-

19

mate. Her natural charisma, education and aristocratic background opened the doors of social circles. Should I try to see her now? Telephones were unreliable. The command car closed on Nichols Field. What was going to happen to Pilar, and to us? I knew I woujld not be going to the Baroque Bar at the Army Navy Club tonight for a restorative, rolling the dice or eating off the 50-foot-long free buffet.

Two-man tents dotted the landscape as we drove up, and some foxholes had already appeared. Moffit strolled over to inform me that I was a captain. "All officers were promoted one grade." The first sergeant suggested that despite my promotion, I start digging a foxhole, because "the Nips are scheduled soon."

That night we got a detailed report of the damage at Clark Field. We were stunned. Our precious Flying Fortresses, the B-17s, had been caught on the ground refueling. By chance, the Jap bombing raid from Formosa had been delayed by fog for three hours. If there had been no fog and the Japs had come on schedule, the field would have been empty. Luck was with them. Our losses were 18 B-17s, 53 P-40s, three P-35s, and 30 miscellaneous aircraft--half of our Air Force. On the first day of the war, the Far Eastern Air Force was eliminated as an effective fighting unit by a second Pearl Harbor.

Our turn was next.

3. FILIPINOS AND THEIR ISLANDS

The Philippine archipelago, 1,500 km. long, extending from near the Equator northward, counts 7,170 islands; average rainfall 50-200 inches, the majority from June to October, the monsoon season. There are 87 dialects, but only three major languages--Cebuano, Ilocano, and colloquial Tagalog. Americans appeared on the scene in 1898 when Admiral George Dewey sank the Spanish fleet in Manila bay. Self-government was given to the country in 1935, and Manuel L. Quezon became the first President and Sergio Osmeña Vice-President, and later the second President.

The carabao, a water buffalo, must be the national animal; milk fish (*bangus*), the native fish, raised privately and commercially in ponds; sampaguita, the national flower; *tuba*, the native drink from coconut palms; and gecko, the native bug catcher (a lizard which hangs on the ceiling gobbling up mosquitoes; consequently, it is not molested). *Lechon* (roast pig) or chicken *adobo* should be the national dish. Native fruits are abundant, including my favorite, mango (*manga*).

The Philippines, where the best beer in the Orient (San Miguel) is made, the sweetest mangoes grow, the grandest sunsets usher in the lush nights, the swingingest musicians play, the most elegantly dressed girls sway, plus, by far, where the most beautiful people, inside and out, live in the world. They have everything but freckles. When I arrived there, it seemed the average Filipino had only two simple wishes--to feed his family three meals a day and to send the children to school. At times the oldest daughter dutifully went to Manila and worked the streets to help provide clothes and education for her younger brothers and sisters.

Large families, six or eight children, were then the rule. Postwar road signs boldly state, "Three is enough," taxes are levied on children after the third (farmers are allowed more). Credit for the signs belongs to Imelda Marcos, wife of President Ferdinand

Marcos, deposed in February 1986.

It is the Americana of the Orient. Our record in this paradise is good. We sent educators and economists to assist this fledgeling democracy. Hot sunny days, 95° average daytime temperature, are followed by balmy evenings. The countryside nurtures jasmine, orchids, bougainvillea, hibiscus, acacia, fire trees, *banyan* with buttress of roots, and ever-present palms of multiple varieties. The flat land, chiefly rice paddies, is dotted with lush plantations of banana, papaya, mango, pineapple, guava, *kalamansi*, durian, *makopa* (curacao apple), *pasion oryo* (passion fruit), Spanish plum (*sineguelas*), and star apple (*kaimito*).

Few Americans have discovered this paradise as other than a battleground. The United States has always been more important to the Philippines than the Philippines to the United States.

The Mexicans have their *mañana*, but out in the Filipino land it's *bahala na* (God will take care). The government attempted unsuccessfully to discourage this philosophy--by brainwashing the masses--but the splendid result was a mixture of friendliness, warmth inside and out, loyalty and a charm found in such abundance in no other people in the world. The U.S. might profit today from importing a whole bunch of "*bahala na.*"

The Filipino girl uses rice powder sparingly on her face. Her beautiful tanned complexion requires no coverup for freckles or pimples. Coconut milk in her coal black hair and gumamela flower petals for lipstick completes her cosmetics. It is said that a Filipino playmate is noisy in bed. She motions with her dainty hand--go away; but in her custom this means come closer. Her body looks like a girl, sways like a girl. She loves being one. She stands close and smiles at you.

Filipinos must be the cleanest people in the world, since every day they spend hours on the banks of a river doing the laundry by pounding it on a rock with a short club.

Filipinos are naturally friendly and not war-like. They lead a simple life and don't seem to mind the inferior role in their relationship with Americans. Courting is universal and encouraged. You are addressed as "Sir" and "Joe" with a smile and "*mabuhay*," meaning, "glad to see you," or "welcome." A Filipino wants a big funeral with a parade and a jazzy band which may cost him ten years' wages. Some older women from the provinces chew betel nuts and gambier, which stains the teeth dark brown, and also smoke cigarettes with the lighted end inside their mouth. GIs never spent too much time mastering either custom. Filipino children do not cry or fight.

The Filipino, good-natured about his country, makes a satire of the Spanish rule and our succession as "300 years in a convent, and then the Americans gave us two generations in Hollywood." As one Filipino said, "It's a banana republic, but don't worry, the top banana won't live forever." This was the country and these were the people where my war was to be waged.

4. BOMBS AWAY

The scream of the falling bombs destined to explode 500 meters away woke me up at 0200 hours, on 9 December. First the whistling crescendo; a few seconds pause, then a flash; next a jolting *harrump,* followed by a rolling fireball. Nichols Field was under attack; the whole flight line was ablaze and exploding. The Filipino-American-Japanese Armageddon had started. The shrieking crescendo filled me with terror. My heart pounded wildly. My whole body shook. The explosions seemed not to crack in my ears, but to shake my insides. My body jumped in the air, making it impossible to lie flat. Hundreds of bombs exploded and then the drone of the attacking planes gradually faded. Soon a second and a third wave of attacking bombers swept the field, adding to the widespread destruction.

Flames illuminated the whole area. The barracks and the tower were silhouetted against the fires. The remnants of our Air Force were disappearing in front of our very eyes. If there was any anti-aircraft action or fighter challenge, it went undetected. I apparently dove from my cot through the mosquito bar, landing on my belly in the cogon grass outside the tent. Not being able to see well, I decided to stand up for a better view. More bombs continued to fall, whistling louder, apparently aiming for a closer target.

Wow! Those exploded about 300 meters behind me, demolishing the Pan Am Communications Center.

With bombs bracketing me, I finally decided to start on my foxhole--just like the Sergeant had suggested. By this time the sound of shovels crunching in the soil was clearly audible. Images of the digging soldiers were etched starkly in the night sky by the roaring fires from planes, gas stores and barracks. One soldier dug with a spoon and a mess kit lid. Just shows what a little motivation can do. Damn it--in my panic, I couldn't find my shovel!

Deep shudderings and whomps of the bombing ended as the drone of the planes faded away. The sky seemed to be on fire.

24

Explosions continued throughout the night. Our unit had escaped serious casualties this time. My heart finally quieted enough to allow me to crawl back onto my cot and sleep until dawn.

On inspection the next morning, we found a clean hole in the mosquito bar, just enough for my body, apparently torn during my reflex headlong dive from the cot. Hunkins never let me forget the escape hatch trick in taking cover from the first "shrieking bombs."

He suggested that we inspect the remains of our Air Force. Nichols Field was in shambles, covered with greasy smoke, fires burning out of control and collapsed buildings. The planes on the ground, the barracks, fuel tanks, repair shops--all lay in complete ruins. The last major U.S. airfield in Luzon was destroyed. Obviously, we were going to have to fight the rest of the war without any significant air power. The stroll past the Pan Am Communications Building revealed that a near-miss by a bomb had demolished the place and killed the operator.

"A funny thing;" Hunkins said, "he was a civilian."

The horrible whistling, explosion, fires, and the resulting destruction from the bombing set off an emotional reaction among our nurses back in Sternberg Hospital, ten km. away. Almost all of the women reported a cessation of their menstrual cycle beginning in December 1941, and lasting for months or years. This observation, suspected before, had never been reported in such a traumatic incident or in such a large group of women. Pregnancy was not considered in the differential diagnosis. Although the men failed to report any physiological consequences as vivid, they also suffered emotionally.

By 1100 hours, on returning from our inspection, low-flying Jap planes came winging in, bombing and strafing, giving us our first close daytime look at our adversary. Suddenly the cogon grass began to swish as the bullets from the strafing Jap fighters ripped through our bivouac area. Spying a carabao wallow, I dove for it and found myself on top of the heap with a carabao and two other soldiers underneath me. After the clatter and roaring had quieted down, I turned over to note my south end was arched high in the air. This gave me some insight as to why there were so many wounds in the fanny. No one moved, including the carabao, until I scrambled off the top. We really needed a referee to unpile

25

us. Right then the plans for my foxhole number one matured. Incidentally, the final score read 25 moves and 24 foxholes dug.

Some of my most profound thinking was done while crouched in a foxhole staring at the muddy walls. This situation seemed to stimulate my personal philosophy and provoked questions like, "What in the hell are you doing in this pickle?" Incoming shells set the pace for these extravagant mental aberrations. The main theme was survival.

Another wave of Nip strafers, Mitsubishi type 0 fighters, better known as "Zeros," interrupted the beginning of construction. One Jap strafer, not over 200 feet in the air, banked right over me, providing me a good look at him. His front teeth glistened in a big grin. He seemed to be enjoying himself. The big red "rising sun," the national emblem, beamed from the rear fuselage. (The nickname of flaming asshole substituted in the common vernacular, henceforth.) This plane, obviously very maneuverable and reasonably fast, was in charge at this point in time. Fortunately for us, we made great improvements in our aircraft as the war progressed while the Japs stayed with the Zero, the Zeke and the Hap, low-wing aircraft. These planes never did have armor or self-sealing fuel tanks.

More Zeros dove over me so I stumbled down a ravine, and inadvertently came onto Lt. Tooley manning his telephone switchboard. Despite the strafing, Bill was still plugging the lines when a bullet, which barely missed him, went through the middle of the switchboard.

"I've lost some of the outfits and got some busy signals," he allowed. Bill continued to hand crank the magneto in an effort to contact other units. He performed under all conditions. If the squeaky wheel is the one which gets greased, Bill must have been running on dry bearings. He had a penchant for keeping out of sight, even when present and not echoing his voice in conversation. His medium build, thin face, black hair, and neutral expression--not far from a smile--were reasons for underestimating Bill. He was physically unremarkable except for an inner toughness. He always said he only wanted to be a second lieutenant and after accidentally dumping the unit's only radio in the Pasig River while on earlier maneuvers, he took a giant step towards his goal!

26

Later that afternoon we spotted a Zero on the tail of a B-17, both clattering away at each other with no apparent effect. Our bomber continued its flight south to the sanctuary of Mindanao.

Just at sunset, the men, still jittery and trigger happy, spotted a low flying observation plane. A dozen of our machine guns opened up. An order for "stop firing" was ignored, and even in one instance the officer had to drag the gunner away from his weapon. Suddenly we spotted the floating white umbrella of a parachutist. I grabbed a first aid kit and took off running. The pilot and I hit the landing spot about the same time. He was an American fuming mad and badly wounded.

"I've been flying over the Japs all day, but never ran into a barrage like this. The bullets started going between my legs, so I decided to get out," he said.

Wounded while in the parachute, a bullet had gone completely through his left lung, so he was hurried off to the hospital. Incidentally, he recovered and returned to active combat before the war was over. I don't know if he made it home or not.

This shooting mistake really bothered the troops. I shook with frustration. All day we had been shot at without adequate weapons to retaliate. And now we shot down one of our own planes and damn near killed the pilot. Our inexperience and panic was showing. After the ambulance left I strolled slowly back to my tent. I thought I was going to puke.

On 8 December 1941, the Asiatic Fleet of five destroyers and 27 submarines were based at Cavite Naval Yards in Manila Bay. The flagship, *Houston*, a heavy cruiser, was berthed in Iloilo and the light cruiser *Boise* was cruising off Cebu. The ancient cruiser *Marblehead* was in Borneo. Before the first whistling of the bombs was heard on the 10th of December over Cavite Naval Base, the fleet was chugging south for Australia and that day cleared Philippine waters. Later, the *Canopus*, a submarine tender, was scuttled at Mariveles. This comprised our superannuated naval fleet. Too bad the fleet didn't stay for the big bonfire the Japs were planning and the "squirrel hunting" in Bataan.

On 10 December, the primary target of the Jap air raids was Cavite Naval Base less than ten km. from Nichols Field. By 1100 hours, simultaneous attacks began while I enjoyed the protection of my first foxhole and a seat on the 50-yard line. The deep

27

drone of the Jap bomber formation heralded the enemy over-head. I could see the bomb bay doors open, then the bombs glistened in the sun. They seemed to tumble wildly. Soon, as if on command like puppets, they lined up in the sky in perfect formation, plunging earthward with a spine-chilling crescendo. I hoped none of them were destined for me. They struck with a *harrump* and an earth-shaking explosion.

The air attack shifted to Cavite, continuing for two hours. Soon, black, greasy smoke engulfed the whole south bay, flames leaping toward the black clouds. The fires burned out of control for days afterwards. At Nichols after the bombers passed, we were entertained by strafers--Zeros which came in to complete the destruction of any planes or warehouses overlooked during the high-altitude attack.

We had just witnessed the complete and final destruction of our primary naval and air bases in the islands. The Japs attained military supremacy in a short 24 hours.

Two hundred torpedoes stacked at dockside and two subma-rines lying alongside were lost. The 25 submarines representing our remaining naval attack force cruised out of Manila Bay. Rounding Bataan peninsula and entering Lingayen Gulf, they en-countered the whole Jap invasion fleet bulging with troop trans-ports and men of war. Our boys touched off a couple of torpedoes aimed at prize targets only to hear a dull thud on impact but no explosion. The ancient warheads did not detonate, so the subma-rines sailed out of this beautiful bay for Australia. Only the dog-faced soldier remained--up Predicament Creek.

Why were our planes lined up like sitting ducks?

Why were they caught on the ground?

Why was crucial navy equipment, i.e. torpedoes, not dis-persed and protected, and tested for malfunction?

We obviously were digging an awful deep hole--not foxholes either. To me, we seemingly were waiting for the enemy to at-tack us, for them to be the aggressors. The record will not indict us as warmongers. No, siree! History will be clear as to who started the war against the United States. Unfortunately, we had to do this at every airfield and navy base in the Philippines. I thought that the destruction of just one airfield, not the whole damn air force, would have been sufficient. A second Pearl Harbor was unnecessary. The "don't shoot first" policy ruined us.

It is sad but true, some of the newly arrived P-40s were not yet outfitted with armament, some guns had not been fired, some of the planes had no ammunition aboard, and some pilots were untrained in aerial combat technique. There was no anti-aircraft protection other than three-inch guns with a ceiling of 18,000 feet while the Jap bombers cruised in at 20,000 feet. The Communication Center lacked a foolproof and backup network. It was also true that the Jap attack was no surprise in the Philippines. The Communication Officer was "at lunch" at the critical time at Clark Field. No counter-attack was ever carried out; and, also, according to a Navy file, half of Cavite could have been saved with a good fire department.

Lt. Joe McClellan, one of the Whiffenpoof Boys, told me of trying to mount armament on his newly arrived P-40, hand loading ammo belts. He couldn't do it fast enough in the face of attacking Jap planes, so he took off and flew away from the action until the gas gauge registered empty, then flew back only to see his plane blown up on the ground a few minutes after landing. Joe, a relative of another great soldier, Gen. George B. McClellan of Civil War days, later was given a rifle and transformed into an infantryman almost overnight. He did a creditable job.

Soon after dark on the 11th, the Battalion moved back into blacked-out Manila to bivouac in the Luneta as paratroop guard. This huge park, bounded by the Army Navy and the Elks Clubs on one side and the Manila Hotel on the other, closed by the Bay on the sunset side, presented an ideal place for a sky drop. Hopefully here we could get this war down to a one-on-one confrontation.

The Army Navy Club was the most fashionable gathering place for officers of all branches of the service. It offered several bars, dining rooms, and a popular free buffet every night. Dinner was delightful on the broad veranda overlooking Manila Bay, streaked with the moonglow. Drinks cost 15-20 cents each. The Filipino bartender poured from the bottle until signaled to stop.

A few days of war had dimmed my memories of past life and my old apartment only a few blocks away. To revisit never entered my mind. The tower and the buildings across the park, the route of my evening stroll to the Army/Navy Club were vaguely outlined. The darkened city remained quiet until around midnight, when suddenly the clock on the huge tower lit up. Unbelievable! A few shots rung out and then our machine guns opened up and blew the clock to smithereens. It was dark again.

I often wondered how the mistake happened, but felt confident that the keeper of the tower never experienced such a traumatic response to merely pushing the light button!

Numerous rumors of spying and signaling the enemy circulated at this time but almost none proved to be true.

Manila's eyes were closed. All was quiet; maybe everyone was not asleep but just waiting and wondering what the U.S. could do and what the Japs had in mind. Acrid smoke drifted across the city fed by fires from Nichols Field, Cavite, and numerous hulks half sunk in Manila Bay. I wondered where Pilar was tonight.

Less than a week before, we had played golf at Wack Wack. The yellow-plumed acacia trees dotted the rolling green hills offering a real challenge to golfers. Pilar was a good player and clever enough not to beat me. She played in a very proper outfit since shorts were sternly frowned on by the staid Spanish colony. We retired to the 19th hole and were promptly hailed by several people, indicating Pilar had not been on the links recently. What with her job as editor of the woman's page for the *Herald* and teaching English at Philippine Women's University, and a very busy social life, her golf had been neglected.

As I leaned back with my helmet as a pillow and a six-shooter at my side, it was hard to believe the events of the past few days. Less than a week ago, Pilar and I had been out to dinner at the Embassy Club. Afterwards, we stopped by my apartment for a brandy. Although she was not a big drinker, she agreed. We talked and talked. Pilar described her flight home on the Pan Am Clipper. It was the thrill of her life. She left San Francisco on 4 October 1939, stopping at Hawaii, Midway, Wake and Guam. On 10 October she was in her beloved islands, never to leave.

The hour was late, and our conversation turned to the threat of war. We couldn't manage anything but depressing stories. She finally stood up abruptly and, shaking her head, said, "This is not our night to palaver. Take me home."

5. BATAAN

Off to Bataan!! The order came after midnight to pack up and start the long dark trek to our haven. This was Plan WPO-3 for the defense of Bataan, the traditional war department masterpiece going into effect. Never having been there, I nevertheless figured a little change of foliage might serve a purpose.

It soon became obvious that the 2nd Battalion medical detachment lacked adequate moving equipment. Our transportation allotment was two Willey's taxicabs. Also, the detachment assumed a low march priority, being the last unit to be loaded. Generously, two Filipino drivers went with the allotment but in less than half an hour both cabs broke down. We then piled into a commandeered school bus, which soon rolled down the dark road, the first of many blackout rides.

Everybody dozed, and suddenly we awoke with a terrific jolt and crash. Someone yelled, "Take cover, bombers!"

We soon discovered that instead of bombers, our bus had smashed into the truck ahead. No serious injuries were sustained except for an augmentation of my nervous tension. I decided to find Hunkins and ride with him for the rest of the night--something less exciting. A precedent began with this trip and continued through the war with Dwight and me sharing an open, two-seated command car, sometimes moving towards the front for an imminent battle and other times driving on random missions. We usually rode in silence and often at night with a full moon above. I soon learned how not to sleep.

Tonight the narrow gravel road, just wide enough for one car, wound through the barrios on our way to Bataan. Lining the road were nipa shacks, raised on bamboo stilts, with sides and roofs made from the broad fronds of the nipa palm tree. Nipa thatched the roof and walls of most huts in the rural Philippines. The villages were dark. An occasional home-made candle, wax poured into a section of bamboo, could be seen. Sometimes natives waved to us as we went by.

31

We turned into Bataan Peninsula at Layac Junction near Dinalupihan. I didn't realize this little barrio would be the scene of our first front-line combat with the Japs in early January. The sleeping barrios of Orani, Abucay, Balanga and Pila slowly disappeared to the rear.

Just before dawn our command car developed engine trouble and finally stalled while passing through a ''''no-name'' barrio. Our driver and mechanic said he couldn't fix it during the night with the tools at hand. Nothing was going right. With the first light, Dwight spied a nice shiny Packard sedan under a *balete* tree.

"That ought to make a pretty good command car," mused Dwight. We were unable to find the key or wire up the ignition, but were determined to commandeer the car. About that time the owner, a handsome little Filipino, appeared, excited but willing.

"It's perfectly all right," he said. "In fact, I'll come along and drive you. I know the road well."

When daylight came, we discovered that the driver had not even stopped to change from his pajamas. Never had a cabbie driven me any place in pajamas. The Filipino, anxious to help our effort, continued as our chauffeur for several days and was reluctant to go home. I finally ordered him to leave, not because of violation of our dress code, but simply because there was no reason for him to get mixed up any further in this dirty mess. He disappeared down the road, walking slowly towards home, leaving his beloved Packard with us.

In 1955, the War Claims Commission wrote inquiring about Mr. Guzman's Packard. "Did I have any knowledge of a car, a Packard, gas, tools, and even a pig, being commandeered on or about the 10th or 12th of December 1941, near the town of Abucay? If so, please give the details so that the U.S. Government could repay Mr. Guzman." The incident had been completely forgotten for years. Yet, with this jogging, I was happy to confirm the incident and hoped this fine Filipino patriot was compensated. I didn't remember the pig, but figured Mr. Guzman needed one to get started again. Most Filipinos in Bataan never lived to file a claim.

At 50 km. milepost across the viridescent rice paddies, the foothills of Bataan could be seen in another tone of green. The soaring central spine of mountains and extinct volcanic peaks loomed ahead. These formidable mountains--Nahib, Samat, Bataan and Mariveles--the highest at 1,400 meters, became more rugged as we approached. The malaria-infested steamy jungle covered 90 percent of the entire peninsula from Manila Bay on the east to the China Sea on the west. The city of Mariveles on the southern tip of the peninsula provided piers and navy installations. This jungle bastion was to be our home for four months. Now the enemy, at a disadvantage, would have to come to us.

"We have run far enough. We'll stand now and take them on," I thought.

Only 80 km. long and 30 km. wide across its narrow waist, Bataan presented an ideal infantryman's defense. With the jungle as camouflage--it was possible to walk ten minutes and never see the sun--the mountains commanded a field of fire, and the numerous streams and deep ravines that cut the peninsula offered great natural defensive positions.

Bataan was laden with snakes, bugs, and mosquitoes, dwelling in an impenetrable entanglement of creeper ferns and kava brush laced with mile-long rattan vines. This mantrap of jungle was thick enough to hide any army and provided a sanctuary for our weaker forces. Our protection was the foxhole and the jungle. We felt good, morale was high. The Japanese air superiority and naval guns would do them little good in this setting. We would sting their little asses as they came through the jungle.

Unfortunately, WPO-3 (Orange Plan)--the American defense of the Philippines--ordered a retreat of both North and South Luzon forces into Bataan. That kept our backside towards the front and encouraged snafu at every move. The Jap plan called for total conquest of the country by 15 January 1942.

Our regimental mission was to develop the main line of resistance. The MLR from Abucay to Mauban extended along the foothills with fields of fire across flat ground and rice paddies in front of Mt. Natib--1,405 meters high.

After ten days of feverish work, real human labor on the MLR, the 2nd Battalion moved back to organize and disguise the defenses of the reserve line of resistance--RLR--15 kms. to the rear. Only one established gravel road tunneled through the jungle along the perimeter of the peninsula.

33

We moved many times in the next three weeks. Another move, another foxhole. The architectural and engineering design improved with each move. My production had not reached the pinnacle of success with catacombs and laterals but was functional--getting my head and my fanny below ground at the same time, providing a sanctuary from bombs and artillery burst. My confidence expanded with each day of toiling and escape from enemy fire. My confidence was shaken somewhat when I spied our anti-tank weapon, a one-pounder, with a two-meter long slender barrel. It was on a two-wheel cart, and looked to me like a toy. The gun crew reassured me that with a direct broadside hit, it would demolish a small- to medium-sized tank. Also, the Japs were reputed to have poorly built tanks of "paper mache." I was glad to be reassured.

As the Japs moved closer to the entrance into Bataan, the 31st Regiment moved up. We took a position forward of the MLR near Olongapo at Subic Bay on the South China Sea coast, where a U.S. Navy base had flourished for years. With the onset of the war it had been abandoned by the Navy with an order to destroy everything.

We decided to make a visit the day before the windy road out of Olongapo was to be blown up. Our inspection, to our surprise, rvealed a lot of "confidential and secret" papers scattered all over the compound and in the barracks.

While we were looking around the place, suddenly three dive bombers came over. These were identified as Vals. Built by Aichi, these single-engine fixed-landing gear planes had a gunner in the rear seat. Decker and I dove into a concrete irrigation ditch; another soldier followed suit behind us. The two-meter-deep ditch presented an ideal shelter from the string of falling bombs. Soon several went off in front and then behind about 30-40 meters away. We all bounced in the air with the detonations. A huge slab of concrete bounced over our heads. The planes soon vanished and we took stock of our situation. No one had been hit. The soldier behind us had braced his rifle crossways across the ditch against the concrete slab. He kept inspecting his rifle, sighting down the barrel, and handed it to me. There was big *Wow* in the barrel. The pressure against the concrete slab had bent the barrel. We thanked him for his quick thinking with the reassurance of getting him another rifle upon return to our bivouac area.

That night the engineers detonated the dynamite charges on the hillside road. The explosions blew off the whole hillside, obliterating the road from Olongapo into the interior. Another entrance was sealed. Although we were bivouacked more than a km. away, huge boulders the size of buckets sailed over our heads and rained down among the troops. There were no serious casualties. In a few days our patrols spotted the Japs moving into the Subic Bay area. We avoided contact with them.

Having been in the jungle for almost three weeks, our hair was getting long and shaggy. We needed a barber. At detachment meeting one evening, I suggested that we find a barber. No volunteers were immediately forthcoming but after a more urgent plea, good old Cpl. Irving Beattie held up his hand and in his rather effeminate voice said he would be the barber. Beattie, an unassuming type of fellow of medium size, alert and easy going, turned out to be one of the bravest and most capable soldiers in my detachment. He always stood tall with me.

"Have you had any experience in cutting hair?" I queried.

"No, sir," he answered.

"Well, how do you cut hair?" I continued.

"Just as long as it lasts, sir," he quipped.

That's the way he did it. The next day, supplied with a pair of scissors and a comb, he started in. By evening his first production was on line. He had cut and shaved the heads of seven soldiers, one letter each, to spell the word *victory*. We had a good laugh, which sounded odd to me since we hadn't done much of that recently. The dress code on Bataan had been trimmed.

With each move, the motor pool attempted to transport to the nearest road junction our foot lockers containing medical equipment. From there, my men carried them, usually two or three lockers, several kms. down the trail to our bivouac area. All too often some of the equipment was lost. I notified Major Clarence White, my immediate superior and the regimental medical officer, that our equipment was dwindling, abandoned at the trail junctions. Otherwise, our supplies consisted of a musette bag and a small first aid packet across our shoulders.

Three ambulances available to us remained at regimental motor pool. In most of the big battles no roads were close by, so other means had to be utilized to evacuate the wounded.

Hunkins suggested that we take a ride into Manila for a little sightseeing and foraging. We left before dawn on the 24th of December, planning to cruise north on Highway 110 to #7 to San Fernando and #3 along the narrow bay towards Manila. At daylight we were in Mabatang, a small barrio. We slowed to drive through a narrow one-lane road, hard by native palm huts. A small Filipino boy darted between the *bahays* (huts) and rammed the side of our open command car. He span down the road doing flip flops. Our driver stopped immediately. I jumped out. The boy, screaming bloody murder, jumped up and ran full speed. After chasing the supposedly wounded lad between the shacks for about 100 meters, I gave up and came back to the car protesting that even with an injury he was faster than I was. A crowd quickly gathered in response to the screaming and the screeching of our brakes. I was relieved when one older Filipino repeated, "Okay, okay, Joe." After my apologies and reassurances of assistance to the crowd, we proceeded on the deserted road to Manila. I thought later, if I could have caught the little Filipino boy and patched him up with band aids, he would have been eligible for a Purple Heart.

Japanese observation planes and strafers hit us twice as we moved out of the jungle into the open rice paddy country. We spotted a speck coming at us, leaped into the ditch as the bullets sprayed wildly on both sides. We soon concluded that Mitsubishi's best, marked brilliantly with the flaming asshole; did not present as formidable a weapon as supposed. A lot of space existed between the bullets. A foxhole added greatly to your safety and unless he dropped proximity bombs or got a tree burst, chances of knocking you out were only fair. One other strafing attack was avoided when our driver spotted the strafer in his rear view mirror. Fortunately, the road curved into a coconut grove, leaving the Zero without any visible target.

We drove straight to Pilar's lovely mansion and she came running out anticipating a big hug, but my natural shyness cut it down to a little peck on the cheek.

6. GOODBYE TO PILAR, MANILA, AND OUR AIR FORCE

Manila on 24 December 1941 presented an extreme contrast to its usually bursting activity with huge traffic snarls, including *calesas* (pony-drawn high-wheeled gigs), limousines, tricycles, bicycles, man-drawn two-wheel produce carts, and rickshaws. The nearly empty streets were lined with barricaded stores. We proceeded to the dock area and the *Manila Herald* building, where I jumped out. The piers were in shambles. Some fires were burning out of control There were 30 to 40 hulls and masts of sunken ships in the Bay. "I'll pick you up at your old apartment," Dwight yelled as he continued on to the Quartermaster to get us some frozen turkeys. I bounded up the stairs looking like a soldier with gas mask, side arm, World War I helmet, and a hand grenade, which Dwight had insisted I fasten on my belt. Abruptly breaking into a large room where 30 people were studiously plunking on their typewriters, my sudden appearance startled everyone, including myself.

I searched anxiously for Pilar and heard her yell. My heart leaped. She was not quite as undecided how our greeting should take place. She took my hand as we scurried behind a bamboo curtain. We hugged. Our conversation was in hushed tones since everybody's trumpet was out. "Boy, it's good to see you, Petie," I said. "Pilar whispered, "Let's go; my work is about finished. Besides, the building will be cleared soon because of our daily bomb raids." The bomber's target, the dock area, was not very far away.

Pilar drove us to the Spanish Club where her family had been charter members. A liveried man opened the huge ornamental door. On entering, we found ourselves quite alone, except for a bartender who recognized Pilar. We sat at a little round table. I felt a bit restrained and the conversation was somewhat forced, even after a gin and tonic. She smiled, but I avoided her big brown, soulful eyes. I didn't want to start blubbering like a lovesick fool. All I could do was squeeze her hand.

About noon, Pilar remarked, "They're on time."

Air warning sirens wailed in the distance and the falling bombs began to whistle, exploding in the dock area. The docks were still being secretly worked by American details trying desperately to slip food to Bataan and Corregidor. Fires were permitted to burn as a coverup.

We arrived at my San Carlos apartment, nearly bare except for the rattan furniture and a few wall hangings. Dominador was nowhere to be seen. I turned abruptly and asked Pilar, "What happened?"

"I loaded up all the valuables in your footlocker and hid them in the attic at my home," she confessed with her head lowered. "Is that okay?"

"Sure, Petie, that's fine. It was great of you to do it," I said, trying to hide my alarm.

Neither of us realized that this little affair would sentence Pilar to bitter experiences with the Kempei Tai, the cruel Japanese secret police. Stenciled on the top of the locker in bold letters was **LT. RALPH HIBBS, M.D., U.S. ARMY**, a red flag to the Japanese intelligence service.

"You'd better take off for the hills, Pilar," I said. She responded with a faraway, noncommital look, but did not say anything.

Hunkins honked. We stood up and hesitated in the doorway. Finally, after an awkward moment, a hug and a wave. I muttered, "Take care of yourself, Pilar."

What a lousy way to say goodbye to the prettiest Filipino patriot in the whole damn archipelago--and a real sweetheart. About halfway to the command car I stopped, turned around and went back. She put her arms around my neck as her tears moistened my face, her soft body pressed close to mine. My heart pounded in my throat. My mouth was dry. We kissed and she whispered in my ear, "Be careful--I want you to come back." I looked at her in alarm and pleaded, "Don't get mixed up in this mess. Don't worry about me." Feeling warm inside, I waved weakly, looking the poor actor. I was afraid of showing my true feelings.

Memories came flooding back of another parting after a private party at her home. She had entertained five bachelor officers and five lovely Filipino women. They left, and Pilar and I lingered in the shadows of the garden trying to say good night. A pink strapless dress outlined her every contour. She moved closer and tilted her face upwards. Her lips pouted so I kissed her full on the mouth.

"It's about time," she murmured, jauntily cocking her head. I liked that.

The driver eased us down the narrow alleyway into A. Mabini and my old apartment to see Dominador, my no. 1 houseboy. The emotion of our goodbye gripped me. I never saw the apartment again. We were on our way north to view the destruction at Clark Field.

Dwight had secured four frozen turkeys and to this day my memory doesn't relieve me of the horrible thought that I never did pay for them and maybe he didn't either, since about that time the Quartermaster warehouses were thrown open to the public with an invitation to "come and get it."

Highway #3, Luzon's main north/south road to Clark Field and Ft. Stotsenburg, was free of traffic, except for a few lazy carabaos pulling two-wheel carts filled with rice straw. We spotted no dive bombers or Jap observation planes on this 150-km. stretch of road. Unbeknownst to us, our good fortune was not by chance, since on this very day, the 24th of December 1941, the major Japanese landing in the Philippines was in progress at Lingayen Gulf. Gen. Masaharu Homma had just stepped ashore. All of their attention and airplane support centered around that area, some 50 kms. north of our destination. We passed the lone mountain, Mt. Arayat, in the middle of the rice paddies. In the next week it was to provide a great observation point to watch the bike-pedaling slant eyes swarm Central Luzon.

Dwight was quiet, but good company at that. The four frozen turkeys were cuddled under a tarp in the back seat out of the tropical sun. The two-hour ride seemed short, probably because our minds were consumed with the uncertainty of our military chances. The outline for our future was very indistinct from where we stood.

We arrived at Clark Field and drove through the gate and guard station without challenge, an indication of the complete abandonment of the field. At the same time, as an added attraction, two Japanese strafers swept the air strip with just a few remaining rounds before they returned to their base. Not a shot

39

was fired at them. I believed. Oh, boy, did I ever! Something other than our airplanes would be needed to give us a chance in this battle.

Lazy spirals of greasy black smoke dotted the landing strip giving vivid testimony to the death of each precious and proud U.S. airplane. Before us was almost the total bombing strength of the Far Eastern Air Force--smoking, twisted metal derelicts destroyed on the ground by "Tojo's gallant warriors." The burnt-out, mangled airplanes lined the strip as though parked in a junkyard. A few smoldering junkers were nestled in separate revetments or in cul de sacs. Because of the havoc, it was difficult to distinguish a burnt-out B-17 from a P-35. Apparently, many of the planes were hit just after refueling, leaving nothing to salvage. The planes with the scorched poached egg emblem had had their day.

Our command car moved along the road parallel to the landing strip behind the barracks buildings. We stopped and watched two more Zeros strafe some target, certainly not a very good one. At best we could see there was nothing worth shooting at. We took no evasive action, watching the procedure from the back seat. After their noisy sweep, we decided to move out. We didn't bother to tour Ft. Stotsenburg, the adjacent Army post--we had seen enough. Our hope, at least in part, died a little more that afternoon. The crucible of survival offered little hope.

Later, Lt. Sam Maddux, a B-17 pilot, told me of watching the plane he had nursed across the Pacific go up in flames on this field at 1240 hours on 8 December 1941. He had been ordered to land for refueling just as the Jap aircraft appeared. He heard the warning siren, took cover at the corner of the barracks just as the Zeros swept in. Suddenly, his beloved plane was a ball of fire.

My reaction after viewing the garish scene at Clark Field was similar to my feeling at Nichols FIeld weeks before. I thought the Air Force could have and should have done better. A third of the planes might have been up in the air, one third refueling, and pilots of the other planes taking a siesta. But not the whole damn Air Force to be caught on the ground!

Later, Lt. Col. Rosy O'Donnell, another B-17 pilot, gathered 30 or 40 grounded pilots from the squadrons on Luzon, found an old banana boat and sailed off for Mindanao to fight again.

Sam reported, "It was a hairy trip. We were bombed and hit, but after putting out the fire, we made it to Cagayan, a barrio on the north shore of Mindanao. In looking around we found a select and undamaged wine cellar at Lake Lanao Resort. Since we lacked medicine, I 'borrowed' some brandy and Scotch for medicinal purposes. I duly recorded the transaction by nailing a note to the door of the cellar reading something like this: 'To whom it may concern: This is to acknowledge that on 20 December 1941, the U.S. Air Corps acquired from Lake Lanao Hotel one case of Scotch whiskey, and one case of Brandy. Signed: S. Maddux, 1st Lt. A.C.'"

Both Sam and Rosy later became general officers.

We were soon on the road back to Bataan. The command car was equipped with hand grenades hooked over a bar on the back of the front seat. The pins, firmly in place, were eyed frequently as we cruised along. After bouncing through a chuck hole, one grenade rolled under our feet. Dwight calmly picked it up and pulled the pin and alleyooped it to the rear. In eight seconds we were safely separated from a loud report. Dwight shrugged his shoulders as I looked questioningly at him.

"It's going to be a long, tough war," mumbled Dwight.

Layac Junction, the bottleneck into Bataan Peninsula, loomed ahead. The light of day was rapidly replaced by the gray of sunset, then the blackness of night. Within 30 minutes we were in the jungle near Limay, on the shores of Manila Bay, only to discover our unit had moved. It was Christmas Eve 1941. Still separated from my unit at midnight, exhausted and damned discouraged, I lay down on the ground in a banana grove up trail #2 and slept.

On this day, the USS William L. Maclan, a hospital ship out of Manila Bay loaded with 224 wounded Americans headed for Australia--the last ship to escape. What a Christmas present!

The four frozen turkeys had been deposited earlier with a 1st Battalion mess sergeant. He had been given orders to save one for his company and deliver the remaining three to companies in the Second Battalion. This didn't work. I never saw the turkeys again.

At dawn of the 25th I found Maj. Moffit, who suggested we establish the first aid station in the old church in nearby Abucay.

41

My men began to dig foxholes. Their expertise had improved considerably since the first attempt at Nichols Field, but they soon discovered human bones. Unfortunately, those bones did not "rest in peace." Lots of them! We were in the process of excavating a cemetery. We soon moved our digging project to the rear of the church.

That Christmas night my stomach began to gnaw. Someone finally slipped me a can of sardines, not turkey. With difficulty, I opened the can with my mess kit knife. Standing ankle deep in a pig sty, I suddenly surprised myself by shouting, "It's Christmas! By golly, where are my turkeys?" We laughed and relaxed.

"A better Christmas is coming," someone muttered.

The mystery of the three missing and forgotten turkeys was solved several weeks later with the confession of the mess sergeant of the 1st Batallion. He cooked them but he didn't quite understand the desired distribution of this unusual Army generosity. At least my friend, the 1st Batallion surgeon Capt. John Wallace, enjoyed it. Sorry, John, no cranberries!

By the 5th of January 1942, all of our troops had safely slipped into Bataan through the bottleneck at Layac Junction. The bridges over the Pampanga River at Calumpit and the Culo River above Layac Junction were blown up and the door slammed shut in the face of the Japs. The plan, WPO-3, had worked perfectly. Fifty thousand Filipino Army and 100,000 Filipino Reservists, plus 12,000 U.S. servicemen, the combined north and south Luzon forces, had successfully executed the simultaneous withdrawal into the Bataan Peninsula. Thousands of civilians rushed in also, aggravating the food supply problem. Great credit was due the commanding generals, Parker and Jones of the Southern Luzon force and Wainwright of the North Luzon force, for this brilliant and complicated maneuver.

7. OUR FIRST DEFEAT

The battle at Layac Junction in early January was our first battle, and our first defeat. With the first acrid smell of burning nitrate, gunpowder behind me, I rested when it was over. A profound exhaustion swept over me. I personally had done nothing exept to panic in my foxhole, cowering like a rat burdened with the helplessness of our situation. My intense dislike for artillery was etched forever on my memory in what seemed the longest day of my life. It was six hours of hell, which at the time I thought was impossible to live through. I had struggled to die bravely.

The quiet of the hillside ravines during the lull from the bombardment and the noise of battle was profound--almost oppressive--on the ears. Something was missing. Do you know what the first sound was? After another 15 minutes, the silence was broken by a single chirp--a hesitant and uncertain sound. It seemed to ask, "Is that horrible clatter over? Can I go back to my usual songfest?" Soon other birds chimed in, followed by the shrill whistle of locusts, the trill of geckos; the jungle sounded normal again, accenting the craziness of war.

We had eaten nothing all day long. My guts ached, but not for the rations. The urge to run had dampened my appetite.

I wondered, What happened to the kid with the snake bite? He soon appeared looking about as sheepish as I. Examination revealed no swelling, no tenderness or pain at the sites of the two fang perforations. He was not venomized and nothing further was necessary.

"You're entitled to a Purple Heart as a result of enemy action," I jokingly reassured him.

He allowed it was a little rice cobra, about three feet long, a bright green snake, and very poisonous.

"That's not our real enemy; it's those yellow guys over there!" I pointed out.

At dusk a dry ration was distributed. Just like rats, we waited until dark to make our move. Not only was the time consistent but our attitudes were appropriate. With my mouth about as dry as the biscuit, I had difficulty swallowing the food.

A withdrawal order was issued by early evening calling for general retreat from our line beginning at 2200 hours. Specific instructions as to the order and time of withdrawal of each unit were issued and the line of march specified. The unit on the left flank (west), the 26th Cavalry, was to withdraw first, proceeding each behind the other units. They were Philippine Scouts, a highly trained mounted group. The rest of the line, although badly mauled, was to evacuate to the east down Route #7 to 101, the main north/south road along the Manila Bay.

The jump-off time for our unit was 0100 hours. the 71st and 72nd Philippine Army Divisions on our right flank were to hold until we had passed behind them to the main road. Well, it didn't work out that way. We soon found the road clogged with personnel of the two Filipino units. The holding shell had disappeared prematurely. The order of withdrawal dissolved into a melee of confusion and rabble. Intermittent small arms fire from Jap patrols peppered us along our line of retreat.

It was a tragic and painful sight of men and equipment clogging the road. All night, Filipino and U.S. units struggled toward the rear. Many of the Filipino soldiers shuffled along with a bewildered expression on their faces. At least darkness provided a coverup for our lack of discipline. The poor 26th Cavalry found themselves without a route of withdrawal, necessitating a scramble to the south through the trackless jungle. They abandoned a lot of their equipment, but regrouped five or six days later, ready to fight again.

Our two footlockers of bandages, splints, medicines, syringes and needles and a few litters for the wounded, were carried back with our unit. At times we waited along the narrow road jammed with soldiers, unable to move. We finally threw our footlockers into the empty back seat of the last command car. I didn't opt to jumb aboard since the speed of travel was almost the same whether you were in a car or on foot. There was still some roadside first aid to do.

We had lost nothing vital on this retreat, but each move meant a dwindling supply. Usually the medics were the last to get the word and the last to be loaded. The way I figured it, the supplies wouldn't have to last too long if the outcome of the battles wasn't different from the the one at Layac Junction.

Among our meager supplies, the most merciful were morphine syringettes--disposable--easy to give to relieve the suffering of the wounded soldier. Nothing was more important on the battlefield. There were two things to do. First, tell the soldier he was not going to die, which was usually his first question ("Am I hit bad, Doc?"), and secondly, ease his pain.

The dawn of the 7th of January found all three battalions of the 31st safely behind the MLR. The 2nd Battalion was in position outside the town of Abucay--the site of my ersatz Christmas dinner and also our grave-digging escapades. The troops languished in a huge bamboo thicket at the edge of a hillside banana grove, licking their wounds and trying to find something to rebuild morale. Fortunately, the Japs failed to follow up their advantage.

The performance of the 31st had not been outstanding. We had lost the battle, our line had been temporarily breached, but our analysis emphasized the poor judgment in selecting this defensive position. Col. Harry Skerry, from Portland, Oregon, the Chief Engineer of the North Luzon forces, strongly opposed this line, pointing out there was no natural concealment or commanding terrain. The enemy artillery with longer range and greater accuracy because of the efficient use of unmolested observation planes, unmercifully punished our batteries and troops. In addition, our line and the short protecting ridge faced northeast. This permitted enfilade fire from the west. The Japs were quick to exploit this advantage with withering lengthwise shelling.

The medical detachment, all 28 of us, had performed well. We seemingly functioned better in combat, never backing off from our mission, regardless of danger. When a problem arose, it was not a question of ordering someone; there were usually volunteers, "Oh, I'll get a couple of men and take care of that." I was proud of this great bunch of essentially untrained first-aid soldiers. They were always innovative, fun-loving, but not always honest, which is not necessarily a detriment during war. My two Filipino soldiers, Juan and Ruperto, who were attached to us, performed in a soldierly fashion. Not highly trained, but with unfaltering loyalty and always available, they moved quickly through the jungle or enemy fire.

The lesson from this experience was to locate the aid station clear of the artillery. The final score in my book was three shrapnel wounds, minor; one cobra snake bite, non-venomized; a fundamental dislike for artillery barrages; and a conclusion that "we can't even make a good retreat."

On the 9th of January, Cpl. Paul Decker and I wandered to the rear to check on the evacuation of casualties. Paul was from Oklahoma, and was always my close companion, kind of like an aide. How I selected him, I never knew. When I looked around, he was there. He was muscular, with a medium frame. He had sandy hair and freckles, tough, but rather retiring and always agreeable. He was at my side at all times, usually packing a long rifle. It was proper for him to accompany me even though the rifle was not part of the equipment for a non-combatant.

We had not gone over a couple of hundred meters across an open cogon grass hillside when dive bombers, Mr. Mitsubishi's finest, started firing. Quickly, you must determine whether his dive is on your personal disaster course. The best clue is to sight up at the line of the propeller, and if it held steady, begin the game of "hide and seek." A series of foxholes was nearby, so we borrowed one from some kind soldier who had vacated it. The planes laid several strings of bombs fairly close, but again missed us.

Suddenly Decker yelled, "Look over there." Sure enough, strolling across the open hillside came Gen. MacArthur, Gen. Albert Jones, and his staff. I jumped out of the foxhole and without thinking gave a rather clumsy salute, which was not necessary in the field. MacArthur waved to stay put, and swinging his riding crop vigorously with great strides, moved across the open meadow as more Zeros came winging in. A couple of his aides were tugging on his shirt tail telling him to get down. He shrugged them off and kept on walking. Not looking up at the dive bombers, he surveyed the troop deployment and the terrain. As he passed us, one of the officers pointed toward the thicket where 155 mm. artillery pieces were hidden.

MacArthur reportedly said, "I don't want to see them; I want to hear them."

The bombs landed fairly close, but the general was completely

46

oblivious to them. Me—I was in my foxhole! "There is really a brave man!" I thought. "He's no showoff. He's desperately trying to help his troops win this campaign." From that moment on there was no doubt in my mind about the sincerity of this brilliant and brave soldier. His life's concern was his soldiers and the corps. "If I ever stumble into another war, I hope MacArthur is on my side," I told Decker.

The dive bombers faded away and so did MacArthur—scrambled eggs and all. It was a long, long time before I was to see him again.

We licked our wounds until the 15th of January, bivouacked in a bamboo thicket—an ideal place to hide. The tall canes provided a steeple about 20 meters in the air giving dense concealment, shade, and self-ventilation. The breeze constantly swayed the crown, fanning us with a melodious murmur, like the deep bass of an organ.

We busied ourselves with care of our feet. Jungle rot—dhobie itch—was a continuous problem because of hot sweaty marches. Sometimes we had gone two or three days without taking off our shoes. The troops were advised to sun their feet and to walk around barefooted, having no hookworms in the area to our knowledge. A stream of cool, clear flowing water nearby was a great luxury in which to sit and soak our feet. It was the nearest thing to a Jacuzzi that we had. The shoes were aired in the direct sunshine to decrease the fungus family hibernating in them.

About this time, MacArthur's famous communique dated 15th of January 1942 filtered up to the front lines:

"Help is on the way; thousands of troops and hundreds of planes are being dispatched. The exact time of arrival of reenforcements is unknown as they will have to fight their way through Japanese attempts against them. It is imperative that our troops hold until these reinforcements arrive. No further retreat is possible. We have more troops in Bataan than the Japanese have thrown against us; our supplies are ample; a determined defense will defeat the enemy's attack. It is a question now of courage and determination. Men who run will merely be destroyed, but men who fight will save themselves and their country. I call upon every soldier in Bataan to fight in his assigned position, resisting every attack. This is the only

47

road to salvation. If we fight, we will win; if we retreat, we shall be destroyed."

This meant something, even to soldiers whose bellies were empty and whose ammunition would not detonate. They seemed to fight with more determination even though the skies were filled with enemy planes and the Emperor's navy roamed the waters on three sides. Openly, nobody doubted the general's message, but secretly we questioned it. MacArthur was not criticized for trying.

In mid-January 1942, when all of our messages from outside were coming by submarine, a Stateside telegram was delivered to me with a message from home:

> Dave (brother) Capt. Dental Corps at Fort Ord and Betty and Ginny (sisters), in the Red Cross in Texas. Okay. All's well on the home front.
>
> Dad

With this reassurance, I decided not to send a C.A.R.E. package home. Several submarines sneaked into Corregidor during the first five months of the war, bringing medicines, specifically quinine, and some 90 mm. fuses for A-A ammunitions. One submarine took a dozen or so nurses off the island.

8. THE ABUCAY HACIENDA BATTLE

The Japs, attacking since the 9th of January, were having some success near the Abucay Hacienda. They'll be calling for us soon, I thought, and by the 15th orders were received to advance to the hot spot. We were part of USAFFE, United States Armed Forces of the Far East. Our job on Bataan was to be the reserve, the King's Elite, MacArthur's Palace Guard. This was our mission. We were never in a permanent defensive position, but always the relief unit to go when there was a breakthrough, confusion, disorganization, and the enemy shooting from all directions. The night of the 16th of January we moved up and deployed in a thicketed ravine with complete ready-made foxholes nearby. This was about the 16th move and the 15th foxhole that I had had so far in this campaign.

Strangely, but customarily, by the time the order arrived at the detachment, everybody else had moved out. In the rush, one of our footlockers was lost. I left my glasses hanging on a branch of the *balete* tree above my head. I never saw them again. After a few hours, my eyes adjusted fairly well, at least for long-range vision. At about 0300 hours, we bedded down in the darkness without the foggiest idea of the terrain. Just as I was about to lie down, a terrific muzzle blast turned me around and knocked my helmet off. We had inadvertently set up the aid station directly in front of a 155 mm. rifle. We moved.

By dawn of the 17th we were ready for a counterattack. We hoped to re-establish the MLR in advance of the Abucay Hacienda overlooking the Balantay River on the eastern slopes of Mt. Natib.

The original planners of our defense of Bataan had figured Natib mountain was too rugged, the jungle too impenetrable to have any offensive potential, and therefore did not extend out MLR up the mountain side. In reality, the Japs had scaled the mountain peak and were sneaking down the eastern slope in sufficient numbers to threaten our flank.

49

The peaceful morning of the 17th was soon shattered by a thunderous barrage from our side as a prelude to our infantry counterattack. I moved my detachment into the shade of a mango grove along Trail #12, about a kilometer east of the Abucay Hacienda. I was always partial to mangoes, my favorite fruit, but soon learned the folly of seeking shelter under them. It wasn't long until the Japanese artillery opened up.

After a couple of tree bursts scattering shrapnel in all directions with heavy casualties, we came charging out of the grove and moved pretty much across open ground toward our advancing skirmish line.

At the same time, a hundred meters away in the 3rd Battalion position, Capt. Tom Bell, "M" company commander, and Capt. Jim Brennan, the surgeon, dove into a trench as the Jap 105's detonated above their heads. Shrapnel covered the area like an umbrella for a couple of hundred meters. A large piece hit Bell in the left groin, severing the leg and the femoral artery. After two pumps of the wounded man's heart, each shooting a column of blood the size of your thumb into the air, one pint each heartbeat, Jim lunged over and grabbed the artery with his bare right hand between his thumb and second and third fingers. Holding the artery firmly, he slid his first aid pack off his shoulder, fumbled around with his left hand, found a forceps, slipped it under his clinched fingers, and successfully clamped the artery. Six or eight more pumps would have heralded the end. Tom lost his leg in the mango grove, but lived through Bataan and prison camp. Jim was awarded the Silver Star for this brave act. He did what he had to do despite continued shrapnel raining all over the place.

The shouts of litter team, as small arms fire heated up, were coming from all directions. We scampered forward, and discovered an unconscious moaning figure in a ravine. We turned him over, but in the excitement, I couldn't be sure whether he was a Filipino or a Japanese. It really was not very important since at that point in time I was in the healing business, not the killing business. We tried to stop his bleeding. We finally decided his wounds were so serious that he was going to die anyway, so we hurried forward, kind of hypnotized by the first casualty of the battle. Later reflection identified him as a Filipino.

About 1000 hours, Maj. Moffit sent a runner instructing us to

50

set up our aid station near the command post, since we were needed on the front line and not in the rear. As we hurried across open cogon grass fields, several single shots rang out and one of my men went down. He was hit in the upper right chest, bleeding profusely. I dispatched three of my men to move him back. They picked him up and got him into an ambulance parked near our mango grove. Despite strafing and an open road, the ambulance took off hell bent for the hospital,. We later learned that he, along with dozens more, died that night.

We concluded there were snipers in the huge sausage and teak trees curtained with vines and tree ferns. The battle was raging up front so it took a little time to get Maj. Moffit's attention. We told him that if he'd like the detachment to function, he had better get rid of the snipers in our backyard.

Soon a special detachment of three shotgun-toting soldiers showed up. I pointed saying something like, "That son-of-a-bitch sniper must be over in that direction." The three crawled off through the cogon grass. Within an hour and after several shotgun blasts, a Jap came tumbling out of the tree, bedecked with a fine net full of green leaves, camouflaged as well as a chameleon. Apparently our anti-sniper unit had drawn fire from the sniper, then they blazed away at him. This cleared the rear for evacuation of an increasing number of casualties.

Capt. Bill Montgomery, a line officer with a Philippine Army outfit, later told me of his experience with snipers:

A Philippine scout from the 57th Regiment sneaked into his headquarters one day. "Snipers in the thicket," he muttered. Following closely they crept out. "Careful, sir," whispered the scout. Soon he motioned for Montgomery to lie down in the *talahib* grass and stay put. Five minutes, ten minutes, fifteen minutes went by and then "kersplam!" from a 30-06. There was a rustling ten meters up in the monkey pod tree 200 meters away. This proved to be a Jap sniper dangling from a limb. His holding rope loosened and he fell dead to the ground. The Filipino scout moved over him and with the butt of his rifle smashed his skull. "The Filipino was madder than I was," Bill concluded.

51

Different degrees of savagery emerged. Japs killed by 45th and 57th Filipino Scouts were shot in the head. Many of these scouts were descendants of Chief Lapulapu of Cebu, who waylaid Magellan in 1521. They were the first defenders of the Philippines against a foreign invader--Spain.

Soon, we scooted forward 300 - 400 meters into a ravine where the command post was set up. Maj. Moffit was flailing his arms in all directions, giving orders. It was one hell of a fight! At one time the Battalion Commander ordered a litter team to go forward across a cane field in front of the skirmish line. Both of my men were wounded--fortunately, not too seriously.

I strode over to the major and declared very stoutly, "Damn it! I wish no one would order my men forward for casualties without my approval. What do you want them to do, kill the Japs, advance the line, and at the same time pick up the wounded?"

The major, his face sweaty and deeply seamed, nodded but never did declare himself.

At times, the corpsmen were charging into the battle lines and taking undue risks. A little breathlessly, one litter team reported to me they had found a casualty, but the man weighed almost 300 lbs. He couldn't walk, and they couldn't stand up to shoulder a litter because of the intense small arms fire. He seemed too big to drag. Fortunately, he was not bleeding. I instructed them to cool it for the time being, but before long I spotted the wounded man's buddies dragging him back to our aid station.

I could see our men charging forward, hitting the ground and crawling. Were they hit? Suddenly, one would jump up and run pell mell straight towards the enemy, spraying lead core with their submachine gun or automatic rifle, then drop down spread-eagled on his elbows. Another soldier would charge forward. This was what bravery was all about.

At first I lay on my belly just above the aid station on the edge of the cane field. It sloped downward into another ravine about 200 meters away. This was occupied by the Japs. Their cries were clearly audible after each mortar explosion. In the midst of it all, I was trying to figure out our evacuation route. As the rifle and machine gun fire intensified, I slid down the bank into our aid station.

Soon casualties filled the ravine, requiring immediate treatment and emergency decisions. Shock was treated by controlling hemorrhages, relieving pain and swift evacuation. This meant transporting the wounded across open meadows, hopefully to a waiting ambulance. They nearly always made it to a collecting company five to ten kms. to the rear where IVs and transfusions were available. We never had IV fluids in front-line combat situations. About a dozen of my men were in the station--tagging, applying tourniquets, compressing wounds to stop their bleeding, giving hypos and oral medications, washing and bandaging, fitting slings, assisting litter teams from the front and those sneaking to the rear. The remainder comprised four litter teams of four men each. I don't remember how many first aid packs I tied on. My hands were bloody all day.

The wounds were varied, usually small arms fire--25 caliber, from rifles and mortars. Fortunately, few were abdominal or head wounds. Bleeding from the jagged shrapnel wounds was more profuse, but easier to control.

The fighting was intense with mortars, artillery, dive bombers, and automatic weapons fire. Crack troops of both sides had bumped headlong into each other. By 1500 hours our troops were prevailing. Unfortunately, we later learned to our everlasting chagrin, that at first a great deal of the exchange of fire on our right flank was between us and friendly troops of the 45th Philippine Scouts. In this impenetrable jungle, communication was difficult--physical contact was almost impossible, and the line was irregular and mobile. Confusion was inevitable. I still believe that if the first-day counterattack on the 17th had been well coordinated, the 31st would have overrun the Japanese and the MLR would have been reestablished at the Balantay River.

Night came and about the same time, silence. A hot sultry haze lay over the cane field. Even the Japs didn't mount their nightly counterattack. The ravine was full of wounded with a few drifting to the rear. Those who were unconscious or dying were segregated a hundred meters down the ravine in their own terminal thicket. Moans were heard from the unconscious men, otherwise, everything was quiet.

Ambulances began moving up the narrow roads in the dusk, crossing the open slopes, making contact with our litter teams, so that after an hour or two of darkness, most of the wounded had been evacuated. We made judgment calls on the patients' prognosis, which determined priorities for evacuation. Our main effort was directed to those we felt would recover. I was proud of my detachment. We had one dead and one seriously wounded, but never once did personal danger prevent them from doing their duty.

That first death in the detachment came from bullet wounds to the head, suffered as the corpsman was walking along, helping a wounded soldier.

Our evacuation policy was relatively simple. If your legs were all right, and you were not shot in the chest or belly, not bleeding and were able to walk, we encouraged you to drift to the rear along the trails and gullies where you could be picked up by support units and transported to the collecting companies and then to the hospital. A field tag describing the wound and medication given were hung around your neck. There was a pat on the fanny, and the admonition, "I'd get the hell out of here if I were you--this is dangerous!" was usually sufficient instruction for the wounded soldier to take off in the "line of drift."

We improvised litters by taking two bamboo poles about seven to eight meters long, tying them together with vines, stretching a blanket between them on which the wounded was tied. One end was secured to a collar on a calesa pony, while the other end slid along the ground. It was dubbed the "Bataan Ambulance Service." It did a magnificent job when there were no roads. In lieu of an ambulance or calesa pony, two soldiers would drag the bamboo litter, each grabbing a pole with one hand, leaving the other free to throw grenades or fire at the infiltrating Japs.

Darkness brought a soothing welcome that blanketed much of the agony of our first attack on the Japs. Small fires burned in the cane field in front of us. The burnt powder smell had drifted away. The silence hurt. The moans of the wounded were gone. No calls for litter teams were heard. The blood was dry. Soldiers with bowed heads sat about in quiet groups. A real dejection was evident, but not overwhelming. No one was bragging. We were fast becoming hardened soldiers, accepting the fact that death was close by, at least for the fellow next to you--maybe not yourself.

The 2nd Battalion had been badly mauled. The enemy in front of us was annihilated. The number of our dead and wounded had been high, about 100 casualties, with just over 600 effective soldiers remaining--almost 15% in one day.

Rumor had it that the Japs were waiting to face the American infantry. Well, they got a pretty good taste of it today. Maybe tomorrow, with a better organized and coordinated offense by the 45th Filipino Scouts and the entire 31st Infantry Regiment, we could save our line.

What do soldiers do after they have survived a day of fighting? Usually they gathered in small groups--two or three--the smaller the better. Some wandered off by themselves in profound solemnity. No one wanted to be the life of the party or defend his actions in a large group. The mood was subdued, a time of personal reflection--"boy, was I scared"--or sharing with one's buddy. The post-mortem was brief and soon replaced by less combative topics of conversation. It was not like a Monday morning quarterback club. One was not likely to hear laughter or phrases like "Hope we get to play them again." I believe only the scared win medals for valor.

The cry "chow now" brought me back to reality. Miraculously, the kitchen crew produced a hot meal that night, served several hours after dark. I wandered slowly back in the darkness to the open meadow. In the pitch black, with only a faint blue jet from the field kitchen, the crew was serving a meal of rice and corned beef. It was welcome, since the butterflies in my stomach had disappeared with the firing. I ate because of hunger. With a full stomach, I thought, "Tomorrow we'll get 'em."

Much to our surprise, after the meal bugling was heard. It was the martial tempo of a single bugle. The bugling was to become routine each night about 2000, the call for the Japanese artillery batteries to ready the breach, swab the tubes, and commence firing. With the first few rounds, I started looking for my foxhole. As it turned out, these barrages ordinarily were not intended for us. It was interdictory fire aimed at main roads and road junctions to the rear.

I wandered in the dark to headquarters on the forward edge of the small ravine just in front of my first aid station. Capt. Buster Conrad, the F Company commander, was giving a volunteer

55

final patrol instructions.

Befitting his nickname, Buster was stocky and broad-shouldered. He swaggered as he approached, looking like a policeman about to arrest you. But there was a pleasant face and pleasing voice that contrasted with his macho physique. He was one man who matched his bravado with action. The four soldiers of the patrol were heavily loaded with crisscross bandoleers of ammunition. Each carried a belt full of hand grenades and an automatic weapon. The sweat on their faces glistened in the burning cane field fire. They stood hunched over listening, probably reflecting that the day's battle was not over for them. They would be crawling around in the sweltering jungle most of the night looking for the enemy.

"Bring back a dead Jap," Buster said. "We're curious about his equipment, what he looks like, and particularly his 25 caliber rifle. Bring back one of those bastards--dead!"

On this night, the grandeur of the sunset ablaze with crimson and yellow had faded to purple silhouetting the jagged Zambales mountains. After this bizarre day, my mind flipflopped to Pilar and the typical evening scene of a Filipino family. The nipa palm *bahays* were separated by banana, palm and papaya trees, lining the narrow gravel road through the barrio. Chickens and hump-backed pigs patrolled the ground underneath the elevated bamboo floor. A single coconut oil lamp burned on a rattan table in the center of the room while a candle lit the crucifix on the wall. All sat in a circle on their heels with their arms wrapped around their knees. Laughter and smiles depicted a happy group. The children, the girls clothed, the boys only with a top, sprawled just outside the circle of yellow lamp light.

Many of the adults smoked. When the thin black cigarette had burned down to an inch in length, it was tucked on the tip of the tongue and flipped backwards into the mouth and the lips were closed. The smoke is savored in this fashion for a minute or two and then the mouth opens, the tongue uncurls with the butt still smoking. I never tried it. The custom seemed to be practiced by the old folks, both men and women. A mahogany bowl filled with bananas, mangoes, and *calamansis* in the middle of the circle measured a prosperous farmer. A carabao tethered in the rice paddy nearby was further proof of well-being. This was the typical family scene.

After several lengthy conferences during the night, orders came to move forward to make "physical contact" with the 45th Philippine Scouts, making a solid line of troops. Plans called for a one-hour rolling barrage, preceding our advance. It opened up on time at 0800 hours, but was so far in advance of us that it was ineffective. Artillery shells were whistling high overhead, hitting at least 600 meters in front of our lines.

By mid-morning, we were stalled again. The Japs tried their Val dive bombers around noon. A whole bunch of them came over, screaming down on top of us. I could see them as they peeled off and hurtled down towards us. My eyes were glued on the propeller of one aiming directly at me, or was it shifting off to one side or the other? Still standing, I froze on the prop of this airplane. He's got me in his sights, I thought. Where was the nearest foxhole? Spotting one, I ran for it, hoping it was designed like the gold vaults of Kentucky. Watching, I could see the bomb falling with me as the apparent target. My heart pounded wildly, waiting for the explosion. This time it was close, but muffled. The bomb buried itself. The explosion pushed up a mushroom of earth which almost caved in my foxhole. Fortunately, the shrapnels were buried in the soft ground.

After similar bombing experiences, my bladder became conditioned to the scream of the planes and the explosions. This urged me to make an emergeny pit stop with each attack. They continued to dive bomb our area most of the day. Obviously, we were the target and the main resistance in this battle. They were on the offensive, and so were we, and we hit head-on again today. The bombings gave my bladder a real workout.

The Vals finally went home, but not without inflicting casualties. Several of our men were killed. About mid-afternoon a corpsman brought over a complete leg that had been severed from a body, covered with one GI issue pant leg and an infantryman's shoe. We made out the battle casualty tag as "unknown soldier," probably from E Company of the 2nd Battalion. The piece of anatomy was buried in a marked grave just to the rear of our area, much to the consternation of the graves registration unit at division headquarters.

The next day a colonel from that unit showed up. "You must

not have isolated burials in the jungle," he insisted.

"Okay," I told the colonel. "You send your burial detail up here after each battle and pick up the remains."

He also complained that some of the field casualty tags were inappropriate, pulling several out of his pocket, and reading, "shot in the ass." I recognized Pvt. Smith's writing but also some of my own.

"Now," he said, "that isn't very scientific. Can't you do better than that?"

I never saw him or heard from grave registration again during the Battle of Bataan. The problem didn't go away. My rumination on this bothered me. The colonel was right and I knew it but it took time to sort out the important points he had made.

The fight was close-in on the 19th, the third day of the battle. The chief resistance came from machine gun nests dug on the opposite side of the cane field about 200 or 300 meters away. Bayonets glistened and mortars tumbled back and forth. Unfortunately, our three-inch Stokes mortar ammunition, 1918 issue, was so antiquated that only about two out of five would detonate.

We lined up three 3-inch mortars at the command post just above my aid station, with most all the officers of the Battalion watching while the crews started firing. The rounds were slammed down the tube, detonating the propulsion charge. Then the rounds would tumble over and over, landing some distance away. The ones that went off were quite effective, evoking some wild screaming and hollering from the Japanese. Once, when our soldier slammed a round into the tube, the charge was faulty. The projectile went up in the air about 20 meters, tumbled over once, and lit within ten meters of us. There was a yell of alarm, but not enough time to take any evasive action. The shell hit harmlessly --it didn't explode.

"What the hell are you guys doing?" Major Moffit bellowed from his command post.

My delayed reaction was a one-and-a-half backward gainer that I learned on the swim team at the University of Iowa. My God, the whole command of the 2nd Battalion would have been wiped out had it exploded. After that, we were all a little more tolerant of "old Stokes."

Our weapons platoon responded to the low flying planes with

fire 30- and 50-caliber machine guns with tracers. It was impossible to evaluate the accuracy and effectiveness of this fire until we started using tracers every third round. This showed the trajectory of the 30-caliber was badly curved and dropping off below the target. It was about as futile as a small boy with a pail and shovel heading for the beach on receipt of a tidal wave warning.

On the other hand, the 50-caliber slammed into the strafers at times. Although I never saw one downed, supposedly several limped off flying low and crashed a couple of kilometers away. If you were a duck hunter, it was a good lesson in marksmanship. Be sure to "lead 'em" enough. Hunters can remember aiming and firing at the lead duck and seeing one on the tail end fall.

One night after the perimeter guard had reported noises close by in a dense vine-covered *ipil-ipil* thicket, old Sgt. Pentawski growled: "Call in the dogs and piss on the fires. Fix bayonets, we'll settle this with cold steel. The password is *hula hula, hala, hala*. Shoot anything that moves."

This triggered off my own cold chill. Shooting continued most of the night and by morning a patrol found only a dead carabao. The Quartermaster thanked us and issued a fresh meat ration.

After numerous midnight conferences with all the generals in the 2nd Corps, the 2nd Battalion would start off every morning in an effort to re-establish the line at Balantay River. The prejump-off artillery and mortar barrages seemed to get a little less effective each day. Our casualties were mounting. The troops were definitely dispirited. The food was dwindling in quality and quantity.

By the fifth day on the line we found ourselves exactly where we'd started. The Japs reinforced their defensive line nightly so that we were not able to completely dislodge or wipe them out.

About the sixth day of our offensive, a Capt. O'Donovan from the 1st Batallion showed up. He had a submachine gun with bandoleers of 45-caliber shells draped across both shoulders. Excitedly he chided the men along our lines, including the officers, "Come with me and you'll get medals; let's bell the cat." I never questioned his intentions, but figured the reward was more likely to be lead in our fanny. He was sincere, but trying to run a one-man show. He didn't belong to the 2nd Batallion so I didn't worry about a mental evaluation. I think he was killed on Bataan.

At dawn of the 22nd, a patrol pulled in the body of a Jap shot through the neck. The end had been quick and decisive for the young lad. This was death at close range. We looked him over carefully, undressed him, and went through his uniform. His shirt, with sleeves rolled up and with lots of pockets, was of poor cotton; his short visored brown cap with white stars on the side was cloth, of universal size, with lacing behind and a flipper with another star covering the neck. His muscular bowed legs were banded with olive-colored cloth wrap-ons. He wore canvas shoes also of universal size. He had a wrist watch with a black web band on his left arm, a mustache and black horn-rimmed glasses. Fastened with hooks along his web belt were several paraffin-coated cardboard wrapped packages. One ingredient smelled and looked like dried compressed fish sticks. Probably this was to be sprinkled on his ration of rice each meal. Another package of small brown pellets was not identified, along with oyster crackers and small sugar and salt balls.

His 25-caliber rifle seemed rather puny and cheaply constructed compared to our new issue, the Garand 30-06 caliber. The American rifle was almost twice as heavy. The firing report of the two weapons was easily distinguished and so was the ping of the 25-caliber bullet as it sailed by.

There was no question that the Japanese were our enemy, and the best kind--dead! There was some discussion about who was going to bury him. It seemed quite obvious that he would swell up and stink like any other cadaver, so we had some volunteers do the job. This Jap wasn't ever going home. He had done what the Emperor asked him to do. The sight of him didn't make me do any handsprings.

On one quiet afternoon, not a shot was heard along the line. Everybody was taking their *siesta*. My foxhole was of sufficient size so I could lie down in it. I decided to take my siesta in it so it wouldn't be necessary to be jumping in from time to time to avoid dive bombers and artillery shells.

After a short nap, I awoke looking up at the bamboo towering above me, and spotted the green triangular head of a snake bobbing back and forth over the foxhole. About ten inches separated me from his protruding forked tongue. Neither one of us seemed to want to assume the adversarial role. Freezing for a moment, I then moved my right hand slowly, feeling for my gun. Steadying my eyeballs, I suddenly ducked my head to the right, throwing my knees to the left, jumping up and out of the foxhole. In the meantime, securing my 38-caliber pistol in the best western fast draw, I fired three shots at the snake as it slithered away unharmed.

Immediately our machine guns began to rattle their rat-a-tat-tat all up up and down the line.

"What the hell is going on? What are you shooting at?" yelled Major Moffit from the headquarters just above me.

"A snake tried to get in my foxhole," I replied sheepishly.

"You've ruined everybody's *siesta* and at least 500 rounds of ammunition have been wasted. Tell 'em to cool it," he yelled down the line. "It's just that dumb medical officer trying to kill a snake." He asked me later if I had killed it.

"I'm afraid not, sir," I admitted with bowed head.

Reports came in after five or six days that there were dead American bodies bloating in the tropical sun. They were somewhere out there across the contested cane field in front of three Japanese machine gun nests. We had fought over this same ground and knocked out the nests at least three previous times. Supposedly the Japs had withdrawn, so it was suggested that the medical detachment retrieve the bodies if possible. Three heavily armed soldiers from E Company crawled ahead of us as we made our way through the shredded cane field, over the ridge, and on the down slope of the next ridge. Three unrecognizable stinking bodies lay just in front of the Jap dugouts. Half a dozen unexploded Stokes mortar shells lay within ten feet of these foxholes. Bits of bloodied clothing, blown up guns and equipment, were found in the foxholes, evidence of direct hits from our mortars. Our riflemen reported there were apparently no Japs in the area, or at least none who were going to fire on us, so we stood up and examined the bodies as closely as possible. I spotted a helmet lying close to one of the bodies and looked inside. To my horror on the sweat band it read Capt. John K. Wallace III, the Surgeon of the 3rd Battalion.

"My God, John has been killed," I blurted. It couldn't be. "Someone would have reported his death," I rationalized.

With palpitating heart, choking and sobbing, I tugged at the bodies. Perspiration beaded my forehead and my face was contorted as I examined the faces of the dead men.

But the carcasses were beyond recognition. The skin was blistered, bloated, smelly, rotten, and covered with maggots. It would peel off with my tugging. I thought then that all statesmen should have the opportunity of examining a five-day old-corpse. It was almost impossible to turn the bodies without pulling off an extremity. My judgment was the corpses were too badly decomposed to try to evacuate them to the rear. And, furthermore, we didn't have any bags for such a project. I agonized with the thought of leaving John in a jungle grave, but finally ordered the men to start digging. We dug as fast as we could. Shallow graves were the best we could manage in the hard sun-baked dhobie clay. After having stuck a dog tag in their mouths, we rolled them over, covered them up, and placed a head marker on each grave. At least they were buried where they had died.

It was strange, I thought, that the names on the dog tags did not match John Wallace's name on the helmet.

"Has anyone heard that Capt. Wallace was killed?" I yelled as I came back to the unit carrying a shovel and the helmet. No one answered until finally the Executive Officer admitted he had heard that three men in John's medical detachment were missing. I soon had John on the phone.

"Are you sure that is you?" I gulped. I was so relieved to hear his voice. He was a great friend, a good soldier and in peacetime was always good for a roll of the dice for cider and peanuts in the Quartel de España.

"I traded helmets with this lad about a month ago. He was complaining the sweat band didn't work right. I'm sorry to hear that they were killed. It was what we presumed since they had been missing now for five days," John explained. I reflected that some men die early, having contributed their bit, however small.

During the middle of a rather intense small arms fire fight, my corpsmen brought in two bedraggled-looking Filipinos with attire consistent with crawling through the jungle for some time. Their only weapons were bolos strapped on their backs. This was the third time that these two men, whom we recognized, had been behind our lines. We were suspicious that they were spies. The two other times we saw them we were building defensive positions. A decision seemed to be necessary. Major Moffit indicated that he was satisfied that they were spies and should have an appropriate sentence. A few minutes later several shots rang out. The sergeant reported that the two Filipinos started running up the ravine and his men shot and killed them. I never knew for sure who sat on their final judgment. A decomposition odor a few days later indicated that the burial and the investigation of their crime were both rather shallow. The matter was closed and forgotten.

By this time our casualties had reached around 50 percent. Our fire power was down. Each advance was carried out with less vigor. A few more people were killed or wounded. We had been on the line now for over a week.

The food, through no fault of our mess crew, was dwindling. The supply line ended before reaching us. The ration had been cut to one-third.

Customarily, front-line soldiers require around 4,000 calories a day, but our ration had dropped to less than 2,000 and was cut twice more before the end. In truth, but not publicized, the Quartermaster had stockpiled only enough food for 100,000 persons for one month. My weight had dropped from 178 to around 140 pounds. My belt was running out of holes. The weight loss among the troops was horrible. We chewed on stalks of sugar cane, not only for the calories, but to quench our thirst. It was a rather chewy stick which was cut in 6-12-inch lengths and chewed on like a good old piece of licorice. The only penalty for these calories was diarrhea--the raw sugar was Mother Nature's Ex-Lax.

Late one afternoon a Val paid us a visit. He had spotted a wisp of smoke coming up through the dense jungle from the field kitchens, where supper was being prepared. He laid a string of bombs through the area, wounding a couple of men and cancelling our entire meal. Grace, not dive bombers, would have been more appropriate. Our food was served in darkness, morning and night. The chow line was usually quiet. Although our ration was pretty skimpy, no one really complained about the food. It was just a small part of the bad scene. Besides rice, oatmeal and evaporated milk, there was an occasional vegetable stew with Australian beef which had been stored on Corregidor. Fish, rarely potatoes or beans, sometimes pudding, plus a little sugar or salt, were the rest of our diet.

Our morale was waning but, more important, our vigor to fight was fading. By this time I was thoroughly convinced we could not accomplish the original mission, but was positive that the Japs could not advance on us. Furthermore, the acute awareness of the possibility of being killed was blunted. The enemy didn't frighten me and because of the close proximity, their artillery couldn't punish us. A Banzai charge and being run through by a bayonet-wielding enemy was a possibility. I used to confide to Dwight the wish that my executor would not be a dumb, uneducated Jap; at least he should be a college graduate. More often, I did say, "To hell with them." My thinking was changing. We were becoming hardened soldiers.

About this time, swollen legs, sore purple tongues, night blindness, and skin hemorrhages were making their first appearance, indicative of vitamin deficiencies. These men were not evacuated until malaria or dysentery complicated the overall disability. Illness alone depleted our troop strength by two to five soldiers a day, since almost no one returned to the Battalion after being sent to the hospital.

There was one exception. It came on a black night while driving on a tortuous mountain road. We were following directly behind a blacked-out car. Suddenly, it disappeared over the side, tumbling to the bottom. My driver and I scrambled through the brush to discover two unconscious but alive soldiers. I rolled one over, put a flashlight in his face and discovered my old pal, Denny Rees, a dental officer from Oregon.

He regained consciousness in a few minutes, cursing the damned war. His right arm was broken. He tried the hospital for about two weeks and then returned to the front with his arm in a sling. As a dental officer, trained as a non-combatant, he was one gutsy guy. Denny was a slight fellow, probably about five feet, seven inches tall, with curly light brown hair. His gravelly voice was pleasant and he was an agreeable counter-puncher in a conversation. He practiced orthodontia in Klamath Falls, Oregon, before leaving to do his patriotic duty with us in the Orient. In the last days of fighting, Denny was still doing first aid at the skirmish line. He fortunately escaped further injury and was one of the few who survived prison camp as well.

Buster Conrad, by this time heavily bearded, appeared one

night, silhouetted by the fire, his piercing eyes sparkling. He was bedecked with bandoleers of ammunition crisscrossing his shoulders. Slung over the crook of his right arm was a short, stubby 45-caliber Colt submachine gun. They were not general issue, just kind of special for gangsters and tough guys. It didn't have a wooden stock on it, just a metal brace so it could either be shot from the hip or the shoulder.

"The mission is kill, kill, kill!" Buster growled. He seemed to be particularly wild tonight. "The password is a Bob White bird whistle. Anyone want to come along?"

Volunteers with dirty faces stood up. Quietly they trudged off down the ravine on a narrow dusty trail to start the night's destruction. The bramble hook of creepers would resist any movement except on the trails. I was restless all night, listening to the sporadic firing. I wondered how Buster was making out. It was with great relief that I stumbled into Buster in the dark at breakfast.

"We had a pretty good night. No problem on our side. Tojo had better count his men," he advised.

Further attacks by our Battalion and the whole 31st Infantry Regiment were fast becoming futile. The Japs were reinforcing with fresh troops. Our reserves were already committed. There was very little rest at night because of the Japanese dirty tricks and a propensity for attacking at night. Their patrols used delayed-action firecrackers to hide their movements. At times, loudspeakers beamed surrender messages our way. Even their bugling at night had some harassing effect. Our mortar duds were more frequent than live rounds.

By the night of the 21st or 22nd, we were again stalled about 800 meters forward of the jump-off mango grove. This night the cane field ahead of us, shredded by days of intense fire from both sides, burned fiercely. The buildings at the hacienda and the thatched-roof storage sheds of the old sugar central were all ablaze. The fire was no advantage to our side except to put a barrier in front of us so the night infiltrators would have a hot time coming directly at us.

The movement of the Japanese around our left flank up on the slopes of Mt. Natib was becoming more serious. So, after two weeks, a sufficient number of Japs had managed to crawl through

65

the tangle of vines and jungle to present a critical threat.

The order for a general withdrawal, not unexpected, arrived.

The logistics of withdrawal of thousands of troops still engaged with an oncoming enemy in confusing terrain, multiple locations and evacuation routes, and different potentials of mobility and equipment, presented a horrible problem to the staff. The pullback would take four days, commencing with heavy units moving out on the 22nd under the cover of darkness. The withdrawal would continue each succeeding night until all the troops were out by the morning of the 26th. Only a few would remain the last 24 hours. The 31st was chosen to be the last unit out.

The last day on the line, the 25th of January, was a hot one. It was the day that taught me to step on ants. The Japanese buildup in fire power opened with small arms fire early on this morning, which was somewhat unusual. By mutual agreement, we charged forward in the daytime, leaving the killing to the Japs at night. The little pellets from the 25-caliber rifles whistled overhead snapping branches close by most of the day. Their fire, fortunately, seemed to be going over our heads. Apparently, this is what happens when you are shooting downhill; you overshoot the target. Thank God! A well-trained soldier shoots low.

Shortly after noon, Japs were spotted coming towards us down the narrow one-way lane from Mt. Natib to Abucay Hacienda. The trail was flanked by the encroaching jungle. They were less than 300 meters away jogging four abreast calling the cadence when our Battalion, plus the 1st Battalion on our left, opened up with everyone firing. Several of my corpsmen asked permission to get into the fray. The Japanese column was cut to ribbons. It was, indeed, a great day to step on ants.

I had even looked at a Garand left by a dead soldier, with the idea that I might go out and pop a couple myself, but I never got around to it.

After a couple of hours, another column with reckless defiance came down the trail trotting along--chop, chop--yelling, trying to keep up their courage, I suppose. The Jap soldiers seemed bent on suicide as they dove into the grass along the trail. If you held your sights on the spot, in a few minutes the soldier would rise up exactly where he had disappeared, making him an easy potshot. With a little elementary infantry training, a soldier

66

should learn never to rise up in the same spot where he had disappeared. Hit the ground and roll, I believe is the tactic.

Shooting was great from our side since it was very close range with little return fire from the Japs. As yet, their artillery had not zeroed in. Their observation planes had difficulty picking up our lines. Red cloth strips 10-15 meters long were stretched along the tops of the bushes. Apparently, they were ground markers for their spotters to direct the artillery fire. They must have gotten their signals mixed up because they couldn't find us that afternoon.

About this time, two U.S. self-propelled SP 75's sneaked into our ravine and commenced firing. The artillery piece was mounted on the back of a half-track truck. They would hustle out of the ravine, fire a dozen pointblank rounds and roll back to the bottom under the concealment of kava brush.

This withering and effective fire must have mauled over a battalion or two. This fire was critical in our successful escape from their enveloping action. The Jap dive bombers buzzed round and round, trying frantically but unsuccessfully to spot those SP 75s.

Late that afternoon, a couple of my corpsmen brought over a half-opened wooden box containing some smelly fish which they had found on the battlefield. They smelled a little strong. The texture was soft and the palatability rather questionable. The safety of ingestion was in serious doubt.

"I will try one," I stated magnanimously. And with a Joan of Arc flair, I shook off the worms and took a bite. With a questioning expression, I continued as the men grabbed the box, and started tossing fish to everybody in sight, not waiting for my medical report. The fish, probably left by a withdrawing unit, were soon devoured without any ill effects.

As the sun dropped behind Mt. Natib, a shout went up. "Here comes another column of Tojo's boys." They were not over 300 meters away. With a tremendous roar, the artillery, mortars, heavy authomatic weapons, and rifle fire blew the Japanese column to smithereens. The road on the hillside, and the cogon grass meadow to the north of the trail, were littered with hundreds of dead Jap soldiers. It must have taken the Japanese two weeks to bury all of them. That little punch must have delayed their advance a day or two, requiring new units to resume their offensive. They had started their bayonet charge about 300 meters too soon and exposed themselves to the destructive fire from the muzzles of all the weapons we had. Even after that, there was sporadic small arms fire over our heads most of that night as we started our final withdrawal from Abucay Hacienda.

It had been 11 days of front-line duty. Boy, it would feel good to take my shoes off and put my feet in some cold water. The battle of the Abuday line was nearly over. We had not won the war, but had completely decimated the enemy units in front of us. Despite the Japanese discipline of a glorious death for the Emperor, their fanatics and suicidal maneuvers failed. The good old 2nd Battalion had fought gallantly. No one in my detachment had ever refused or even questioned an order to go forward to get a wounded buddy. In fact, they were guilty of overexposure at times.

During the night of the 23rd and the 24th of January, most of the artillery and noncombatant elements along with one company of each battalion, withdrew without incident. The final covering force consisted of one rifle company and one machine gun platoon for each battalion plus a battery of 75-mm guns.

At midnight the pressure on the line again increased just as our withdrawal began. We fell back to the mango grove where Capt. Tom Bell had lost his leg 11 days before. Our machine guns, both the 30- and 50-caliber platoons, clattered incessantly. Our protective shell was holding. Thank God for the brave and determined men who remained behind. Twenty-five caliber pellets from the Japanese rifles were peppering all around us inflicting some wounds. A slug clipped a branch off a bush about head-high--others slammed into the tree trunks.

"Jeepers," I said to Cpl. Decker, who was near by, "that was damned close!"

"Yes, Captain, that went right between our heads," he replied matter-of-factly.

Oh, well, I thought, they're never going to get me now. I was thoroughly convinced of that. "Let's ease down this road," I said.

We continued to drift slowly back to the rear road, checking to see that all our wounded had been evacuated this far by the "Bataan Ambulance Service." We were soon caught up in a great mass of milling Filipino soldiers. Many of them had had very little military training. Many were clad only in breech cloths. They clogged the road and ditches, with a complete loss of identity of units, disorganized, stumbling along, at times dragging their rifles--probably old Enfields. Incidentally, the stock on these rifles was so long it was difficult for the small Filipino to shoulder. We bandaged some bleeding wounds, encouraging them to move out. We soon caught up with my ambulances loaded with wounded. They were barely able to move in the jam of troops, sometimes halting as long as an hour.

I spotted a command car near the junction of the back road and the Abucay Hacienda road. After clearing everybody out of the car who could walk, we started reloading with the more seriously wonded. First, those who could sit up got in, but we soon found that there were more seriously wounded. In the end, only the litter cases were allowed to ride. Using litters we crisscrossed them from front to back and side to side on the seats of the command car. Many wounded soldiers lay in the ditches after dropping out of the march. I ordered any passing troops to pick up the wounded. Sometimes rescue came after spotting a pair of legs protruding from the dark jungle. A soldier would pull the man out, shoulder him, and slowly lug him away in the darkness. Even dead soldiers were carried to the rear. At times two men were necessary to carry the wounded man, and other times it took four men, one on each extremity.

"Don't leave any wounded along the road. Don't pass anyone who needs help," I yelled repeatedly--at times face to face with a stunned Philippine Army soldier.

The pace was so slow there was no reason to leave any living soldier behind. The firing behind us faded as the column inched down the single-track Hacienda Road. We needed a long night if there was any chance of breaking up this road jam and getting the troops back behind the reserve line of resistance at Orion. Fortunately, the Japanese did not unlimber their artillery that night. The buglers must have been down to the barrio drinking *tuba*.

At about 0300 the morning of the 26th, the last of our covering force--the rifle company and machine gun platoons from E Company, 2nd Battalion, supported by heavy fire from the 194th Tank Battalion and the 75-mm self-propelled guns--pulled back. They staggered out of their positions looking like walking dead men. They kept the enemy hordes in check, and I gave them an overwhelming thanks.

"They had a blank stare in their eyes," wrote an officer of the regiment, "their faces covered with beards lacked any semblance of expression."

My men were also dirty, hungry with sunken eyes and gaunt bodies from lack of food and two weeks of battle. It had been ten or eleven days since I had had my shoes off, and twice as long since my last bath. My beard was so long it curled and turned velvety.

"We don't look like a very efficient fighting force," I mused, "but their appearance belied the true grit of real American GIs.

We inched down the road, jostling and shoving a little bit. Generally the troops were quiet. At times a hand would reach from the ditch begging for help.

To my knowledge, no wounded were passed that night--dead soldiers, possibly, but no wounded remained along the road.

"Father, you've got to give us more darkness," I prayed. "Please, oh, God, please don't let the sun come up yet."

Our machine gun boys were still clattering away back up the road, effective enough to keep the Nips off our backs. The false dawn appeared over the mountains of Legaspi and Cavite across Manila Bay. A mantle of smoke covered Manila 40 kms. across the bay.

"With a little luck we can still make it," I mumbled.

We turned into the main Manila Bay road, providing room for five or six men to march abreast, allowing us to lengthen our stride. The road was bordered by *ipil-ipil* trees about three or four meters tall. The small green leaves provided a visual screen. We're gaining, I thought.

"One of the men is dead in the car there, Captain," Beattie reported.

"Okay," I ordered, "pick up the next wounded who can't walk and put him on top of the dead man."

The motors are turning over on the Jap dive bombers, I thought. Time is running out for all of us, yet our pace is quickening. We are stretching our legs now, striding down the road as the first streaks of dawn appear across Manila Bay. We'll soon, in probably less than an hour, have Val dive bombers coming at us for their greatest kill of the war. The pace quickened--the column thinned. The sunless jungle thickness closed in on us. We disappeared into the welcome arms of the steaming jungle as the first observation planes hovered overhead.

The dive bombers were too late. We had escaped.

By 1100 hours, "E" and "F" Companies were in Balanga hiding under *nipa* huts. We established headquarters, the aid station, and set up our defensive lines across the main road. Then we waited once more for the little yellow soldiers to attack us. Our backs were to Corregidor and our feet almost in salt water.

"Major Moffit requests an officers' call in 15 minutes," a runner announced.

Baloney, I thought. I'm ready for chow call and a little *siesta*. After all, we have had neither for about 36 hours.

The officers squatted in the dirt, Filipino fashion, under a deserted *bahay*.

"How many soldiers do we have left?" Moffit asked me solemnly, looking at the ground.

"About 350, Major. I can't be sure," I replied.

Moffit, shivering and obviously struggling with his emotions, got up and began to pace. He was mad, crying and swearing. I'm sure the disappointment of not accomplishing the mission on the Abucay line was having its toll. God knows he tried.

Pray leaned over and whispered, "The major must have got a fart stuck crosswise."

Moffit began to talk in short staccato bursts.

"We've got to hold this road, the main road. It's the only chance of establishing another line and the survival of the whole corps. There are no effective troops between us and the Japs at this time, just stragglers."

He whipped out his revolver, a Smith and Wesson, and brandished it in the air, pumping his arm up and down.

"Damn it, we must not fail this time.!" With that he jammed his revolver towards the ground and a shot went off. I was sitting about three meters from the end of his foot. The muzzle blast came close to knocking me over backwards. Conrad let out a grunt. Pray hollered. "Hold it." Sauer looked wild-eyed. Moffit winced. He stopped for about two seconds and then continued his tirade.

My eyes were glued on his feet. I could make out what appeared to be a hole in his right boot. The shot had apparently gone through his foot.

"You've got to hold, that's all!" he concluded, his fists tightly clinched.

Hunkins and the others moved away in a somber mood, unmindful of the major's self-inflicted wound. I stayed behind, wondering whether I should start sick call or ignore it. Moffit looked at me and I looked at his foot as if to say *well?*

"I shot my damn toe off," he blurted, red-faced.

"Well, let's take a look at it," I suggested, reaching for the shoe string. He pushed me away. When he unlaced the boot, we found the shot had completely severed the terminal phalanx of the second toe. After stopping the bleeding with compression, I applied a bandage which was small enough to be accommodated by his boot. I volunteered some pain tablets.

"Naw, I don't need any. It really doesn't hurt that much," he grumbled resignedly, his face grim and drawn.

In my estimation he grew a foot and a half and appeared as a tough, seven-foot soldier. He limped away. No one else in the Battalion ever knew about this, nor was he awarded a Purple Heart! The wound healed promptly without complaints from him.

I leaned against a corner bamboo stilt of the vacant *bahay*. The midday sun filtered through the bamboo slats of the floor above. Quiet engulfed me, the tension melted, the gut ache subsided as I relaxed. Our exhausted but determined troops straddled the road in borrowed foxholes. We were still on front-line duty.

In the twilight of sleep, I tried to analyze my role as a soldier embroiled in a jungle war halfway around the world. My loyalty and bravery unevenly divided, stemmed from love of country and home. One fought for freedom and the good life of homeland. Sacrifice and duty were accepted as the price of freedom. Surrender offered nothing but an unknown. Liberty was our mandated destiny. I prayed for the strength to fight or die like the man I wanted to be. If I were to die, my wish was to die bravely.

My mind tottered in the haze of sleep--we escaped again but the road seemed endless. The quest for immortality dulls with adversity and terror. Even honor, loyalty and duty ring ever so hollow after weeks and months of a death struggle with an enemy who disregards life--trading it to be an Emperor's pawn on the battlefield.

The principals in this jungle consist of me and an ugly enemy --nobody else--not even Roosevelt, languishing in the purple room of the White House with his back to us. Furthermore, Mac-Arthur's two refrigerators; the Chinese *amah*; young Doug's mentor, Ah Chuh; or his gritty wife, Jean, evoked no resentment from me.

As far as I was concerned, it didn't matter if MacArthur had five refrigerators, and an even dozen *amahs*, as long as he was on my side. Completely committed to defeating the Japs, this general prowled the battlefield tortured by our failures. Give him another refrigerator if it adds to the general's comfort. What makes us persevere? Fight on? Americans' love for their country towers above anything else.

It was dark and quiet when I awoke, still leaning against the bamboo stilt. No Jap artillery, mortars, dive bombers, nor rat-a-tat-tat of small arms had awakened me. Not even the pigs and the chickens whose home I was occupying had bothered me. I wondered how long I had slept. What day was it anyway? My watch said 2000 hours. My God, I thought I must have slept at least eight hours since the officers' call sometime before noon. I'd even missed chow call, whatever that slim ration might have been. Missing meals is not very wise, particularly on one-third rations. Gradually shaking the numbness out of my body, I staggered out into the narrow passageway between the *bahays*. Stumbling onto one of the corpsmen, I queried, "*Que tal?*"

"Nothing doing, Captain," he responded. "The Japs apparently are not following us very closely. They've got a few wounds to lick also."

"No one called me for mess," I complained offhandedly.

"You didn't miss anything," he snorted. "Fish and camotes."

All's quiet on the Balanga front, thank God! I went back to my own private ground-level bamboo quarters, took off my helmet and for the second time in one day in over two weeks, I peeled off my shoes. The olive green GI socks enameled to my macerated feet came clean with a few tugs. I lay down in the dirt, cupped my head in the helmet and waited for sleep, feeling as limp as a

73

noodle. My thoughts wandered to the wounded along the road coming out of the Hacienda. Some had staggered into the jungle and were missed. For sure some were dead, and if they were not, they soon would be. I hope the good Lord lets them die quickly. Those who stretched their hands to us were rescued as best I could tell. Struggling with my thoughts I drank the dregs of bitter defeat.

Is it really necessary to have doctors on the front line? The battalion surgeon of infantry troops is placed in the most forward position, almost on the very skirmish line. Couldn't highly trained medical corpsmen do the job? Are lives saved by the presence and expertise of a doctor at the scene of the fighting? Probably not, except in the rarest circumstances. The battalion surgeon has very little equipment and can hardly use it under most combat conditions. I believe he is stationed on the front lines just as much for morale purposes as for his medical contribution. The soldiers feel that "even if I'm hit, the Doc will pull me through." Good corpsmen can probably do the job. The battalion surgeon commands the medical detachment, but he never commands infantry troops unless all the line officers are gone. A good soldier should not ask too many questions.

The next day we waited. It was the Japs' turn. I wondered how they liked it now. Hours went by, and other than Zeros flying overhead, nothing happened. We stayed three days at the advance post in Balanga, waiting for the Japs to come down the road. Apparently they didn't want much more now. Years later we read Gen. Nara's account that the "65th Brigade had been severely mauled while in extreme stages of exhaustion with very few effectives left." We had seen the Jap soldiers piled up and blown apart.

With no reports of even light patrol action detected on the front, the 2nd Battalion was ordered to withdraw behind the reserve line of resistance (RLR), to our haven back up on the eastern slopes of Mt. Samat.

The RLR, the Orion-Bagac position from Manila Bay to the South China Sea, was 10-12 kms. narrower than our first line of resistance. It protected an area 50 percent smaller, anchored in the center by 640-meter high Mt. Samat, five km. to the rear and overlooking Mt. Natib. It afforded excellent observation of the entire battlefield. Rice paddies stretched north from Mt. Natib snuggling against the shores of Manila Bay on the east. Further retreat was impossible.

The next day Jap observation planes flew around, dropping propaganda leaflets promising great rewards.

"You are doomed." "Who is sleeping with your girlfriend while you're suffering in the jungle?" They even dropped free passes to "surrender." I used mine in lieu of toilet paper.

With the break in combat, I soon discovered that time and memories were the only commodities in good supply. My mind drifted back to peacetime military maneuvers, which usually involved a plethora of snafus, hurry-ups and waits, pick it up and set it down, and high adventure. The 31st endured two such outstanding episodes. The first one came in an overnight camp out in a coconut grove. In the middle of the night a mini-typhoon whipped the nuts off the trees and peppered the tents of the sleeping troops. A couple of soldiers received glancing blows. The colonel said, "Hold tight," until a huge cannonball-type coconut crushed his own tent. He came out shouting, "Get the hell out of here!"

The second episode, probably in November 1941, came after a 20-km hike. The troops ended up on the beach of Manila Bay and promptly dove in. In a few minutes, cries for help were heard. They had splashed into the middle of a school of purple man-o-war jellyfish. Over 30 men were evacuated with huge red splotches covering most of their bodies. Two almost died from bronchospasm before being resuscitated from the acute allergic reaction.

The image of other pre-war times flashed by--the Filipino hawkers who plied their pink, white and even black pearls on A. Mabini St. in the Ermita district of Manila, a few blocks from the Pasig River. You were expected to haggle about the price--"Muy caro" (very dear), since the quality remained even more obscure--a piece of shell, glass or a precious pearl? On the premise that a real pearl could not be crushed, the ruse of stepping on it was tried by some. This might bring a remonstrance from the merchant which ended the feint and supposedly meant he was offering a counterfeit. Research among my jewelry friends indicates that this is not the case at all. Good pearls, depending on their age, varying from four, five, six or more years, possess different thickness and consequently vary in toughness. The thickness of the nacre (shell) before World War II by good commercial standards was 1.5 to 2 mm. or .008 inches. After the war thinner-shelled pearls were marketed. These crushed more easily.

Without any effort, I drifted back to a day and a drive down breezy, palm-tree-lined, posh, Dewey Boulevard in Manila. I encountered a huge crowd of people spilling from the shores of the Bay onto the street, obstructing traffic. After parking, I pushed my way to the inner circle where an ancient *amah* and a Filipino fisherman were haggling over a huge turtle at least one meter in diameter. Money changed hands, the crowd cheered and then the *amah* gently guided the sacred turtle back into the sanctuary of the surf, hopefully to escape the fisherman's net for another one hundred years.

In the good old days, the Army and the "sunshiners," the ones who had missed too many ships to the States, would harmonize in singing "The monkeys have no tails in Zamboanga." It was a popular ditty sung by GIs in those years before 1941. It presented the Filipino as an object of ridicule--a wild, dumb, naked jungle savage--a monkey. This, and rightly so, evoked a bitter reaction from the Filipinos. The song was in bad taste and, to my knowledge, completely abandoned before World War II times. The song originated from the practice of the young native boys scaling the tall, stately royal palms. Twice daily they emptied the buckets which filled with sap from a plug high up on the trunks. Tuba was made from the sap. No wonder we don't sing the song anymore--not after seeing the young Filipinos dead along the trails.

9. OUR BAMBOO CATHEDRAL

Narra or monkey pod, called Philippine mahogany, and the mango and acacia, were the tallest trees dotting the sharp ridges of Bataan Peninsula. After the fall of the Philippines, the Japs cut down all of these precious trees. The *talisay* tree with thin lattice leaves and tiered limbs bordered small openings providing shade and cover. The jungle brush was of *ipil-ipil* and molave plants enmeshed with rattan vines woven into an impenetrable barrier. Narrow bushy ravines 30 to 50 feet deep separated by *cogon* and *talahib* grass two to three feet tall, landscaped the approaches to the velds of Mt. Samat.

Another huge tree, the *balete*, its flying buttress roots big enough to hide three or four men, gave us shelter. The Filipinos believed that evil spirits and ghosts inhabited the recesses of these trees, but they seemed congenial to me--spirits and all. Huge vines hanging from the tops of the trees provided escape routes for the fast disappearing resident monkeys who, as long as they lasted, provided some variation in our diet. Due to their raucous cry and hoarse voice they were named howler monkeys.

I tried monkey meat on a couple of occasions. The color and texture looked rather appetizing. One might have imagined it was braised tenderloin tips. After chewing on a piece it seemed to increase in size requiring resting the masseter muscle. Most monkey meat got placed back in our mess kit pretty much undisturbed. After the chew test there was no difficulty in distinguishing between monkey and beef.

We finally withdrew to a huge bamboo thicket, which crowned 20-30 meters in the air and provided several shaded open spaces underneath as big as a football field. The forest was our friend now, and we could move freely on the shady trails, even in daylight. In the open our troops lived like rats, hiding in holes only to venture out after dark.

With a slight breeze, the bamboo tops would sway gently back and forth, producing a soft melodious tone. The fluted whispers and lilting music of this bamboo forest were like the wind section of a huge orchestra. At times there were higher tones from vibrations but more often the bass came through. It was delightfully airconditioned, the forest cool underneath, the warm air escaping from the pinnacle high above you--Mother Nature's escape from the steamy jungle.

This was to be home, our Valhalla, for almost two months. A cool, clear flowing little stream meandered down the side of the mountain through our rest area. It provided the moisture for the bamboo grove and the greenery of the jungle. The location of the stream, high up on the mountain side above most other personnel, military and nonmilitary, made it quite potable. In other bivouac areas it was necessary to purify the water by adding chlorine tablets to 25-gallon Lister bags hung from a teepee of bamboo poles.

Even more delightful was the chance to take off your shoes and put your dirty smelly feet in the cool stream, even though we were not sure piranha might be lurking. What a great luxury! All one had to do was to take off his shoes to be ready for bed. Clothes were no problem, since any item could be replaced almost any day from a dead soldier. My only spare clothing was a pair of the ubiquitous olive-green army socks, carried in my hip pocket. Most of us wore wool shirts, GI issue. They provided a cooling effect in the searing tropical sun because the sweat would evaporate. Wool was really much more comfortable than the stickiness of a cotton shirt. Although it was never very cold at night, the wool was welcome.

We did get some cotton uniforms when the Quartermaster emptied his warehouse by issuing 10,000 pairs of trousers, shirts and shorts for the 80,000 men engaged in this mountainous jungle warfare. They were a one-time issue.

Unfortunately, Bataan Peninsula was full of malaria, carried by the swarming Anopheles mosquito. This critter came out buzzing after midnight, but only at less than 800 meters altitude. In strong winds the mosquito might be temporarily blown to a higher elevation. Our more permanent bivouac areas were usually higher than the residence of these blood-meal insects.

A mosquito head net kept free of your face with a short piece of bamboo helped to protect you. Tucking the net inside your shirt and sleeping with the shirt sleeves rolled down and hands jammed in your pockets also helped. The idea of hands in pockets was credited by Capt. Bill Montgomery with decreasing the incidence of malaria by 30 percent in his Filipino outfit.

Despite protective measures, however, malaria increased. During April, the last days of our war, admissions for malaria at our two field hospitals totaled 1,000 cases daily. It became mandatory to initiate some prophylactic program. No more tablets were available, so we were issued the flaky powder of pure quinine sulfate. A teaspoonful was approximately five grains--the minimum daily prophylactic dose. This stuff, the most bitter medicine known to man, doesn't dissolve in water. A teaspoon of the suspension swallowed with water numbs your tongue and mouth for 24 hours or until the next medicine call is heard. It was so objectionable that a quinine roll call by name was necessary. The soldier stepped forward with his teaspoon, which was filled with the suspension. He must put it in his mouth within sight of the platoon sergeant, myself, and his company commander. It was absolute torture, horrible stuff, and was not effective as a cure, but probably would suppress the plasmodia if you had been bitten by the malaria-carrying Anopheles mosquito.

Aedes Aegypti, a dengue-fever carrying mosquito, resided here also. This illness resembled a flu with severe aching of the bones and so was dubbed "break bone fever." Although uncomfortable, it was not disabling. I had it one time before the war, but never recognized a second attack in Bataan. One of the peculiar symptoms of dengue was painful movements of your eyes. It hurt even to follow a pretty nurse with your eyeballs, and that is pretty devastating.

At the outbreak of hostilities, most Philippine Army units were ill-equipped. They had tin cans instead of mess kits, Enfield rifles which they had never fired, and pith helmets made of pineapple fiber. Nevertheless, they followed and obeyed the American officers to the bitter end--dying in their foxholes. Many of the Philippine reservists had less than three months' training.

These troops are not to be confused with the Philippine Scouts, who were regular army, the 26th Cavalry and the 45th and 57th Infantry Regiments. They, along with the 31st, were the toughest soldiers we had. Together, we made up the Philippine Division, commanded by Brig. Gen. Clifford Bluemel. He was quoted as saying, "The poorly trained Filipino enlisted men seemed to be proficient in only two things: one, when an officer appeared, to yell "attention" in a loud voice, jump up and salute; the other, to demand three meals a day." This was a poor evaluation of their worth.

Nevertheless, whatever they lacked in training, they made up with *esprit de corps* and personal bravery.

This bivouac area, our bamboo cathedral, afforded the rest we needed to recover from a battle-weary exhaustion. The respite offered me time to take stock of my own position. My values were changing. Wishing to survive and be the last man alive on Bataan became less attractive after frontline warfare. The 31st Regiment fought well, but gained little for themselves but the right to starve slowly, try again and probably fail.

After a few weeks of rest, necessity mothered an invention, a home-made bamboo aqueduct. Some of the larger bamboo stocks measuring five or six inches in diameter were split in half; the partitions were knocked out, making a continuous pipe. It was laid in a stream 500 meters up on the side of the hill and carried water into the center of the camp area. We thanked the Italians for spawning the original idea nearly 2,000 years before.

During the lull in the fighting during March, an invitation to visit came from Capt. John Wister Haines, Topside, Corregidor.

By barge, I crossed the five kilometers of water to John and his roommate Emil Merkle, another medical officer. Between air raids we sat on a sand bag outside the tunnel entrance and sipped our concoctions, grapefruit laced with grain alcohol lifted from the shelf of the Malinta Tunnel Hospital. He was another medico, and a University of Iowa graduate. A large fellow, John moved and talked with dignity but his handsome face was always close to a smile. When you met him, that face would always light up with the joy of a man spotting the last turn in the trail before reaching the campfire. If he suffered from the horrid conditions and prospects, he never voiced it. John Haines was my kind of fellow.

It was a far cry from a pre-war visit to John's island quarters when we had been "songsters off on a spree." As I recall, the highlight was using waffles as frisbees. I left Corregidor, glad my duty was in the jungle of Bataan. The tunnel was depressing to me.

Our paths crossed again in Bilibid prison after the surrender of Corregidor. He still remained the uncomplaining fellow and good soldier. In 1944, he drowned on a Japanese POW ship sunk by U.S. Navy bombers. He was a fine gentleman and a man I chose as a close friend. Our dream of putting up a Far East medical clinic vanished with his death.

The food ration decreased. In January it averaged roughly 2,000 calories, then dropped to 1,500 in February and 1,000 during March. It apeared that both the issue from the Quartermaster and the distribution of food was responsible. At times, the men on the trucks would throw off cartons of canned food and other goodies to their buddies at a prearranged destination. Even military police assigned to ride on the trucks didn't help. They had friends, too.

Although not issued regularly, complaints about Class C rations vintage 1918 were common, particularly about the biscuit or hard tack, bleached chocolate, caramelized coffee, and bully beef in the lower half of the tin can.

I finally sampled a can and thought it was gourmet. It just took time to dissolve the coffee and gnaw on the biscuit, but I had plenty of that. We were never fortunate to get a class C ration in the front lines. Only a small quantity had been stored on Corregidor.

By now a day's ration, less than 1,000 calories, consisted of two handfuls of rice, a small portion of canned fruit, a couple ounces of canned fish, an occasional hunk of meat, and, rarely, a few ounces of evaporated milk. An attempt was made to buy fish--perch and *bangus*, a native favorite--from Filipino fishermen in Manila Bay, but the Japs soon discovered this and the supply was cut off by Japanese patrol boats.

A few tropical birds, including cockatoo, macaws, parrots and other unnamed loud screeching birds, were hunted with shotguns, but were never offered to me. These guns were better used in routing snipers out of the heavy foliage. All of the native-owned carabaos and pigs on the Bataan Peninsula were funneled through the abbatoir and quickly devoured. Also gone were the choice calesa ponies used to pull two-wheel carriages for dray or human transportation.

The crack troops of the 26th Cavalry (Philippine Scouts), after withdrawing into Bataan, were soon dismounted by the

81

Quartermaster to provide us a few rations of mule meat.

Ranking the meats in order of palatability, calesa pony was first, mule second, horse third, carabao fourth, and monkey a poor last. Later in prison camp we had a chance to evaluate other smaller animals, including dogs, cats and rodents. The competition for palatability became academic as your hunger increased.

March slowly slipped away in a stalemate. Both sides were reeling from the casualties inflicted at Abucay. Our troop strength was decreasing at the rate of three or four per day from malaria, dengue fever, dysentery, jungle rot of the feet, and starvation. After the battles of Dinalupihan and Abucay Hacienda and a month in bivouac, our battalion had less than 300 effective soldiers. Our greatest enemy was fast becoming the three horsemen of the apocalypse--war, pestilence and starvation--which one were we ride to our doom?

The troops didn't complain about geckoes, iguanas, or snakes, but there was a real bitterness generated in forcing them to swallow the quinine sulfate and by the food disappearing in transit from the Quartermaster. Padding the unit roster to increase the number of rations was an old trick, but not practiced by the 31st regiment. The weight loss of the frontline troops had been dramatic--from 20 to 30 percent of their body weight. A 180-pound soldier would now weigh about 125-130 pounds. This was not necessarily so with the military police, quartermaster, and service units in the rear.

One night I was stretched on the ground asleep when I woke up to feel a snake slithering across my mid-section. It didn't pause but kept right on sliding across my belt line. I didn't raise my head nor move to identify the creature, but tried to calculate its length by the time it took for it to clear me from left to right. It must have been three to four meters long. Reputedly Frank Buck captured his boa constrictors in the Bataan Peninsula some years previously. I could only surmise that he had missed one. Later, a dead boa constrictor was on display in the rear area. It must have been over three meters long and three to four cms. in diameter. A pretty creature, and, they said, rather choice eating.

The story is told of the Filipino who was losing all his chickens to animals that plundered his flock at night. He decided on a strong woven wire cage to protect his two prize hens. One morning he went out to the pen only to find the two hens gone and a big boa constrictor curled inside the cage.

Capt. Art Wermouth ("One-Man Army," they called him) came by our bivouac area one day. Carrying an automatic weapon and bedecked with a bandoleer of ammunition, the swarthy fellow was followed by his own small heavily armed patrol and his beautiful Filipino sweetheart. I can still see her waist-length flowing black hair. He was a brave man--inflicting heavy casualties on the Japs with his night forays behind their lines. Later, even in prison camp at Lipa he stepped between a guard and a poor POW who was being beaten to death. He pushed the guard back, shouted, "We take care of our own," and got away with it.

His girlfriend reminded me of Pilar and the moonlight night we drove up the canyon to Pagsanjan Falls for a picnic. The water sparkled as it cascaded down the lip of the canyon. She spread a checkered cloth, covering it with a meal of braised chicken adobo, rice, warm bread wrapped in banana leaves, and mangoes. Over the wine, we talked of "the States"--my lifetime home, and hers for three years. Pilar's long black hair tossed in the jasmine-scented breeze. She was beautiful silhouetted in the moonlight. I couldn't wish for Petie to be with me now.

Once, Sgt. Smith, Cpl. Decker and I hiked down dusty, well-worn trail No. 2, the main foot thoroughfare from the frontline to the rear in the 2nd Corps. We wanted to see how regimental headquarters was doing and to visit my medical commander, Maj. Clarence White, the regimental surgeon. Clarence was a professional soldier, a good no-nonsense man, and a fair and capable person. even in this hurry-up-and-wait situation, he appeared to dislike interruptions or having his time wasted. Smiles and animation came hard to him as well as idle conversation. I admired him and felt that he would not use me carelessly. I did not expect him to give me orders that he himself would fail to carry out.

I wondered at times whether I would be relieved from frontline duty. Clarence never promised; I never asked. Not so with a little pipsqueak in the departmental surgeons office, whom I knew quite well and played golf with before the war. I happened to run into him back at regimental headquarters. He seemed rather embarrassed with our meeting and muttered, "I'm going to get you out of the front lines, Ralph, as soon as I can."

Time proved this to be a damned lie, and unnecessary from my standpoint. I felt that being on the frontlines with a good outfit was as good as any other assignment. If you are not there, you worry about moving up, so you might as well stay there and fight it out. I ate a meal with Clarence, far better than our battalion was offering. He had very little to say. He offered no encouragement nor "You're doing a good job," or "We're going to strike a medal for you," or other drivel.

After scouting the Jap landing behind our RLR on the west coast, during the Battle of the Points, we were put on red alert, but not committed. Instead we joined the fighting of the Battle of the Big Pocket and the Tuol Pocket, the two most serious threats. Some 1,000 Japanese had gotten in behind the reserve line of resistance, lost their way, and were encircled and trapped.

The battle went on for seven or eight days, the Japanese putting up a great deal of resistance since they had no place to go. The 2nd Battalion helped close the circle as fire poured in.The "head-hunting" Negritoes and bow-hunting igorots, primitive tribes from the northern provinces of Luzon, who were loyal to our cause, were hoisted on top of our tanks. They hung on and plowed through the entangled jungle throwing grenades and shooting revolvers with their free right hand. There was so much killing the jungle stank with the odor of the dead.

The Igorots and the Negritoes taught survival in the jungle to our boys and, incidentally, ate their own dogs. Another custom was eating a dog's stomach which had been gorged with rice before sacrificing it. The warm rice mixed with the mucus of the stomach supposedly was a delicacy.

When resistance was nearly ended in the Battle of the Tuol Pocket, the Japanese, carrying their wounded on poles and on their backs, started across an open ridge, presumably to surrender to a Filipino unit. They selected this particular unit since they had been less effective in firepower than any of the other encircling units. As the Japanese carried their bandaged and wounded buddies and the last straggling survivors crossed the ridge, the Filipino troops opened fire, killing many of them. Several hundred Japs finally escaped to the north, reaching their own lines after four days of wandering in the jungle with almost no food or water.

After the surrender, one of the first questions the Japs asked prisoners of war was, "Were you at Tuol Pocket?" I answered emphatically, "No, sir, I was clear at the other end of the peninsula. In fact, I've never heard of it."

Gen. MacArthur with a party of 21 persons stealthily departed from the Philippines, leaving Corregidor on the 20th of March 1942 in four PT boats. Lt. John D. Bulkeley's passengers included Jean MacArthur, the general's brave and charming wife; his son, Arthur, and the child's Chinese nursemaid, Ah Chuh. The rest were staff officers of the Air force, Navy, and Army. The departure became public knowledge on the front some three or four days later. The news was of no great moment. I thought it was pretty jolly. I wished him a successful trip and hoped he could get some re-inforcements in Australia and furnish us with some fighting equipment and regular meals.

Most of the troops on Bataan never really resented "Dugout Doug's" leaving. There was nothing he could do here except write more letters to Roosevelt and Gen. George Marshall, the Army Chief of Staff. To us, neither of them seemed particularly interested in the war in the Pacific. My notion did not hold his departure as fleeing in the face of the enemy. A direct order from the President finally compelled MacArthur to depart. The general said, "I shall return," which he did two and a half years later. Incidentally, he only made it once and I've returned twice. The sequel and last sentiments by the Battling Bastards of Bataan was, "I shall never return."

A story which circulated in Bataan found the first soldier talking to his new acquaintance, "I've been in Gen. MacArthur's mess," he boasted. The second retorted, "I was in a mess with him also."

Capt. George Campbell popped into our camp one day, quite unannounced. I hadn't seen him since before the war. He was from California, a medical officer with whom I had shared duties Stateside and in Manila. Spotting me, he said, "Let's have a little talk about getting off this peninsula when we surrender." I hesitated. It startled me and he noticed my reaction.

"You know damned well help is not on the way," he chided.

"You might as well accept it." George was a realist and rather persuasive.

Bill Tooley joined us as we became serious in our plans for hiding food, compass and a native boat. George had already spotted a double outrigger banca in a small cove below Calibobo Point on the China coast. We ended by promising George we would do our best to cache some canned goods off the main East-West road below Lamay. Cpl. Decker who later was invited to join us, managed to secure some supplies, including a flashlight, and a few weeks later hid them in a musette bag in a deep thicket just south of Lamay.

Several more planning sessions were held on the slopes of Mt. Samat. The plans helped our morale but I always harbored serious doubts as to their feasibility.

One day, as George Campbell turned to leave he asked, "Did you hear about George Williams?"

"No, not a thing," I responded.

"Well, he was killed last week in front of the church at Lamay. He was riding his crazy 'mortalcycle,' stopped to chat, leaving the motor running, when a dive bomber spotted him and laid a bomb almost on top of him. With the motor noise he never knew the plane was diving. He was killed instantly.

I hadn't seen George since our Fiesta Pavilion dinner the night before the war started. He was the first of our Whiffenpoof Boys to be killed. George, his wife and his mother and I all had dinner together in San Francisco before sailing. I choked at the thought of the news reaching them, I couldn't stop swallowing.

Campbell shrugged his shoulders, said we had better get ready to go, and disappeared down the trail.

Our foraging for food was rewarded by finding a banana grove on the slopes of Mt. Samat. Unfortunately, the discovery was shared with other troops, who stripped it, leaving only the purple-plumed embryo blossom of the immature banana. It grows out like a head of German cabbage. When diced, it is similar to coleslaw--quite tasty and sweet. The foraging crews also found an old deserted pineapple field well hidden by cogon grass. The pineapples were runted, sour little creatures, about the size of an orange with some nutrition in them, but the resulting diarrhea gave us a negative nutritional balance.

Huge isolated mango trees were scattered all over Bataan. The luscious and sought-after fruit ripened in March. It was a first-come, first-served proposition. Several of the trees were spotted in our many moves, but a particular one behind Abucay was loaded with fruit. Decker and I set out one afternoon and after an hour's hike, we spotted the tree, only to find the fruit all gone, save for one mammoth mango perched on the very top limb. I threw rocks and sticks for two hours trying to dislodge it. Decker kept encouraging me with words like, "Come on, Captain, you'll never get it." Finally, my favorite fruit came tumbling down. After three days of ripening, it was consumed with not just a little satisfaction.

As the stalemated siege continued into April, we decided to build a lean-to as protection during the rainy season, three months away. Ten-foot bamboo poles were split lengthwise, and after knocking out the partition, they were interlaced like a Spanish tile roof. Fortunately, the campaign did not extend into June, the start of the rainy season.

"The Japs have a new weapon," reported Sgt. Lawton one day. "A balloon in the sky. You can only see it through an opening in the steeple of our bamboo thicket."

He led me to a dense thicket where the towering stalks crowned 30 meters above us. A small chink remained in the cathedral tower. By maneuvering around, we could see a small shining round object seemingly fixed in the sky on the Jap side of the battlefront. The report spread rapidly and widely, "Keep under cover." After tracking the "balloon" for a day and into the night with the help of an amateur astronomer, the "balloon" was diagnosed as a star with daytime sighting. The sky visible through the towering bamboo made a natural telescope, which sharpened our vision. I remembered Dad reported this phenomena when peering out of a well. I wished more of the enemy weapons would have disappeared into the universe.

However, the Japs did possess an observation unit that used real balloons. Later, one was clearly spotted over Lamao along Manila Bay. It was used as an observation post for an artillery spotter during the bombardment of Corregidor.

Spectacular sunsets over the China Sea were offered almost every evening with majestic billowing cumulus clouds hued with pink and orange, 15,000 to 20,000 meters up. The price of admission for this show should have been free instead of a horrible war. We anticipated the evening display for its beauty, tranquility and because it meant one more day of this macabre war with the noise of battle, the cry of the wounded, the smell of burning powder had been put behind us. the quiet and beauty of the tropical setting sun held sway for a short time. Even the cicadas and the birds silenced by rocking explosions all day, came on with a hum and a lyric. Soon it would be time for the night-time Jap infiltrators and artillery bombardment orchestrated by the buglers. After two to three minutes of bugling, there would be a command shouted in Japanese. "There's the incoming mail," yelled a G.I., and then the earth-shattering explosion of enemy shells.

Darkness also meant supper--and the mosquitoes.

I felt quite well but hungry during this time. My guts ached, the gnaw of hunger was not exhaustive. Each meal lights the flame of hunger like throwing gas on a dying fire. There were too many bugs, ants and snakes but we could live with them.

My guts also ached from the agony of impending defeat. I was a participant in a lousy game. One side hides in holes and starves while the other blows bugles and shoots guns hoping to kill or starve the other so they can occupy a disease-infested, blood-sodden, worthless jungle. Strange people that foster doom on others.

Gen. Bluemel tried unsuccessfully to unlock stores of food on Corregidor to share with troops on the peninsula. We probably would never have received it anyway. The enormity of the un-planned migration of Filipino civilians into Bataan sealed our doom from starvation. In reality, the Corregidor stores of food for 100,000 people for 30 days had long since been exhausted. In all, the ration was halved three times, so in the end, we couldn't live much longer, let alone fight.

10. THE FINAL BATTLE OF BATAAN

Permission was granted to write a letter home, supposedly to be smuggled out by U.S. submarine. So, on 15 February 1942, the following letter was given to our red-headed chaplain, Bob Taylor, for dispatch:

> Life is not too bad. I have a bamboo bed, a blanket, plenty of water, a few too many mosquitoes. The food is fair --carabao, monkey and occasionally mule. Everyone is content and in fairly good health. No need to worry.
>
> We have plenty of room in which to maneuver and fight and we have plenty of it left in us. Turn the calf out to pasture.
>
> I'll be delayed awhile. Ralph.

On 15 March 1942, the above letter was delivered one month later, to Oskaloosa, Iowa. This was the last message my folks would get from me for a year.

Under the title "Things Are Not Too Bad," it was published in both the *Des Moines Register* and the *Cleveland Free Press*. Supposedly, this was to be a morale booster for the home folks.

On the 4th of April, just at dusk, Maj. Moffit queried me, his heavy-browed eyes showing worry: "How many men of the 225 on the morning roster can march one mile with battle gear?"

"Possibly two-thirds--somewhere around 150 to 175," I answered hesitantly. "Forced all-night marches are just beyond the capacity of most of these men."

"Well, the final big Jap offensive all along the line opened yesterday," he muttered, his jaw muscles rippling. "You'll have to count the effectives; evacuate no one who can walk and fight. There's no tomorrow in this jungle fight." Resignedly he turned and disappeared to try to sleep with his heavy burden. I shared his load. This little man had arrived as a leader.

I was kind of dreading tomorrow's job of sorting out sick and not so sick. In reality every soldier knew his condition better than I did. I thought of Civil War times when the Army exam consisted of the nude inductee jumping stiff-legged off a three-foot stool, and if nothing fell off he was in the service. If this criteria was applied to the Bataan remnants, those qualifying would not fill out the bugle corps.

In truth, of the 77,000 Filipino-American soldiers left in the command, 27,000 were reported combat effective and only 7,000 were really healthy.

During the hot sultry night, orders came to move forward. Our line was crumbling. Help was needed now; the situation was desperate. Out of the original 700 men in the Battalion, 128 volunteers stood up, put on their packs and moved out for the front. Everybody tried to get to the front. Some fell out after a few kilometers. Others left their hospital beds and joined us. They said, "Let's die at the front instead of at a hospital." Everybody tried. Bravery was a universal quality.

We put casualty tags on those that couldn't march, assuring them "Someone will help you," a far cry from the proud 31st U.S. Infantry Regiment--Manila's Own--the USAFFE's Reserve-- the King's Guard--MacArthur's Elite--the U.S.'s only foreign legion. The Regiment had never been Stateside. Now was the last time for its leaders to call names, kick ass, and move out. The thin line slowly shuffled up the dark trail shedding the last shards of comfort. We were on our way to help.

During the night many of the men on the march, passing through the cane field, emerged with a short stalk sticking jauntily out of the corner of their mouth like a big cigar or Mr. Roosevelt's cigarette holder. It provided quick energy, fluids, a morale boost, but also Queen Isabella's syndrome--diarrhea, from the raw sugar. We struggled on.

All night my detachment, now down to 16 effective men, trudged uphill. We had nothing heavy to carry. I had a first aid kit over my shoulder, a musette bag and the ever-present gas mask. My extra pair of olive green socks were in my left back pocket. One field locker was aboard the only remaining usable ambulance. Without the moon, and with my night blindness resulting from a Vitamin A-deficient diet, several hours passed before I adapted to the narrow winding jungle trail.

At midnight we bivouacked on the southeast slope of Mt. Samat near the end of the trail. It was virgin country for the second battalion. This night as I lay on the ground, mosquito bar over my head and hands in pockets, waiting for sleep, I heard someone close by say, "Ralph, are you there?" I recognized Hunkins' voice.

"Ya, Dwight. What's up?"

"Oh, I don't know. I can't sleep and I can't get the thought out of my mind. I'm positive I'll never make it through this mess. I miss my wife so much tonight. My grief is I'll never see her again --what I should have told her. And my little daughter, never to be part of my life again."

He sobbed. "This damned army." It was pretty strong stuff for a West Pointer. Dwight rolled away from me. Repeatedly during the night I woke to hear him struggling with himself--thrashing around. I didn't have a wife or kids, but I loved the prospect of them.

The morning sun on the 5th of April blazed dully in a cerulean sky, and the jungle steamed in response. The light on the jungle floor was dappled by shadows from the flimsy champaca trees. It provided glimpses through tangled vines and underbrush of hazy Manila Bay and Pilar's city, 40 kms. to the east. To the west and in front of us were the mountain spines of Mt. Samat, supporting the interwoven green mat of the jungle hillsides. Sheltered most of the time by the deep shadows, we struggled up Trail No. 2 most of the 5th of April to reach the trouble spots.

Along the way, some of our soldiers spotted another cane field down the slope. Defying the Zero strafers, the troops soon emerged from the cane brake with a good supply of all-day suckers; and then they were spotted. Three planes peeled off and dove straight towards our boys, guns chattering. "Take cover," someone shouted and all hit the ground. Three were wounded and lost to our dwindling forces.

We struggled into an abandoned Philippine Army position as Pfc. Jimmy Smith yelled at me. There, slumped in their foxholes, were two dead Filipino soldiers who never deserted but fought until hit. It gave me pause in considering the bravery of our ally. Stories circulated that Filipinos had to be chained to their guns to prevent desertion. Those tales were false. A well trained Filipino was as good as any other soldier in the world.

Funny, I thought, the color of one's skin does not distinguish between friend or enemy.

We approached the frontline just before dusk. The firing became intense, particularly mortars and the Nips' damnable 105s howitzers. We began taking casualties. Darkness brought an end to the shooting. An ominous silence followed with the realization that the frontline and our destiny was near. This ends the whole mess, I thought; the waiting is over. We obviously lose, but some of you yellow-bellied sons of bitches are coming along with us. The stillness pressed too hard on some of the soldiers. Four months of fighting, trying to kill and win, turned into hopelessness, the greatest personal enemy of a soldier. One is never more alone than when without hope. The short-lived tranquility was broken by rifle shots nearby, isolated at first, echoing across the ravine-separated hillsides. And then, strangely, several more.

My God, I thought, no, it can't be, the soldiers are shooting themselves. In a few minutes, two, then one more, self-inflicted wounded limped into our aid station, usually by themselves. They came without buddies, or medics. They were alone and beaten.

The three gaunt, starry-eyed GIs sat in the dirt holding a boot in one hand and a bloody foot in the other. Their eyes were downcast and tearful. They had opted tonight to end their fighting this way. The explosion and the pain brought one soldier back to reality. He didn't try to explain, but ended up head down and sobbing. I understood. No one measured his bravery. After stopping the bleeding, bandaging and a shot of morphine, I turned to Beattie. "Get 'em back to Trail No. 2 and the Road Junction and leave em. The ambulance will pick them up tomorrow."

Poor devils, they could fight but they couldn't endure the waiting. Home was never farther away. Their buddies rot in a cane brake at Abucay Hacienda. Their minds wander to home, the thin protective veneer shielding it from reality crumbles. "Yes, I see it now, Mother coming from the kitchen, smiling, something special for you--date pudding." The remembrance flashes by, the emotion swells in their chest, the voice chokes and tears flow. A voice tells them, "An escape, a way out, settle it now. My 30-06 provides a solution." The options before a battle become vague and restrictive, since a strong and aggressive enemy denies them. The agony of helplessness overwhelms the fear of impending death. Tonight we are crossing our River Rubicon. The sight and care of the wounded GIs gave me something to do, but even more vital, it produced an emotional diversion.

Who knows how a dog-face soldier feels peering over his machine gun looking for his enemy in his last hour of combat?

"I'll rattle it again just to keep them off balance," the gunner may think. "It's quiet now—I'm alone and surely the bastards out there are not sneaking up on me. Just another burst to be sure so I can hunker down and relax. Now I'm sure it's safe—to wander off a few thousand miles to home. Gosh, I wonder if they ever imagine me in a foxhole on a jungle hillside in the merciless tropical sun? Maybe I'm scared but I can't tell you that 'cause I'm supposed to be a brave soldier. Did you ever picture yourself in the same position as a combat soldier? How did you come out? I hope you didn't just turn your back to reality. I hope not, 'cause someone has to do it. I'm alone again. I can hear noises, funny noises in the jungle, not birds, tree climbers or snakes, but just possible enemy noises. I'll clear that bamboo thicket with a spray from old reliable. It's lonely again and boring duty. My gosh! That's mortar tumbling in. I'm in real trouble. Hope Mom and Dad realize what's happening before it's all over. Kersplam. Please God, say goodbye for me."

To die on a battlefield, the glorification by Rudyard Kipling notwithstanding or to fight in a tattered uniform, a long way from home, in a foreign country with a strange tongue, hungry and without any real chance of success, left my dreams unfulfilled. Yet we continued to fight. I figured myself as a poor soldier, but a Class I patriot. What the hell, we made it to the finals and maybe to the last man.

Interdictory Jap fire began at 2000 hours that night, introduced by the damnable bugle corps and then 105 battery fire. Smoke from brush and bamboo fires billowed skyward. An eerie orange sunset haze blanketed the jungle thickets and hillsides of our mountain massif, Mt. Samat. Large sectors of the reserve line of resistance had disappeared, and forward salients existed. Heavy Jap infiltration in the dense thickets made it impossible to distinguish friendly from enemy fire.

After a short break our column struggled slowly uphill on Trail No. 2 until almost midnight. All was quiet when suddenly firing began not more than 200 meters to the rear. Maj. Collier, G-2 from Regimental Headquarters, with a reconnaissance patrol, was ambushed just behind us. We dove into the jungle as the Jap 25-caliber rifle fire came zinging from both sides of the trail. Immediate machine gun counterfire silenced them. I heard a call "medic," and found the major badly wounded but not complaining. One other soldier was killed. With a flashlight, I opened the major's shirt to discover a neat red spot front and back. A 25-caliber slug had penetrated through his right chest.

Maybe he'll make it, I thought as my corpsman carried him down the trail.

Six dead Japs paid the price for that ambush. The order came for the leg-weary troops to fall out for the night. Widely scattered and sporadic small arms fire interrupted the remainder of a fitful night's sleep.

Dawn revealed our position in an old organized defense area with well-used foxholes on the eastern slopes and overlooked by the peak of Mt. Samat. Steep cliffs guarded the approaches to the mountaintop. Plans called for a 0700 hour "thunderous" barrage preceding our counterattack, but all we heard was desultory fire. By 0900 hours, close-range artillery shells began whirring among us. I shuddered with the realization the Japs had secured the top of "our mountain," Mt. Samat, and had placed a small howitzer there to fire down our throats. This was catastrophic. Mt. Samat, 640 meters high, a commanding spikey peak with jagged crags and steep hillsides, was interlaced with trails clear to the summit. At times they were only two to three meters wide, already dusty from thousands of footsteps. They were the perfect route for movement of the foot soldier.

Companies "E" and "G" advanced 400-500 meters over a couple of small ridges. The fire and resistance became intense.

"Give 'em 25 rounds of mortar, and then take cover. This is a retaliatory weapon, you know," said Col. Charles L. Steel, who had just come forward from regimental headquarters to assume command of the 2nd Battalion.

Soon our three-inch Stokes mortar shells were landing among the Japanese, now separated from us by 150 meters of brambled ridge. Each explosion evoked great cries of anguish. Japs yell and writhe when hit while an American clinches his teeth and lies quiet. I wonder why.

Our barrage ended and, sure enough, the Japs returned the

fire. They were masters with mortars. Reportedly, they used a small knee mortar capable of catching up with a man running at full speed. Later that day we were startled by a swishing sound of an overhead projectile followed in a few seconds by a huge explosion in the enemy lines. It was the shriek of rotating bands on a12-inch mortar tumbling through the sky. They were fired from Battery Way on Corregidor at a range of 20,000 meters. The killing radius was 400 meters, but as it turned out these mortars were the only heavy armament still capable of firing. Without any advance observation posts, we doubted their effectiveness.

A large dug-out, four meters square and over a meter deep, was the first aid station. No one was ever tried for stealing a foxhole; we just borrowed this one. Shrapnel wound casualties appeared. They were bandaged, then moved down the trail to a road where hopefully an ambulance might show up. We traded mortar fire until about 1200 hours. Soon the whole hillside shuddered with incoming artillery and mortar explosions, crackling with murderous small arms fire. Heavy smoke blanketed us. Both sides were slugging it out.

While talking to two GIs just outside the first aid dugout, an explosion turned me around. I really thought it was my hip pocket. Patting myself and finding no blood, I realized that both soldiers were hit. The soldier on my left received leg shrapnel. The soldier on the right was pointing at his neck. Blood was gushing from a clean, transverse laceration which had severed the trachea, inflicting a tracheostomy (surely without informed consent). Leaning him forward to prevent a bloody aspiration, and with pressure on both jugulars, the bleeding soon stopped. Advising him not to eat or drink anything until under hospital care, we bandaged the bloody area and pointed him to the rear. He was glad to go and be able to walk. A swarm of flies followed the poor devil down the trail. Later in prison camp he identified himself, pointing to the collar scar and admitted, "I never missed a meal." A medical officer told me they discovered the lad in chow line even before he got to the medical officer.

Overnight we inherited a new Battalion Commander. Major Moffit was replaced by Col. "Bud" Marron, tall, straight, and grey-haired. A good soldier. No explanation was ever given. Possibly the failure to win at Abucay and establish the MLR was a factor but no one ever hinted it was command failure. Moffit had developed leadership qualities and his performance was consistent with them.

Col. Marron, thrown into an impossible combat situation under intense pressure, pleaded on the phone to regimental headquarters for orders to withdraw. We had failed to make friendly contact on the right and had denied the Japs our left flank with only the jungle protecting our position.

By 1500 hours we were receiving fire from three sides, the most damaging and intense coming from our left, down the ridge from Mt. Samat. Tearfully, the colonel begged for retreat orders. It looked to me as if the old 2nd Battalion had just about had it.

"Do you want the second battalion destroyed here?" he pleaded in a quavering voice.

I felt sorry for him, and wondered if Maj. Moffit would ever have made a personal request for relief. Later Bud became violently ill and had to be evacuated.

In this battle, I saw several good soldiers who crept forward, firing from a different location to quiet yet another machine gun and then--it happened to them--the searing numbness, the fainting, the last call of "I'm falling. Litter team, litter team." Another brave soldier finished the course.

Men wounded by 25-caliber bullets and mortar-shrapnel wounded staggered into the open pit first aid station. The grim-faced GIs suffered quietly, hoping for another crack at the Japs.

"How long have you been bleeding? Can you walk?" I asked. "The last bus was ambushed trying to get out, so I'd wait until dark and hit the trail to the rear."

By the next morning the walking wounded had disappeared, hopefully to a rear medical unit. The evacuation problem, a serious one now, was eased when at noon an ambulance picked up six non-ambulatory wounded. The drivers reassured me a road-block to our rear had been cleared. They took off and made it, although heavy fire sprayed the ambulance shortly after leaving us. An old school bus loaded with wounded departed a few minutes later but ran into small arms fire and caught fire. All on the bus and ambulance were lost.

"Capt. Hibbs, Captain," someone yelled.

I stumbled forward saying, "Yep, you got him."

"I'm Sgt. Gary Doyle, one of your ambulance drivers. I just want to report that Hospital No. 1 at Little Baguio has gas gangrene in the wounds. I understand it is widespread and pretty bad. Thought you ought to know."

"Thanks, Gary," I muttered, weighing the transformation of that hospital into a pest house. "Don't think I'd want to go there now. . . . Incidentally, Gary, take it easy on the road out of here. The Nips are all over the place," I shouted.

Earlier that day I had examined a lad in deep coma with a shrapnel wound in the head. He had Cheyne-Stokes breathing, a waxing and waning respiration, usually a terminal event. Within a few minutes the breathing would change from fast and shallow to slow and deep. A bloody grey matter oozed from a left temporal wound. The wound and drainage were depressurizing the head injury.

"Leave him in the shade. He's not going to make it," I advised.

Checking him again just before the battalion withdrew I found him alive with breathing more stable and a pulse of better quality. Our plans didn't call for abandoning wounded to the enemy.

I motioned to Beattie.

"I can carry him," he volunteered, hoisting the man onto his shoulders and ambling down the trail

A queer sight--the poor lad's bloody head dangling over my corpsman's shoulders as the medical detachment led the way to the rear down the jungle-canopied Trail No. 44. Both legs of the corpsman's pants were streaked with blood. With each withdrawal the comatose GI, still alive, was lugged towards the rear. Later that night he was deposited in a medical collecting company and forgotten. About two years later, while in prison camp, a GI approached me rather abruptly, but good-naturedly.

"You don't know who I am, do you?" he asked with a smug expression.

"Golly, soldier, give me one more clue," I said jokingly.

"Well, Captain, I'm the guy with the shrapnel wound in the head you were going to leave under a bush at Mt. Samat. Remember?"

Gasping, I responded, "My God, no! Boy, do I remember you.

Your chances were slim. In fact, I thought you were a dead duck."
I paused. "I guess the brain injury just naturally decompressed
itself."

We both slapped each other on the back.

"Just shows you what good medical care will do for a fellow,"
I remarked solemnly. "You've got lead in your head. Most people
have it in their ass."

He laughed and thanked me, repeating his gratitude on several other occasions.

During the night, the battalion was ordered to withdraw. We
woke with the brilliant morning sun casting thin shadows through
the tangled vines like spider webs. The jungle was alive with enemy patrols. A large gap existed in our new line. Our position was
in the vicinity of Trail No. 2 and the San Vicente River. The trail
dropped sharply down a deep rocky ravine to the water. The canyon was so steep the men could hardly lug their machine guns up
the south wall. By now the exhaustion was overwhelming. Hardly
fit for combat they continued to fight without complaint. We had
been on the move; day and night, for over 72 hours. Not much
more could be expected of us. As one commander was reported
to have said, "Even if my troops were unopposed they couldn't
crawl forward on their hands and knees." Disintegration and disorganization of the unit was becoming all too evident. It was fast
becoming a running jungle fight.

About an hour before sundown on the 7th, the remnants of
the 2nd Battalion had struggled up the steep trail, finally reaching
the south rim of the Pantingan River. The trail branched out on
the rocky hillside so that some groups separated and a few of our
dwindling number became lost. March discipline in a running
jungle fight became impossible.

One 30-caliber machine gun crew of three reached a promontory with a shallow dugout overlooking both rocky banks of the
river. An old grim-jawed sergeant, crying and cussing, loaded
with bandoleers of ammo, slammed the gun into the pit and
snarled, "This is as far as we go. I'm not backing up any farther."

We moved down the trail, but before plunging into the ebony
shadows of the jungle, I turned to see the three scanning the
canyon for targets. Soon their gun opened up at the emerging
Jap skirmish line across the river. The first line and then the se-

cond line went down. Mortars from the Japs retaliated, then more rapid fire followed. The noise of the private battle continued for an hour, until just about dark when we heard several huge explosions and silence. Three brave men had seen their duty and did it. They had tried desperately to convert the Japs to our way of thinking. They gave us an hour to regroup and set up a thin line and, thank God, to carry our wounded with us. Some of my corpsmen were separated. We just guessed where headquarters was. That evening our detachment moved again.

Just at dark we rounded a corner of the trail following a pistol-packing officer. He suddenly and without any announcement shipped out his Smith and Wesson and fired one time. We moved forward 20 meters in the growing dusk and found a Jap, dead on the trail with a bullet hole in his forehead. We later learned the officer whom I had never seen before had been on a marksmanship team. He deserved another medal.

One of my corpsmen yelled, "I can see the soles of his shoes."

Just off the trail was a U.S. soldier, dead from multiple chest wounds. After rolling him over, a lump was discovered under his wool shirt--a book, *Look Homeward, Angel*. Scribbled inside the front leaf, punctuated by blotches of blood was:

Janet dear,
I'm not going to make it home. I've looked homeward oh so long. All my love to you and the girls.

Below: "Whoever finds this book, please carry it on and hopefully Janet someday will get it." It was signed, "Tim."

Later, the book showed up in prison camp, but as the unconfirmed story goes, not until after two couriers had been killed.

Cpl. Decker, myself along with two others of my detachment, and the two Filipino corpsmen, Juan and Ruperto, finally quit the jungle trail. We lay down and rested. No one called us for chow. When we awoke, we were alone and lost. In the darkness we had become separated from the main body. My last thought in the twilight of sleep was, Surely my country would not desert her soldiers in the field. Are we who are so far from home privileged to ask where is the help? At that time we were the only American soldiers defending the American flag in combat. We needed am-

99

munition, food and medicine—now!

"Oh, God, help us now," I mumbled. Juan bent over me and asked quietly, "Can I help you, sir?"

"No, I'll make it even if we have to back up and take another run for it."

Dawn of the 8th of April came before I opened my eyes. The sun was still around, the birds chirping and the battlefield quiet. Smoke from the numerous jungle and grass fires swirled around us. We bummed a meal from a medical receiving company which we stumbled on, and took off down a trail for the main east road. Turning north up the road, we dodged dive bombers and headed toward our cache of food and equipment. We found only stragglers moving away from the front.

They warned, "The Japs are coming down this road."

The canned milk, Spam, a flashlight, compass and even the musette bag that had been well hidden in a thicket were missing. With this our hopes for escape were almost gone. We turned back south. Furthermore, our vinta was hidden in a cove clear on the other side of Bataan. Without a compass, our escape by sea was hardly possible anyway. The plan was falling apart. Our options were evaporating.

We arrived at Hospital No. 2, which was mass confusion, overrun with sick and wounded. I found Maj. Clinton Maupin, the able adjutant who warned that "surrender is imminent." He looked mighty discouraged. "We only have one week's supply of quinine left," he said. The medical struggle was winding down. We learned that Campbell was in the hospital with dysentery.

After a 15-minute search of the wards, I found George naked, looking blindly towards the ceiling of the tent. He looked pretty sick to me. His handsome face, crowned by jet-black hair was punctuated by sunken eyes, typical of dehydration.

After considerable talking, I convinced him that he was better off in the jungle with us. He obediently put on his dirty, worn khaki pants and we disappeared down the trail.

On this day, the 8th, the Quartermaster reported to the commanding general of Bataan forces, Gen. King, that one day's food remained for his command. In the past four months, in an attempt to feed 86,000 civilians, 12,000 Americans, 20,000 Filipino regulars, and 100,000 Filipino reservists in Bataan, the

Quartermaster had slaughtered 1,000 carabaos, 250 horses, and 48 mules from the 26th Cavalry and all the *calesa* ponies, wild pigs, chickens that he could beg, borrow or steal. A carabao selling for $200 at the outset of the Bataan campaign soared in value to $2000, if available, by surrender time in April 1942. During the campaign an attempt was made to raise *bangus*, a native carp, in fish ponds. This fish, revered by the Japs as symbolic of courage, reached sufficient size in three months to feed five or six people. Bangus, iguana lizards, and snakes were nothing more than gourmet foods adding practically nothing to the dwindling general ration.

Our little group drifted south along the clogged trail. By late afternoon, men of the battalion straggled by. One recognized me and stopped.

"Maj. Moffit was killed an hour ago. A dive bomber laid one on the trail near him. He died instantly with shrapnel in the head," he recited sadly. Despite being relieved of his command, he had stayed on and died with the 31st.

Soldiers told me later that Moffit had teamed up with Col. Jack Brady, a fearless soldier, CO of the 1st Battalion, in a last-ditch effort to establish a line. They stopped small groups of American GIs, who were straggling down the trails and turned them around. About 100 men from the regiment were rallied together north of Cabcaben for a futile stand. Soon after Moffit was hit.

This brave little man was gone. Everything for him was ended, the race run. I nodded solemnly and silently.

"The surrender order has been announced. We are released to go into the jungle," the 2nd Battalion soldier said and trudged on down the trail. It was "everyone for himself."

On this, the final day of fighting, the Jap artillery seemed to have a lot of excess ammunition and the bombers had a most destructive day as well as starting fires with incendiary bombs in the dry cogon grass. They apparently had figured out the trail grid. Consequently, the bombs repeatedly hit the crowded trails. The Japanese fought like they wanted to finish us off before sundown.

The communique of February flashed back all too clearly, "Help is on the way." The food, guns, planes and men would never reach us. We were alone, deserted, in the last stages of exhaustion, a defeated army. The battling bastards of Bataan were broke and hungry. Those who live on hope die hungry.

Even on 8 April, an effort was made to have Gen. King release the 31st for fighting on Corregidor. I never knew for sure whether an order was issued, but at least we never received it. Supposedly, the plans were for barging us across the five kms. of water from Mariveles on the southern tip of Bataan to "the Rock."

That night, three of my corpsmen, two attached Filipinos, the extent of my detachment, George and myself, rendezvoused in the ditch beside the windy road to Mariveles, the Zigzag near Hospital No. 1. Our location seemed advantageous to either report to Hospital No. 1 and Col. Duckworth, where we could observe the Japs advancing down the road, or slip into the jungle for an escape. I felt weak and choleric from too much walking and not enough food. Weary, footsore, hungry and bewildered, the six of us had been without hot food for three days. My guts ached, yet the realization of the end to this damned jungle massacre evoked a relief.

Even though defeated on the battlefield, I was grateful for my own survival. Bomb craters bordering on my foxhole, hot shrapnel in my trench, bullets clipping bushes above my head, any one of a hundred instances might have been the end of my life. I was well aware of the seriousness, but I figured it was going to get you, and you, but not me. But, if the end comes, I hoped, someone nearby would face Mt. Samat and whisper for me, "Thank you for this life given, however short it may be."

Fortunately, this Filipino jungle combat mission was predestined not to end my life at 26 years.

Suddenly I began to chill, my teeth rattled, my bones ached-- I had malaria! Taking two aspirins, cuddling up in a ball, I realized the door to escape had just slammed shut. Decker said he'd give me some quinine, but he couldn't find any in my first aid kit. I knew there wasn't any. I drank a canteen of water and dozed restlessly. I was pretty disorganized that night.

The Zigzag was clogged with stumbling Filipino and American troops moving to the south away from the frontlines. Several wounded men, bleeding heavily, needed reinforcing bandages which we supplied. We dispensed a few pain pills. Decker and Smith carried a Filipino with a bloody arm of bone and torn muscle dangling at his side into the hospital area. It was just routine for them.

Without warning, a terrific detonation rocked the mountain. A big yellow ball of fire rolled up less than 500 meters away up the trail beyond Hospital No. 1. Rocks and shells, duds and live rounds, came hurtling down. It was the beginning of the destruction of the ammunition dumps by our own demolition squads. The air rocked for several hours with gigantic explosions. Still chilling, I finally found safety in a ditch. With each blast my body would bounce clear into the air.

The sky, mountains, and the whole countryside were illuminated. It was the biggest fireworks display, the Iowa State Fair notwithstanding, I've ever seen. A harbinger of the end and surrender. Duds landed around us, but I didn't worry because these were American made. This was the final destruction of USAFFE --the United States Armed Forces in the Far East--108 tanks, 12,000 U.S. servicemen, 20,000 Filipino regulars, and 100,000 Filipino reservists.

Later that very night I woke up with the earth shaking and the trees swishing. "You'd think it was an earthquake,"I muttered, raising up on one elbow. There was no ball of fire or ear-splitting explosion to associate with a man-made destructive weapon. My faithful Filipino runner answered, "Sir, it *is* an earthquake." I settled back into the sleeping position, then did a doubletake and jumped up. After a few moments of consideration, I lay back down, quite resigned to this seemingly harmless situation. Earthquakes, God-made, seemed mild in comparison with man-made frontline tricks.

Before going back to sleep, I called my two Filipino corpsmen, Juan and Ruperto, and chatted about the impending surrender. We squatted there in the dark with the explosions lighting up our faces. Ruperto, a handsome lad, was a *cafe au lait*-tinted native with the instincts of a bloodhound. I gave them the choice of becoming guerrillas or surrendering with the unit. Difficult as it was to maintain the will to fight, they still did not want to surrender.

"They both cried, "I will not surrender."

"You'll do more good to go into the jungle," I counseled in a low voice.

They talked together, shook hands with me, then moved off into the night, the jungle and the unknown. I never saw them again. Their loyalty was never exceeded by anyone else's in my detachment.

Smoke from the destroyed ammunition dumps swirled over us, intermittent explosions disturbed our sleep, the smell of death permeated the jungle.

The Japs will soon come charging, I thought. Let the worst come; after four months of jungle combat I really don't give a damn. I've seen it and lived it from all sides. A tomorrow (probably tomorrow) will see the end of this struggle, which has become a living death. Who yearns for survival when tomorrow holds no promise? I've been struggling long enough to keep from slipping into the inferno.

Capture, moving inexorably closer, seemed impossible to avoid. I prayed, "Forgive me, oh, Lord, for my worst sins."

11. SURRENDER

Dawn of 9 April found the east road still jammed with demoralized troops stumbling south away from the frontlines. The ditches were cluttered with burning cars, jeeps and an occasional smoking tank. The explosions of the ammo dump had stopped. My chills had subsided, leaving me weak and my clothes drenched.

By mid-morning, the Jap dive bombers zoomed over us with the hospital, although well marked, apparently the prime target. With the scream of the falling bombs, I dove into a roadside shallow ditch--my "26th" funk hole--peering anxiously up at the propeller shaft of a diving bomber, which seemed to be veering away. Apparently my attention was fixed on the wrong plane. Two huge explosions bounced me into the air. The concussion stunned me, but I felt no pain.

"Are you hit?" yelled Decker.

"Can't tell for sure," I grumbled, examining myself with a pat of the hand.

In a few minutes we were all accounted for. Fortunately for us the bomb had detonated on the hard-surfaced road. Radial shrapnel marks were scratched in a complete circle, gouging the pavement, but the explosive had not penetrated it. A thousand bits of hot metal had swished over my head. The second bomb exploded in a nearby ward jammed with patients. We heard cries for help as we hurried to the unbelievable carnage. I had never seen so many bodies with so missing parts. At least 30 were killed and 50 men suffering from malaria and dysentery now had fresh shrapnel wounds. Father Bill Cummings, a Jesuit priest, who was standing up in the middle of the war praying, was badly hit. His left arm was blown off. He stood there, his frail body quivering as blood flowed down his left side still reciting the Lord's Prayer: " . . . for thine is the kingdom . . ." A tourniquet stopped the hemorrhaging and saved his life.

"Don't worry about me--I'll make it," he advised us, and he did.

I strolled by the operating room and observed Dr. Adamo and

Dr. Weinstein in the process of a leg amputation and treating an abdominal wound. I could see the surgeons' hands jerk with a close explosion, but neither interrupted the cutting and sewing. They're pretty well battle-conditioned at that, I thought.

About mid-morning we positioned ourselves a few hundred meters down the trail between the hospital and the ammo dump. Our revolvers, two rifles and ammunition were stacked in a shaded clearing along the trail surrounded by charred stumps and shredded trees at the edge of the obsidian black jungle. We waited. Soon, at 1100 hours, trotting down the trail came the Japanese. To us, they were ornery yellow bastards yelling and muttering, with bayonets fixed. They were unshaven, dirty and smelly, combat-crazed frontline troops. Their lower legs were bound with ragged khaki puttees. These men were so young, so close to death, and drunk with their success. They were sated with the belief of invincibility predestined by a military system resulting in uncontrolled belligerency. Cruelty and bravery were synonymous in the mind of the Japanese soldier.

Finding no challenge as we stood quietly and unarmed, not obstructing their advance along the trail, they charged back to examine us more closely. Two came over to me, slapped my pockets and yanked my first aid packet off my shoulder, breaking the strap, dumping the contents onto the ground. They grunted, indicating with their thumb and second finger pointing towards their own shoulder. The message was deciphered to mean, "Get medicine from bag and give me shot." I shook my head vigorously, "No, no!" One cruel-mouthed son-of-a-bitch lunged towards me with his bayonet. This was hardly a fair match. Was I to be run through by a private? Was I to face the Great International Harvester now?

Hurriedly I grabbed a bottle of apomorphine tablets, an emetic, and slapped it in his hands, motioning for him to swallow them. He gave half of them to his pal and swallowed the remainder and within a few minutes they were both sick as dogs, vomiting their guts out.

About this time, three bespectacled Nips looking for more excitement, let out a whoop and jumped into a parked ambulance. The keys were in the ignition. A driver's license was not mandatory. Unfortunately for them, as well as for our motor

106

pool, the engine started and they raced down the narrow road, rolling through the parade ground of Hospital No. 1. We last saw the ambulance turning down the Zigzag toward Mariveles. Some days later our troops proceeding up this road on the death march, discovered the overturned ambulance and three dead Nips--a great ending for a gallant ambulance.

Bill Galos of the 803rd Engineers told me of the first Japanese troops which overran his position. They rummaged around and found some cans of sterno. Three of them popped open the cans, grabbed a spoon and went off down the trail eating the contents. Later Bill found them dying with generalized convulsions. Maybe the armament section should have issued sterno as a chemical weapon instead of the antiquated Stokes mortars.

Capt. Herb Ott's veterinary outfit, our meat cutters, had a little different experience. With the help of the Nip artillery hitting animals on the picket line the day before surrender, they slaughtered the last three mules remaining from the Philippine Scouts 26th Calvary. On 9 April, Jap soldiers and a large black bearded Jap officer appeared and set down to talk in fluent English. Herb invited him to stay for a mule supper, which he did. The Jap, educated at UCLA, explained it was impossible to control all of their soldiers and advised the prisoners to hide their personal possessions. He apparently was a decent sort. I never ran into him.

The only good result of the surrender was the discarding of the cumbersome triangular packet under the arm slung on a shoulder strap--the gas mask. The Nips never carried them, but we did until the very end. No general order filtered up to "frontline troops," but the dog-face soldiers chucked their gas masks into the steamy jungle with the first hint of surrender.

Forty-two Jap POWs, all recovering from serious wounds, were in a lock-up ward across the parade ground from Col. Duckworth's headquarters at Hospital No. 1. On this day the wire front door was wide open, the lock dangling on a wire, but no Japs wandered out.

By now the traffic on the East Road had completely stopped. The air was free of planes, the artillery shelling over. An eerie unnatural silence pervaded the smoking battered hilltop. Shortly after 1200 hours, with a clatter, three Jap light tanks burst into the parade grounds. The turret hatches were opened, the guns menacing the whole area, swinging back and forth, occasionally shooting into the jungle. A Jap jumped out of the lead tank as they "circled their wagons." They must have copied that maneuver from a western movie. Amusingly, one of the tanks threw off a track and came to a halt disabled, stopping the circus. The tankers jumped out with a crowbar and pried it back into place.

"Damned cheap equipment," I said to myself. I don't know how they beat us up so badly.

Col. James Duckworth, the ranking Medical Officer, a stocky, powerful man with a grim face, evidencing the lineage of no particular race but similar to that of a bulldog, limped slowly but confidently down the steps of headquarters toward the tank officers. After a few gestures, it was apparent the Jap officer wanted to see the wounded Japanese POWs incarcerated here. Duckworth pointed towards the open door of the barracks. My heart jumped, since our lives depended on this next scene. The Jap officer, a general, his Samurai sword swinging wildly behind him, strode defiantly into the barracks. In a few minutes he emerged scowling, followed by the bowing and bandaged former Jap POWs. They bowed and crawled on the ground at the feet of the general. I'm sure they were in disgrace and feared for their lives also. The Jap officer continued questioning them, apparently to be sure of their treatment since capture. In reality, their food, medical and general care was every bit as good as that given their American counterparts. The general was apparently satisfied as to the adequacy of their care. Col. Duckworth handed the tank commander a prepared statement concerning the Jap POWs and their treatment at Hospital No. 1. After a short consultation with an interpreter, the Jap officer returned Col. Duckworth's note after penciling Japanese characters on the back. The writing was later interpreted in general terms as: "The Jap POWs had been treated and fed adequately under Col. Duckworth's command." We all breathed a sigh of relief. He used this little epistle on several occasions to head off rampaging Jap troops.

Officers, overhearing Col. Duckworth's conversations with the Japanese general, reported the colonel defiantly demanded, "And why did you bomb my hospital which was clearly marked with a Red Cross?"

108

The general replied, "It was too close to the ammo dump."

"There were needless casualties--30 killed and over 95 wounded," Duckworth said.

"Too bad, too bad," the general was reported to have answered.

"Senseless," Duckworth growled in the general's face.

They moved back to their tanks.

Several rampaging contingents of excited Jap infantrymen, usually three or four in a group, searched us later in the day. Most of our personal items--watches, wallets, rings, and money--had been stripped from us. I slipped by the first group with only a once-over light search. By the time the next bunch of Tojo's boys came by, my Swiss-made watch was hidden in a seam of my green wool shirt and five $20 bills were tucked under the insole of my right shoe.

The message to discard anything "made in Japan" spread rapidly by the bamboo wireless. In their minds, possession of such an article meant you killed a Jap to get it. Summary execution was the penalty for possession of these hot articles.

We witnessed a GI being knocked down, then stood up and prodded with bayonets, and finally driven into the woods. Suddenly a shot rang out, the penalty for wearing a "made in Japan" watch.

Several of the Nips peered into the GIs' mouths. I couldn't figure out why until I saw a Jap knock a GI senseless, and extract a tooth with a gold filling.

I saluted and strolled by nonchalantly when accosted by a bunch of marauding Nips. My Red Cross armband was prominently displayed. No one called my bluff. Increasing atrocities by the Japs hurried our decision to move the medical detachment inside the confines of Hospital No. 1. Col. Duckworth agreed, suggesting we would be added to the roll, sleep between the barracks, and answer chow call twice a day.

For no good reason, on the night of 10 April, Decker, another corpsman and I slipped down a trail towards Mariveles. Thousands of troops were milling around. We could hear isolated shots by the Japs which meant the end of some unlucky GI who did something wrong or was caught with contraband. Occasionally, a hand grenade was tossed by a playful enemy into a group of captured resting soldiers.

By the next morning most troops were moving out to the north; a column was forming, the Japanese bayonets prodding the men into ranks. We joined them. Rifle shots rang out frequently to finish off a fallen prisoner. We continued up the road three or four kms. to the Zigzag, a narrow twisting section up a hill in dense jungle. The nature and fate of this march was soon quite obvious. We had seen enough. It was a march of death. We decided to get out quickly.

Fortunately, parts of this tortuous rod were out of sight of the nearest guard. As yet they had not tightened their surveillance. It provided an excellent opportunity to slip into the jungle. I whispered to my two corpsmen my intentions of leaving the column at the next zigzag. We eased over to the left-hand edge, rounded the corner, and disappeared into the friendly jungle. My heart pounded as we crouched and waited for discovery and a shot. None came. It turned out that by deserting the march we had escaped a 100-km. trip of horror and atrocities. We sneaked through the jungle and joined the other two corpsmen at Hospital No. 1 with the firm intention of staying there.

By sheer luck and a sprinkling of frontline savvy, we had avoided the Japanese savagery at surrender. Our luck was holding.

12. DEATH MARCH

The Death March stretched northward 100 km. from Mariveles on the southern tip of Bataan to San Fernando, Tarlac province, then 50 km. in overcrowded railroad cars to Capas and then 12 more km. of marching westward down a dirt road to Camp O'Donnell. The long road was seared by the tropical sun, sometimes dirt, gravel, and then blacktopped pavement.

All of the American and Filipino fighting men were rounded up during the first week and started northward to O'Donnell. Approximately 57,000 Filipinos and 8,000-9,000 Americans marched this route, taking an average of seven days. About 1,000 people died, the majority summarily executed using clubs, bayonets, rifles, swords, or grenades wielded by the cruelest enemy in recorded history. Others were run over or died of dehydration, or starvation. Some soldiers just ran out of gas.

The massacre resulted from the outpouring of hate and revenge imbued in the Jap soldiers by their delayed and costly victory and by their own military system. To die by the sword was their choice, so why not everybody else? The Death March was of their making.

Furthermore, our captors, ignorant of our resolve and military potential, treated us with an attitude which never considered a loser's role.

Surrender was a chance for Japan to show her real colors. Not by wealth or achievements, but by morality in handling prisoners and civilians, Japan was found miserably lacking. To hold out a helping hand to the defeated, not to turn your back, and certainly not to torture and kill the sick and wounded is the mark of a compassionate victor. But their soldiers, officers, commanders, armies and the nation of Japan failed to acknowledge the agony of our defeated army. It is sad that the enemy failed to recognize in us that same courage their victorious troops possessed. They treated us as captives, not as prisoners of war. We had no rights as human beings.

Food and water stops were rare and unplanned. Often food

111

was promised but not delivered. The water supply was scattered irregularly in each barrio, just a single pipe on the roadside from an artesian well. The water flowed very slowly as hundreds of thirsty men lined up. There was a mad scramble as the men pushed toward the spigot, thrusting forward open canteens they hoped would be filled. Then suddenly after just a few minutes the guards rushed in with bayonets, crowding everyone down the torrid road again. Maybe half the people were able to get water.

The majority were thirsty for most of the week's walk. Some drank out of filthy carabao wallows or any puddle in sight. A friend reported to me later seeing a soldier crazed with thirst grab the arm of another GI with a freshly bleeding bayonet wound. He lapped up the blood like a cat cleaning his milk dish. Others crowded towards the water only to have their heads smashed with the butt of a rifle.

Some men tried to walk the entire distance without food or water. All were exhausted from the last days leading to Bataan's collapse. Sick with malaria and dysentery and needing food, rest, medicine, and, foremost, a merciful victor, we found none. Our captors made it a march of torture.

The Japs continually hurried the column along. After a few days, the bayonet wounds were dirty and infected. A bloody, purulent mess developed. This complication sometimes was a deciding factor as to whether the man could continue or not. Stragglers and those who could not keep up were shot in the back or the head, right there on the road. No attempt was made by the Japs to help those men or to give them motor transportation, which was offered and available from our motor pool. One's buddy would help if he were strong enough. Many were carried in a sling made from an army blanket stretched between two bamboo poles.

One old lieutenant colonel, a short, stocky, graying fellow, was becoming weaker, having gone without food and water for several days. He was staggering along the road, slowly falling back in the column. The Japs had bayoneted him a couple of times in the buttocks. His suntan-colored trousers were caked with blood, attracting a swarm of flies. He finally came to a small bridge about ten meters above a rocky dry creek bed. Muttering incoherently, he approached the edge glassy-eyed and threw himself off, headfirst onto the rocks below, ending his suffering.

One of the most savage incidents occurred when a truckload of Jap soldiers riding along the American column spotted a group who were slowly trudging north. With wild yells and obvious ridicule of the Americans, a Jap soldier pulled the pin on a hand grenade and tossed it among the prisoners. A few escaped by jumping into a ditch, but some six or eight were killed, at least twice that many injured. The Japs yelled with glee.

At the end of some five to seven days of walking, the captives were approaching the north end of the Bataan Peninsula and the barrio of Dinalupihan. The column was a mighty sad one. Thirst, hunger and weakness were almost unbelievable. Execution of the stragglers was increasing. That night the Japs did not have a secure place for bivouacking the prisoners, so they decided to herd them into a tin warehouse in the next barrio. After pushing and prodding, the sweltering warehouse was jammed with tired soldiers--standing room only. They were told they would rest here for a short period of time, eat, and then would find some better place for the night's rest.

The iron door clanked shut, and the prisoners were left to stand and squeeze for the rest of the night. By morning some were dead and many could not proceed any farther. Those unable to move out were shot in the head where they lay. Time and time again the Jap guards would fire over the heads of the soldiers in a brutal display of savagery. They also forced marchers to bury the dead. On one occasion, an American was forced to hit a struggling soldier on the head with his shovel to keep him in the trench so he could be buried.

Two Filipino civilians, a man and his wife, were tied to a stake. Gasoline was poured on them and lit. Their horrible screams were never forgotten. Their crime was giving food to GIs who were passing through their barrio.

Four hundred soldiers of the 19th Division, Philippine Army, stationed on the reserve line of resistance on the China Sea side, never reached the Death March. Instead they were beheaded by saber-wielding Japanese after being marched into the woods with their hands tied together. "Because our men died fighting you," was the only excuse.

After the fall of Corregidor on 6 May 1942, the Japanese

113

field commander, Gen. Homma, was ordered home where he was relieved of his command and placed on reserve status for the rest of the war. His treatment stemmed not from punishment for the Death March in Bataan, but for his failure to subdue the forces of Bataan and Corregidor in less than half the time it took him.

In the U.S. war crimes trial, Homma argued that there were three times more POWs than expected; that the captives impeded his attack on Corregidor; and that their own food supply was meager. He testified that the way his army treated prisoners was just part of a harsh military system; the Japs had no idea the defenders were so sick and starved, with so many "old timers"; and that the collapse of the resistance came suddenly, precluding preparations to handle prisoners. To charges of inhumane treatment, Homma pleaded ignorance and extenuation. Pictures and testimony at the trial showed him riding past the Death Marchers. The defense produced official orders which directed "friendly spirit" treatment of the captives. Even his wife testified he was a kind man. He was found guilty and executed at Los Baños, Philippines, on 3 April 1946, exactly four years to the day of his last offense against Bataan.

Of the 86,000 Filipino civilians caught in our battles, the majority were new arrivals in Bataan who fled the peninsula in December when the war broke out. Only 31,000 were listed as living and accounted for after the siege. They took greater casualties than the combatants. The 55,000 died of starvation, accidental gunshots, or were killed by Jap shelling, bombing and the post-surrender slaughter. Theirs was an unspoken tragedy. The Filipino civilians' options, limited by our lack of food and medicine, dwindled during the four months. They suffered quietly in their jungle camps along with the fighting men and women. They didn't even get to fire back.

We stayed at Hospital No. 1 from 9 April to 24 June. This included the 26-day siege of Corregidor.

Daily there were terrific artillery duels between "The Rock" and the Jap batteries on the Bataan Peninsula. The Jap guns were placed near us, but a greater concentration was in the region of Hospital No. 2. Neither hospital was allowed to evacuate their wounded at this time, so the Japs could position their guns nearby hoping to avoid counter fire from Corregidor.

They lined up their 105s wheel-to-wheel just at the very outer perimeter of Hospital No. 2, some within a hundred yards of the buildings. The poor patients, in constant terror, were almost blasted off their cots. Firing went on almost all of the 26-day siege, sometimes for 24 hours at a time. Corregidor received a terrific shelling plus considerable bombing from the Jap air fleet.

Although the Americans on Corregidor possessed accurate grid maps showing our hospitals on Bataan, several shells strayed into the hospital area, killing American soldiers and rewounding others. I later talked to artillery officers from Corregidor who stoutly defended the firing. They knew they were taking a risk, but felt it was necessary to return the Jap fire. Our effectiveness fell as the electric trolley cars hauling ammunition from the battery vaults to the gun pits became inoperable due to twisted rails. This meant the big guns had to be supplied by hand carts.

Stimulated by the reports of starvation and an almost unbelievable death rate for our troops at Camp O'Donnell, end of the Death March, George and I searched the jungles for edibles, ranging from the slopes of Mt. Mariveles to Cabcaben. We had no assigned duty. The Nips never stationed troops in the hospital or demanded a head count.

We wandered out of the hospital area almost every day. Generally we avoided the east road, which carried heavy military traffic and just foraged for food in the old USAFFE bivouac areas. Much to our bitter disappointment, the Japs had gone through the same areas, puncturing the canned food and strewing all packaged rations on the ground. Most of the cans had been open at least a week and the hot tropical sun hurried the rotting process. We searched and searched unsuccessfully for one little overlooked can. We even sampled some of the smelly decomposed offal, but just couldn't stomach it.

We searched through the jungle looking for native food as well. At times we were quite successful, but our activities were limited by the constant moving of Jap forces around and through this particular area.

Native foods like bamboo shoots, breadfruit, *lomboy, siniguelas, ubod* or hearts of palm, and star apples (*kaimito*) were discovered and eaten on the spot. We managed to avoid the Japs despite longer distances we were compelled to travel.

Our greatest find was a huge banana plantation about a mile

115

away. The access was a hidden path from the hospital. We immediately started cutting the beautiful stalks, digging a cave and hiding the bunches. In the dark warm pit, the orange-skinned bananas would ripen in about a week's time. By cutting three or four bunches every few days, we kept a ripe supply usually sufficient so that George, my three corpsmen, and I could eat bananas for an hour almost any day. Some days, with Japs in the area, we stayed away. While most people were losing weight, we were able to maintain ours. It was a Godsend, involving a risk which we didn't mind, and a little cunning which we had.

From our banana plantation vantage point, we could clearly see Corregidor 10 kms. away, a rocky island shaped like a tadpole. Most days "The Rock" was covered by a constant pall of black smoke from the bombardment. One day, during a heavy Jap barrage, a massive roar and earth-shaking explosion occurred. With the quake, a plume of smoke rose about 15,000 meters in the air. The main magazine of Battery Geary had been breached. A one-in-a-million lucky shot. The Jap shell pierced the hinge line of the steel protective door to the magazine, destroying the Battery. A ten-ton barrel from a 12-inch cannon was blown 150 meters over a hill onto the golf course, another into the ocean.

I often wondered how the Topside golf course handled this unnatural hazard--a cannon barrel--an unplayable lie, or a free drop.

· Almost all of the crew were killed except Lt. Lester I. Fox, a diminutive medical officer who lay in the rubble for two days, blackened and unrecognizable. After digging around under blocks of concrete and mangled equipment they found him, still alive. He lost an arm and an eye, but lived to regain his usual happy demeanor and to tell us about Corregidor under siege.

One day in our wanderings, we found a cherry tree, a *duhat*, similar to a farkleberry or our bing cherry, except that the seed is larger and the skin almost black. The tree was at the west end of the old American airstrip at Cabcaben, about two kms. from our hospital area. We found the place strewn with old wrecked U.S. airplanes. This airfield was the last remaining strip on Bataan. It had been used by two or three crippled P-40s until the surrender. The planes were hidden in revetments completely covered by the jungle. Despite handicaps the mechanics successfully mounted bombs on them. On two occasions they bombed Jap ships in Subic Bay, just over the mountains, about 100 kms. away. They reported the sinking of two ships. The Jap observation planes buzzed around unsuccessfully for days trying to find our "bomber."

That effort was almost as primitive as the early bombing by the pioneer U.S. Air Force. Their first bombs were pewter, weighed three pounds, shaped like big shotgun shells, with spring hammers, and pins that detonated on impact. On the very earliest runs a two-seat plane was used, the pilot in front and the bombardier behind holding a bucket with the bomb. Communication was established by a string tied on the bombardier's foot and held by the pilot. When they had maneuvered over the target, the pilot yanked the string and the bomb was promptly emptied over the side. I never heard that this technique was used in Bataan, but the poor mechanics tried everything.

George and I climbed up the *duhat* tree, fitted ourselves into a comfortable crouch and proceeded to eat the delicious cherries. I would imagine we ate for an hour. I was so full I was unable to climb down the tree, so slid and fell the last three meters. It was a most pleasurable sensation to have my tummy that full.

On our way back that afternoon, we foolishly walked up the airstrip toward the main road. Suddenly, before we could duck, we were accosted by a truckload of Japanese soldiers. They were obviously curious where we were going, who we were, and became rather surly by the minute. Ominously it appeared a trial and sentence were going to occur on the spot. We stood our ground, pointed at our Red Cross armbands, and acted as though we knew what we were doing.

We stood at attention and held our salute like good soldiers. After some quarreling among themselves, they waved us on down the road.

George and I walked briskly along the shoulder while the Japs argued some more. After a few minutes, down the road came the Japanese truck racing along. We moved over to the edge of the ditch as it approached and then they swerved in an effort to run us down. I jumped into the ditch as the truck careened past. There was wild laughing and guffawing at the fun. I think they'd have had a much better time if they had run over us. I've often wondered why they didn't shoot us. It was bad judgment to expose ourselves like that.

During the campaign, on this same airstrip, Rosy O'Donnell and Sam Maddux had been cruising along in a jeep when they were spotted by a Jap Zero. Bullets peppered the ground around them as Rosy yelled, "Abandon ship!" Rosy dove to the left, Sam to the right, while the pilotless jeep continued erratically towards the end of the runway and into Manila Bay.

One morning I heard a sound only audible once before, the shrieking of the rotating bands on the projectile from the huge 12-inch mortars. They tumbled over our heads, fired from Battery Way on Corregidor. We heard it while on the frontlines at Samat. *Shoo, shoo, shoo* it went. After the shriek there was a pause, and then ten seconds later--*kerboom*, landing as far as 20,000 meters up the East Road. It seemed rather desultory compared to the thunderous barrage of the Japanese batteries. The little stubby 12-inch mortars traversed sufficiently to hit targets on Bataan Peninsula, yet they were never a factor in our defense. The huge 16-inch rifles (the largest armament in the world at that time) on Corregidor, fired to ocean-side only and were never engineered for covering the Bataan Peninsula.

Within a few days everybody in the Hospital No. 1 (including doctors and several thousand patients) turned yellow, but no one was particularly sick. An endemic hepatitis, probably Type A, had hit the entire population. The jaundice was most noticeable in the whites of their eyes. It disappeared without complications in a couple of weeks.

One morning, we were moving cautiously through the jungle when we came upon two newly mounded-up graves. At the head of each was a marker with Japanese characters, a little cross and three cans of American Vienna sausage. The story was easy to unravel, as far as George and I were concerned. Food was left so the two dead soldiers would be able to have something to eat as they journeyed to the Promised Land. After deliberations lasting a few seconds, George and I decided that our trip was also arduous, and we should avail ourselves of this very generous handout. So we took the cans of Vienna sausage, wandered into the woods, ate the contents, and placed the empty cans on the graves. We felt that the friends of the deceased would undoubtedly interpret this to mean that the trip was longer than anticipated and that more food was necessary. We returned in a few days, but the dead men's friends had apparently not interpreted this as intended.

George still had his beautiful camera and a dozen rolls of exposed film, even though the Japs had ordered all cameras turned in immediately. We finally decided to hide the camera in some safe place in the hope that it could be retrieved after we had been freed. We wrapped the camera in a leather bag, inside of a two-pound coffee can which was filled with rice, sealed the top with adhesive tape, and placed it inside a hollow narra tree. We found a little shelf-like projection up inside the tree about two meters off the ground. Mentally we both marked the exact site of the tree--about 400 or 500 meters south of the headquarters building of Hospital No. 1 along the highest ridge parallel to the main road.

In April 1967, on the 25th anniversary of the Fall of Bataan and Corregidor, I returned to the Philippines, making a beeline for Bataan to search for the camera. I not only didn't find the camera nor the tree, but was never quite sure where the 3,000-bed hospital was located. The Japs had raped Bataan, cutting all the mahogany trees and torn up the jungle beyond recognition. I wandered around, hopelessly lost. Our treasure was gone forever. George never went back to look.

Corregidor shuddered from the ever-increasing bombardment. On 4 May the Japanese fired 16,000 shells, the heaviest of the campaign. We watched from our vantage point four kms away. The black shrouded fortress evidenced its final death throes.

On the night of 5th and 6th May, the shore battery fire of the Japs suddenly stopped, heralding the invasion. Amazingly, one roving searchlight from Corregidor had survived to light up the entire invasion flotilla. The light was soon destroyed by shore fire, but not until our few remaining guns, including the last operational 12-inch mortar of Battery Way, plus guns from Fort Drum on El Fraile Island and Fort Hughes on Caballo Island, blasted the advancing barges. The killing and drowning were terrific, with death rates of 50-75 percent in most units, but, too late, for a Jap beachhead had been established at Cavalry Point.

119

By noon on the 6th of May, a quiet crept over the tadpole-shaped rock. The Japs clambered up the hillsides. They approached Malinta Tunnel and its 254-meter deep tunnel and laterals. The smoke settled. Corregidor had fallen. A white flag flew atop the flag pole. Then it was replaced by the rising sun.

Brig. Gen. William Sharp held out in the southern islands for four more days. He was a personable, jolly good fellow with obvious leadership qualities. He joked, seemingly at ease with the troops. We had both come out on the same ship in June 1941, when Sharp was still a colonel. I liked him, for he seemed to grow in greatness instead of arrogance.

Soon after arrival, he assumed the command of southern Philippines--Visayas-Mindanao--with headquarters in Mindanao near Lake Lanao and the Del Monte pineapple plantation and airfield. A story circulated that when the Japs pushed towards him in April 1942, he wired back, "We'll hold until Lake Lanao freezes over!" The lake is not far from the equator. A few days later his message arrived, "Ice is forming." The Japs probably never decoded that one. His forces in Mindanao surrendered on 10 May 1942, after very little resistance.

A story is told that Gen. Sharp observed a Filipino stealing pineapples from the quartermaster dump one day and promptly yelled at the would-be thief. The Filipino jumped up, looked skyward, and yelled, "Air raid!" Whereupon, the general took off running, while the Filipino shouldered his bag of loot and took off.

After the fall of Corregidor, the Japs began to pay more attention to us. They put troops into our area and informed us we should prepare ourselves to evacuate the patients on short notice. We were going into Manila to Bilibid prison and not to Camp O'Donnell, the terminus of the Death March. Continuing reports of horrible treatment at Camp O'Donnell were delivered by Americans driving Japanese trucks, reporting the death rate was unbelievable--something like 500 Filipinos and about 50 Americans every day.

Again my luck was holding out. The reports from Bilibid, although meager, pictured a more stable and livable prison.

13. BILIBID

On 24 June, the Japs appeared at our hospital with their rickety old ton-and-a-half trucks and started loading our patients for the trip to Manila. They allowed us to take nothing from the hospital. I threw my first-aid kit and scruffy rucksack over my shoulder and climbed onto a truck filled with patients. Decker and the other three corpsmen scampered into another truck. My first ride in several months was fun.

"Beats marching, eh, Captain?" joked a patient.

George Campbell yelled at me just as our truck was departing for Bilibid, "Take care."

I responded, "Welcome to the Philippines."

"Go to hell," he answered, the same response he gave me on arriving in the Philippines. George went to O'Donnell with the hospital unit and later volunteered for outside work details. Our paths never crossed until we met in the States many years later. He was a reluctant but good soldier.

The following day Col. Duckworth and the entire staff of "Little Baguio" Hospital No. 1 (including surgeons Adamo and Al Weinstein) departed from their workshop in Bataan for the hell hole at O'Donnell. Al wrote about his experience in an excellent book called *The Barbed Wire Surgeon*.

There was a certain relief on leaving the blood-soaked, miserable peninsula where we had fought and bled for some six months. This disease-ridden, infested, smelly piece of mountainous jungle and burial ground had been a place of suffering, starvation, and fear of unlimited proportions. The bleak hopelessness was well left behind. The future in prison camp, we reasoned, will just have to take care of itself.

The trip was about 150 kms. and at midpoint we stopped at a small barrio for water. I got off the truck, filled my canteen at the artesian well spigot, and wandered along the street between some small *bahays*. A couple of Filipinos appeared, offering me a rice ball, copra and *sineguelas*, and after glancing furtively around, motioned for me to follow them. No guards were in sight,

121

so I moved behind a *bahay* as they excitedly explained that I should come with them and escape up into the hills.

I had noted that there had not been an accurate count of American prisoners boarding the trucks, so it was entirely possible my escape would have been undetected. On the other hand, I noticed one guard kept his eye on me. There had been no prearranged plan for any of us to try to escape.

My heart pounded wildly. Tempting, but the quick decision had been preempted by a similar one of 9 April, the surrender of Bataan. The challenges of the stockade, an unknown quantity as yet, would be formidable, but so had been the tear of shrapnel, the hole of a 25-caliber pellet or the cut of a bayonet from a banzai charge. No! I'm going to Bilibid with these guys. In the next several years, this decision was challenged many times.

After checking to see that everyone had a drink, I climbed aboard the truck. We continued on after a second water stop, and finally drove through the deserted streets of Manila, where a few breech-clothed natives ran out throwing bananas to us. The convoy turned down Azcarraga Street, and soon pulled up to the huge iron gate guarding the cold grey stone walls of Bilibid Prison. This was to be my home for some five months--until 10 December 1942. There was no greeting committee.

The Navy hospital, first based at Canacao in the Cavite Naval Yards, was captured and moved by the Japanese to organize the Bilibid POW camp. Generally speaking, the staff was a fine lot and, having avoided the rigors of the Peninsular campaign, were in excellent nutritional state and in good spirits. Their uniforms looked pretty clean to me. Tall, slender, taciturn Commander Lee Sartin, the commanding officer and a kindly grey-haired doctor, supervised an excellent medical staff. His mild manner belied the hardships and horrors of war surrounding him.

Bilibid, in active use for the worst Filipino civilian criminals, was built in 1898, the same year Admiral George Dewey sailed into Manila Harbor to destroy the Spanish fleet. The compounds were separated by stone partitions like spokes of a wheel with the high dirty grey stone walls encompassing the whole circular prison. Many two- to three-story stone buildngs of various shapes were crammed into the 200 X 300 meter area with a no man's land of 10 meters next to the wall. The floors were concrete and the windows were wide open. The buildings themselves were quite clean, although barren, dilapidated old structures. It was possible to keep the areas pretty well policed. An inside toilet, a 12-holer, was available, although the sewer drained out into an open ditch. It functioned satisfactorily, except during flooding from a typhoon.

My assigned bed space was in the old three-story former hospital building, so I took refuge on the third floor with a few fellow officers. The desk clerk assured me it had a nice view--huge, wide-open window--at least over the wall. We slept on the concrete slab which was not very comfortable but I was able to make a bed out of it. Late in the night the concrete seems to start bouncing and pressing up against you, affording quite a challenge. Nevertheless, I slept well. My body apparently tried to catch up for the many sleepless nights in Bataan. One night Sgt. Coventry woke me, shaking my arm. "Take it easy, Captain," he said. He had just aborted my dream of a bayonet charge from a Jap. "Get the bastard," I was yelling.

It was amazing. One could go from a sharkskin dinner jacket to no shirt and tattered pants, and from an innerspring mattress to a bed of rock in six months.

The food was considerably poorer than what we had had at Hospital No. 1, considering the extras from foraging, but not as meager as that in the field. There followed a gradual decrease in the amount of food issued. The ration, same as always, consisted of rice, which we had twice a day. At breakfast it was cooked thin, like a gruel or cereal, called *lugao*, and at the other meal it was steamed dry. In addition, there was usually a ladleful of soup per man. This consisted of a thin, salty concoction about the color of dishwater. Usually floating around in it was a short-stalked native vegetable called *kangkong*. It looked something like spinach or sea weed.

The hunger gnawing at your guts overshadowed the discomfort of poor sleeping accommodations. My bedtime thoughts and dreams centered around food with my left hand steadying a meter-high stack of hot cakes, scooping them in with my right. Hunger is not an eexhaustive sensation until afer a few days of total starvation, when acidosis and aldehyde toxicity ensues. Every meal, no matter how inadequate, lights the flame of hunger. For

123

years afterwards I was hungry enough to eat a rat or a dead horse. To my knowledge, I never ate a rat, but I was never offered any either. Starvation is a slow way of dying.

It was not long before my ankles began to swell (edema) and my tongue became sore (pellagra). It was unbelievable to me that I was developing evidence of malnutrition so soon. I didn't think my diet had really been that deficient. My attention had centered on bullets, not butter. My ankles were huge, particularly at the end of the day. This was due to the lack of protein, a condition called nutritional or war edema. My sore slick magenta-colored tongue, atrophic glossitis, and cracked corners of the mouth, heralded Vitamin B deficiency (pellagra and beri beri).

More prisoners were arriving almost daily. A good friend of mine, Capt. Hal Enger, came in with a harrowing experience. He was pretty well beat up but made of tough fiber. He and a fellow officer, captured in the jungle, had been summarily tried by the Japs and convicted as spies. They were sentenced to have their heads chopped off. The entire legal procedure took just a few minutes. His friend was decapitated the same day. The following day he was led into the village square where a Japanese officer brandished his Samurai sword. The captain was made to kneel, placing his head across a log. With much gusto and yelling, the Japanese officer raised his sword but never struck the blow. The Jap repeated his threatening performance for several days but, finally, for unknown reasons, gave up the fun and later Hal was brought into Bilibid. Most of the men captured in the jungle were, in fact, summarily beheaded.

One day the front gates opened and in came four Japanese trucks loaded with American prisoners of war, the remnants of the Batangas work detail. Most were beaten, emaciated, and as sick a group of men as I had ever seen in my life up to that time. Originally, there had been about 125 Americans who had gone down to Batangas to work on roads. Less than 30 survived the three-month ordeal. They related stories of continuous unmerciful beating with clubs, long hours without water, being tied up and harassed by their Jap captors. They slept on the rocky road bed which they were building. Several of the guards--one they called "the Wolf,"--deliberately tried to destroy them with daily beatings, sometimes mutilating a man beyond recognition. They

124

cooked in an old wheelbarrow. No medical facilities were available. They worked 12-14 hours a day on very meager rations. The death rate was at least one or two a day, particularly from dysentery.

One of the main internal problems of this group was to persuade the surviving prisoners to bury their own dead pals. Some reasoned it was more work without more rations. The morale dropped so low that at times the men had to be driven to scratch out a shallow grave. Physically and mentally, they were bankrupt. After every iota of work potential was extracted, the Japs dumped the remains in Bilibid.

I hurried down to help the men unload as they staggered and fell off the trucks. Some crawled on all fours. Some cried, begging for help. Their filthy tattered shorts or "G" strings hardly covered their groins. They were unshaven and smelled to high heaven since baths were nonexistent. A bloody oral discharge oozed from scorbutic gums. Many had large deep ulcers on the shins, the result of malnutrition and poor skin care. Several were blind from corneal ulcers. Never ever had I seen such mistreatment--a sad and tragic sight of beaten and starved Americans. I cried and ached for revenge.

A real but unsuccessful effort was made to help these men. I went to see them lying in filth on the cement floor. I talked to some of them for days in an effort to cheer them up, offering meager extras of food, such as a banana or camote. Most of the 30 men never did recover--they just faded away.

One day a message came that a patient in the dysentery ward wanted to see me. I went over and there was one of the Whiffen-poof Boys, Lt. Joe McClellan of Billings, Montana, lying on the floor, half covered with bloody fecal excreta and flies. We had not seen each other since that dinner at the Manila Hotel the night of 7 December. Our friendship dated back to the trip over on the SS President Coolidge.

Because of the fever and dehydration, Joe recounted with great difficulty how on the first morning of the war he had taken off from Iba Airfield in his unarmed P-40 in an effort to avoid the oncoming Jap air raid. This saved his plane for awhile. Mentally Joe was still flying his P-40. He would drift in and out of consciousness and stare at me blankly. His dysentery, severe and

125

completely uncontrolled, accompanied by chills and fever, resulted in a critical condition. I scrounged a few vitamin and morphine tablets from my Navy pals and stuck them in his mouth. With great difficulty he swallowed one of each, the morphine to control the bloody flux oozing from the rectum and the vitamin for severe malnutrition. After that I helped him with his meals, begging him to swallow.

After three to four days of treatment I gave him both bottles of the precious medicine, suggesting he take one of each several times during the night. The next morning the open bottle and the pills were scattered on the filthy floor. Crawling on the floor, I recovered and cleaned up each pill of the priceless medicine hoping the next time to save a life with them.

His emaciated body with protruding ribs, spindly arms and legs, sunken glassy eyes were all that remained. He went rapidly downhill, and died in my arms by mid-morning. And now there were only three Whiffenpoof Boys. His death was tough to take. I hoped I wouldn't be losing more of my friends after the shooting stopped. Joe was a good friend who also represented the epitome of our fighting forces--a fighter pilot. He was one of over a hundred who were given guns when their planes were destroyed and transformed overnight into infantry soldiers. His death pointed up very strongly the hopelessness of the situation. A few pills would not bring back a patient that far gone with malaria, dysentery and starvation. To survive this ordeal was going to be a real struggle needing more than a little luck.

I helped bury Joe in our rapidly expanding cemetery, located in the corner of the compound. Daily I passed his grave marked by a small wooden cross bearing his name. It was just a few yards from my barracks. Was there any real hope for the rest of us?

Bilibid presented my first strict confinement. Previously I had been able to wander off into the jungle. Here we were thrown together in confined quarters where there were no partitions between our assigned spaces. Only an imaginary line on a slab of concrete outlined your castle. One man drew chalk marks and announced that no one was to enter unless permission was requested and granted. At least in his mind he had some privacy. One had to create his own solitude, albeit imaginary. Nor could you complain to other men since they carried the same burden.

Most men were rather silent, somewhat subdued.

At night in the darkness, we would have long discussions of the world situation. Speculation on the date we would be released had long since failed to be an interesting topic since there was no news to fuel the fire. My hunch was it was going to be a long drawn out war with no rescue in sight. At least this prediction eliminated the disappointment from the failure of the early appearance of the Yanks.

Our appraisal recognized the enemy as a fierce fighter, easily deceived, not resourceful, nor well trained, excitable and foolish in the field, brave to a fault and prone to suicidal effort. I was convinced Japan did not have the industrial potential to produce a war machine equal to the American military juggernaut of the future. As it so happened, their top men and best equipment were being squandered in the early part of the war. The ultimate victor was never in doubt to us, only the time of victory.

"The Army makes men" was an oft-repeated saying and I believed it. In peace time the poorly motivated soldier either became the bugler or was transferred to cook and baker school. Combat and starvation produce unknown quantity. Sometimes a real solid man grows tall with the challenges, and at other times a cheater surfaces.

Bilibid produced many varieties of men. Only one serious bootlicker emerged, a man named Provo who turned out to be as rotten as any I've ever known. A turncoat, flaunting himself in a black flowing robe, he was guilty of hitting and kicking fellow Americans, usually in the presence of the Japs, in order to ingratiate himself. He was able to live close to the Japanese prison headquarters and received privileges and, most importantly, extra rations. He squealed on Americans who were stealing food. On one occasion this led to the execution of Capt. Thompson, a veterinary officer. I never spoke to Provo, whom I labeled a dirty rat. Supposedly he was a Japanese Shinto religious fanatic who had an Oriental wife. After the war he was tried for treason. I don't know what happened to him.

Six Japanese nurses visited us one afternoon, unannounced, escorted by male officers. Overdressed in multiple blue and white skirts, big hats, with pasty fixed faces like geisha girls, they always seemed to look straight ahead. They talked to nobody, asked no

127

questions, walked around the barracks and disappeared. At least they could say they visited a prison where those horrible Americans were held.

One day a Jap guard appeared, who ordered me to go with him to the Japanese headquarters. I had a sudden lump in my throat. I couldn't swallow. Where did they get my name? Strange.

"*Kon nichi wa* (good day)," I bowed and greeted him. "*Arigato* (thank you)."

I followed him through the dark passageway. Coming into a bare waiting room, I was greeted by a stocky Catholic priest. His round cherubic face belied the fierce warrior inside. He was about 5'8" tall, wore a broad-brimmed round black crown hat, and moved slowly, with dignity. Speaking in an engaging and reassuring voice, he said, "Ralph, Pilar asked me to come and visit you. In January she heard you had been killed."

There were no Japs in sight so we soon began to talk freely. He brought a note and money from Pilar. This occupation currency which we called "Mickey Mouse" money was issued by the Japs for use only in the Philippines. Dollars were forbidden and stayed out of sight except on the black market. The kindly priest, Theodore Butienbruch, whispered that Pilar had been cycling outside the prison's north wall. This was just out of the back window where I had been sleeping! After about five minutes of encouragement, he put his arms around me, paused and intoned, "God and you are traveling together."

It turned out that Pilar had been riding daily between 1400 and 1430 hours. She was anxious to see me and establish contact so she send me money, food and medicine regularly. Risks played a part in her planning.

The next day I waited anxiously for Pilar to come by. I paced back and forth just like a groom before his wedding, peering out of the large open window of the third floor. My bedraggled, dirty outfit consisting of a sleeveless shirt and khaki shorts partially filled by a skinny carcass presented an unromantic figure.

After several unfamiliar people went by on bicycles, I saw Pilar. My heart jumped--what a thrill! She was easily recognizable, although 75-80 meters away, even wearing a big floppy woven *pandanus* hat. She pedalled parallel with the wall until she was just 40 meters away. Then she turned left going up the street away from the prison. She rode slowly to the next corner, turned and disappeared. There was no gesture of recognition or even a stare in my direction. I figured she was peeking out from under her floppy hat.

About 15 minutes later she rode by again, repeating this same course. Later a group of girls appeared on a screened-in porch of a home about halfway up the block. After a few minutes, I could distinguish Pilar quite clearly, sitting close to the screen and making short waving gestures in my direction. She saw me alive, 40 pounds lighter and as a not-so-confident hardened soldier. I felt warm inside as my morale soared. Then she was gone. There were aftershocks with the realization that Pilar was getting mixed up in this mess. She was a brave girl.

The Japs patrolled the compound at close intervals day and night, usually with squads of four or six men, marching constantly inside and outside the prison wall. There were two squads on each side meeting at midpoint and then marching in opposite directions and aboutfacing at the corners. To my knowledge, no POW escaped over this wall.

In all other camps except Bilibid, a daily head count, "Tenko," was demanded in the Japanese language and supervised by the Japanese. Here, each day, all we did was to report "all accounted for."

The Mickey Mouse money was most welcome, since a few Filipino or Chinese merchants were occasionally permitted to sell us bananas, pomelos (the poor man's grapefruit), rarely breadfruit, and still more infrequently, some soy beans and salt. One ounce of salt cost one American dollar on the black market.

The underground traffic allowed some prisoners to sign personal notes payable after the war to Chinese merchants. The POWs promised American dollars for occupation currency. For once the Chinese merchants made bad deals, since most of the Americans never lived to honor the notes.

After a couple of weeks and another summons, I found Fr. Ted, his soft grey eyes twinkling, again at the prison gate with some money and vitamins. He brought me a note and a St. Christopher's medal.

"She's very fond of you," he thoughtfully remarked. "The medal is for your protection."

I hoped it was not "Made in Japan."

He sidled over close to me, reached under his black flowing robe and produced three pequeñas bananas. He whispered, "From Pilar. Put them under your blouse and eat them later, Ralph. I'll try to see you again. It's getting very difficult, I don't know what the Japs are going to do with me. God bless you."

The priest had to be suspect for catering to the Americans. I wondered, and so did he, if the meeting place was bugged. We stood close and whispered to avoid any pickup. He wasn't afraid of them. Then abruptly he stopped coming.

On a return trip to the Philippines in 1967--25th anniversary--mention was made in the papers of the mysterious disappearance of Fr. Ted. Apparently in 1943 or 1944 he was thrown into Fort Santiago's tidal water dungeons. No trace or grave was ever found. I'm sure he gave his life to our cause. God bless him and grant, O, Lord, eternal peace for him and those like him who lie in unknown graves.

Tucking the bananas around my skinny middle, I strolled by the guards in a nonchalant manner, retired to my third floor slab where I produced the three precious morsels. One felt funny, and after squeezing it fell apart, exposing a tight roll of money, some sulfa and vitamin pills all packaged by Pilar.

Gourds (upo) later became a common vehicle for smuggling. The hollow center was a great receptable for almost anything. Unfortunately, the Japs considered smuggling a crime and an "insult to the Emperor." The penalty was usually death. They didn't seem to have any milder sentences.

One day, while strolling in the dark hall past the mess, I passed a grubby-looking Filipino who muttered, "Ralph." Not stopping, I eased on down to the corner, surveyed the landscape for Nips, then went back to identify myself. He turned out to be the Campos' "garbage man." He sneaked me a package of vitamins, Jap occupation money, sulfa pills and then a note from Pilar detailing a wild plan for meeting at the wall and even a query, "Do you want to try to escape?"

Her plan basically called for scaling the 10-meter walls with a rope ladder. Then I would drop onto the tin roof of a nearby house, change into native dress and the characteristic straw hat. We would head for the provinces buried under rice straw in a two-wheel carabao cart. Earlier, several Americans had been killed in a similar attempt when at a roadblock, the Japs bayoneted their straw-filled cart.

The critical trick would be to avoid the Jap patrols just inside the walls. The out-of-sight time was not more than two minutes in most places. Patrols on the outside appeared less frequently and presented less of a problem. Her other plan involved sneaking out clad in a short-sleeve shirt, a breech cloth, or clam digger pants disguised as the Filipino garbageman or even hiding in the garbage. My skin was the right color, but my shoulders a little too broad.

Pilar made an intensive study of the prison wall. Probably through other friends, she was able to locate a six-inch diameter drainage pipe at ground level traversing the wall. She was able to enter a house on the street, pass through a small lean-to nipa shack behind the house, and reach a tiny hut which adjoined the wall and the drainage pipe. The opening on my side was in a rather exposed position with ten meters of open ground in each direction. Jap guards patrolling along the inside wall passed the area frequently, that is, about every four to five minutes, and in a rather unpredictable manner. Hopefully, this pipe was to be our message exchange route.

To escape and become a guerrilla, getting back into jungle warfare didn't turn me on. The agony of defeat still gnawed at my guts. The noise of incoming artillery shells was still whining in my ears. Also, the commitment to Pilar would become very real and possibly unfair. My investment and survival as a frontline infantry medical officer weighted the argument in favor of staying put and being less heroic. Pilar, a brave girl, was no tactician. If the escape option was bypassed, all was not lost. My chances of survival in my estimation improved in prison camp over both frontline and guerrilla duty. How much good could I do as a guerrilla? Furthermore, the Japs had threatened reprisals on the other prisoners if anyone escaped. Our first need was contact and not escape. The drainage pipe offered a chance.

The plan called for Pilar remaining at the opening for a space of ten minutes or until we made contact. I never did understand how she was going to escape the patrol on the outside, but it was entirely possible the guards' path was blocked by other buildings

131

in the area.

The appointed night arrived. The action began at 2100 hours. Fortunately, it was a dreary, rainy, dark night. Since precision was of the essence, I removed my watch hidden in the seam of my musette bag. It read 2100 hours as I crawled stealthily forward toward the wall. Two of my friends, Navy medics, were lookouts. Lt. Erickson placed himself to the left, with Lt. Black to the right along the hospital wall about 30 meters from the corner of the building. They were to relay the message that the patrol was approaching. We had a series of whistles figured out--one short soft whistle at five-second intervals if everything was all right, and repeating two short whistles when the patrol was approaching me.

After a few cautious steps, I hurried to the opening and whispered, "Pilar?" She was on the other side. She heard me and whispered, "Hiya, Ralph." I groped my hand into the drainage pipe and at arms length clutched her soft warm hand.

I said a few words like, "I love you. You're great; thanks, pal," and kept mumbling, "I'm perfectly all right; don't worry." It was clumsy for me to say that I was more interested in listening for the guards.

She stuck a roll of P20 bills, occupation money, about the size of an orange, into my hand. There were sulfa and vitamins also. I thanked her, again rather clumsily, squeezed her hand and muttered, "I'd better get going." The whistles were becoming more frequent, and a little less distinct in my mind as to whether they were one or two blasts.

A shuffling noise was audible down the wall. Crouching, I scooted back to the hospital building, straightened up, and slowly sauntered around the corner just as the Jap patrol came high-stepping past me. My heart palpitated as I breathed for what seemed to be the first time in minutes. A wry grin slowly crept over my face.

Still clutching my poke, I lay down on my concrete mattress smiling over the bravery and loyalty of this beautiful girl. I was sure that many heroes in the Philippines wore frangipani perfume. I felt pretty smug. There were about P650 in the roll. My newly acquired wealth reminded me of the five U.S. $20 bills under the thin leather insole of my right shoe. Much to my dismay, I found all the bills chewed to pieces beyond retrieval. I had steamed them with the sweat of my foot for some two months. President Jackson's picture was barely recognizable, not good enough to be negotiable, not even to buy a banana. Pilar's gift took on new value after this loss.

She continued to ride by almost daily at 1400 hours in a different attire, wearing a variety of floppy hats. Sometimes there was some faint gesture of recognition. She was able to smuggle notes into the compound with some regularity through the garbage collector. We did not try the hole-in-the-wall trick again. Her notes were folksy and cheerful--a little fun playing bridge or a party with friends, probably at Trophy Ocampo's, a good meal, plans for the future, and even a description of her dream husband.

In an effort not to expose other people another scheme was devised. I tied a letter onto a rock and heaved it over the wall through the open third-story window. I tried to throw the rock so it landed ahead of her as she rode by. The first time the rock rolled in front of her bike, it startled her since she had no warning of my scheme. She ignored it and then after some ten minutes came back and picked it up. This worked successfully six or seven times during my stay at Bilibid. We were never caught at this, although at times the Japs would turn suddenly and look in my direction, apparently never seeing the flying object. The window was large enough so I could throw while hidden inside the building. At least no real names appeared on our notes, so the Japs could not identify the author or intended recipient. She signed off with "Love, Petie."

One afternoon Pilar pedalled by but disappeared around the corner without grabbing the letter rock. Something queer was going on. At least the inside guards continued their routine patrol oblivious to our ball game. Watching intently, I had a start when suddenly an outside Jap patrol moved into sight. They hurried down the street, but marched right by the funny rock with the white paper attached. I started breathing again. It was impossible for me to see the outside oncoming patrols. I had almost conked one on the head. In about ten minutes my little "peasant girl" appeared, riding, and then pushing her bike in the opposite direction. She stopped, moved her bike to the edge of the road,

133

and slowly picked up the rock, slyly peering in all directions out from under her floppy hat. Nonchalantly she pedalled away, disappearing around the corner.

Unbeknownst to me and at about the same time, September 1942, my folks in Oskaloosa, Iowa, were notified by the War Department that I was "missing in action." Soon after this the Japs, after releasing the few surviving Filipinos from Camp O'Donnell, finally declared we were officially prisoners of war. Up until then we were just somebody to beat up, known as "captives." Word that I was alive and a POW was first received by Dad and Mom through the Red Cross in October 1942, six months after surrender. As expected, they received the telegram calmly and without surprise. "He'll make it," Dad was reported to have said.

Life in Bilibid Prison was not too severe. Most of the men, except for the incoming work details, were in pretty good physical condition. Most had escaped the Death March. The Navy unit was in first-class shape. The Japanese garrison was also not of the killer type that we had been exposed to in Bataan. Nor were the Japanese in charge of Bilibid the bestial humans like Capt. Tsuneyoshi, the first Commanding Officer at O'Donnell. He delivered Philippic tirades to all new arrivals, scathing denunciations like "You are enemies of Japan. I wish you were all dead." Purportedly to discourage escapes he also confiscated all shoes. This simple act grounded everyone since the paths were searing hot.

In the War Crimes Trial, he talked himself into life in prison. There were 27,000 Filipino and American POWs who died under his command during April and May 1942 at O'Donnell, witness to Tsuneyoshi's cruelty. Once he proudly displayed one emaciated carabao to demonstrate the generosity of the Imperial Japanese Forces. After two days of exhibition the animal was cooked and divided among 50,000 prisoners.

Nevertheless, the five months while I was in Bilibid, from 24 June until 10 December, found my good luck holding up. My health was fair and stable. The beri beri neuritis and pellagrous glossitis improved, with no more malaria chills, and the dysentery gone. The ankle edema had disappeared because of increased intake of animal and fish protein and an involuntary low-salt

134

intake.

While we waited inside the formidable gray stone walls, we tried to live something more than an existence. We started playing chess, making our own men from narra (pterocarpus), and policing the compound. As my own strength picked up, I was able to play volleyball almost every day. It was an excellent form of recreation, a wonderful morale booster, and served to keep one in fair muscle tone. The amount of the exercise was closely related to the marginal rations we received.

We had one severe typhoon, force seven on the scale of one to nine, while we were in Bilibid. It flooded the entire city of Manila, and overflowed the open sewage canals. Consequently, there was wide distribution of excreta with "legless alligators floating everywhere inside and outside the prison. The high winds and rains lasted for several days. The rain blew in through the open windows, puddling water in our sleeping quarters. It became necessary to sweep off the slab before going to bed and crowding in the corner each time a squall blew by. It was at least a week before we were dried out. Fortunately, the temperature was tolerable--an average daytime high of 95 and an average of 86 at night.

According to reports filtering in, O'Donnell was being closed. The Filipinos had been released to go home and die and all Americans were to be transferred to a new prison camp at Cabanatuan, in the province of Nueva Ecija, by August.

The situation in Bilibid was a thousand times better than O'Donnell. Our indoor privies, flushed by city water, beat the open straddle trenches of O'Donnell. The medical support by the Navy was superior to the poor exhausted Army medic who walked out of Bataan with the entire supply of medicine contained in his first aid kit and musette bag. Even a concrete mattress for a bed beat a bamboo strip floor. The food ration of camote, rice, whistle weed soup, and a sliver of meat occasionally, was about all the Japs issued to POWs at either prison.

Commander Sartin assigned me as a special project officer. My first job was to dry mattresses which were soaked accidentally during the rainy season and by that one typhoon. I hauled the soggy things out with the sun and back inside with each sudden downpour. The job was soon judged to be impossible, at least dur-

135

ing the rainy season. My next task as assistant ward surgeon was to help Chaplain Hugh Kennedy sort out the men who most needed extra rations or last rites. Occasionally, a few cans of condensed or evaporated milk showed up for distribution. Hugh seemed to be better at the latter task.

After the war, the Navy, on Commander Sartin's orders, sent me a letter of commendation. I was never quite sure which one of my jobs earned this decoration. In truth, my association with the Navy in Bilibid was excellent and really appreciated.

About the first week in Decemb er 1942, a message carried by word of mouth from Maj. Clarence White suggested that if possible, any of my medical detachment and I should transfer to Camp No. 1 in Cabanatuan. In a few days a detail of American POWs was scheduled to go north, so Cpl. Decker, one other corpsman and I volunteered. My policy all during the long captivity was to avoid volunteering for small work details. They seemed to disappear mysteriously. Yet I was anxious to see all my old buddies and find out who was still alive. Most of the other officer survivors of the 31st, so I had heard, were at Cabanatuan. I wondered about the two remaining Whiffenpoof Boys--Hunkins and Tooley. It would be great to see them.

The day before departure, 9 December 1942, as usual at 1400 hours, Pilar bicycled by, floppy hat and all. I waved as she steadily approached the wall. No inside patrols were in sight so I tossed my last missile, ignoring the outside patrols.

She rode past, returning in five minutes pushing the bike and swooshed up the rock. In the letter I had written, "I'm leaving tomorrow to rejoin my outfit at Cabanatuan as ordered by my C.O. I'd rather stay here where I can at least see you. Thanks for the help. I'm really OK and not worried other than for your safety. Please take to the hills. Love you--R."

Later I spotted the vague outline of Pilar barely discernible through the vine-covered screen on the porch of her friend's house. She had read my note and was waving good-bye.

I worried about Pilar and the dreaded Kempei Tai. Stories reached us of rape, and the molesting of women and children. Hopefully they would not seize her as they sought out the enemy.

The next day the garbage man brought a pair of prescription glasses that I had requested earlier and a cute picture of Pilar as a newspaper reporter. Thank God the captors didn't discover the picture!

We rode in open trucks to the railroad station. I searched the open streets for Pilar but did not see her. The 100-km. eight-hour trip via the "carabao railway express" took us straight north through the flat rice paddies of Luzon, from Manila to Cabanatuan. About 50 of us were crowded into a near airtight box car. The last few boarded with shoving and prodding by the Jap guards. The journey passed without casualties, although by noon the metal walls were searing hot from the tropical sun. Enjoyably, the ride broke up the monotony of prison life. Cracks in the sliding doors gave us a little air and glimpses of rice paddies, mango groves, papaya, acacia trees, and just plain countryside. I even spotted a carabao, a Filipino's most prized possession, save his family. Bougainvillea, fire trees, hibiscus and poinsettia blurred by, the first color we'd seen in months.

All too soon, our train ride ended. Decker jumped off ahead of me. The column, prodded by Jap guards, started the 10-km. hike to Prison Camp No. 1. We carried all our earthly belongings on our backs. Our next stop: Cabanatuan. A cruel POW camp and uncertain future lay ahead. As we plodded sweltering in the tropical sun, motivated by the glistening bayonets of the guards, I decided not to look too far ahead or I might stumble on my own boots.

14. CABANATUAN

Cabanatuan, meaning a "rock" place, was my home from 10 December 1942 until 30 January 1945. Cabanatuan Prison Camp No. 1 was located 10 km. east of Cabanatuan City (population: 100,000), the capital of the province of Nueva Ecija in the northeastern part of the broad reaches of the flat rice paddies of Central Luzon.

Capt. Mori, the camp commander, was a Jap reserve officer who lived in Manila and ran a bicycle shop before the war. Although many of the Americans were good customers of his, he never acknowledged it in any way. Not as belligerent as some Japanese we came in contact with, he never helped us either. Sometimes, a non-commissioned officer ran the camp--a sergeant in charge of the destiny of 5,000 to 7,000 men!

Activated in August 1942, Cabanatuan Camp No. 1 was a consolidation of the survivors of Camp O'Donnell and Cabanatuan Camps Nos. 2 and 3, which were opened and closed in a few months. It consisted of a total enclosure 1,000 by 800 meters, an old Philippine Army training camp. Surrounded by flat open rice paddies and cogon grass meadows, the area was split by a dead-end gravel road, a spur off the bordering Cabanatuan-Cabu Highway. Our camp road moved gently uphill towards the south knoll with the Japanese section separating the two American areas, general and hospital.

The main Jap headquarters and guard house or "posay bodega," transient quarters, officers and enlisted men housing and the motor pool, were on the promontory pretty much in the center of the camp.

Our barren knoll was dotted with 100 barracks elevated a couple of feet above the ground for air circulation and drainage. Each was 20 meters long, capped with nipa palm thatch roofs. The huts were arranged in parallel rows. They provided two-decker bunk space for a maximum of 8,500 American POWs. Each had a wide open doorway at both ends with an elevated bamboo center aisle, and three small windows on each side,

138

closed by straw shutters. The thatch provided meager shelter from the rains which came from July until October. During the typhoon season the barracks were invariably wet. Up to 125 men were quartered in each barracks designed for 40. We slept on bamboo slats with each man allotted a space one meter wide. Bamboo, versatile as it is, even when split, provided an uneven, hard and uncomfortable bed. If covered with a rice straw tick or mattress, it soon became a homestead for bugs. Small boarded barracks were used for headquarters. Eight to 12 men were crowded into shacks assigned for officers.

The outstanding architectural edifice of Camp No. 1 was a wooden water tower on bamboo stilts, close by the Jap officers' quarters. The other vista highlight was a pond near the main gate with its white geese. The few trees that dotted the barren hillside were soon stripped. Leaves from guava trees were boiled for tannic acid tea, a major ingredient in our famous diarrhea remedy. The bare trees added to the desolation. They never had a chance, and the patients only slightly more. The three barbed wire perimeter fences, with the inner fence slanting sharply inward, locked at the base to the upright second fence, a no-man's land of three meters, and the third outside fence four meters tall, precluded any rational chance of escape. Except for one occasion, the fence proved to be insurmountable.

The camp was organized in a military way. The ranking field officer, Lt. Col. Curtis Beecher, assumed overall command, and the ranking medical officer, Lt. Col. James Gillespie, commanded the hospital. Medical support, in addition to the hospital, included three clinics scattered through the compound, each providing three sick calls a day.

Arriving on 30 November 1941, after five years in Shanghai, Beecher and 750 men from the 4th Marines had been assigned to Corregidor beach defenses. They fought a losing battle. In prison, he returned bloody-faced on several occasions after his morning conference with the Japs. They might have broken a lesser man. He took the beatings but never waivered from his American viewpoint and demands for fairness. I think he would have greeted Doomsday with a wink if he had the chance. He was tough enough to make a Marine sergeant wince.

During my imprisonment the hospital was commanded by me-

139

dical officers Lt. Col. James Gillespie, Lt. Col. William North, Lt. Col. Jack Schwartz, and, at the very end, Col. James Duckworth with me as his adjutant.

By December 1942, when I arrived, the camp held approximately 7,000 people. The hospital consisted of the western half of camp with general living quarters in the eastern half. By spring of 1943, with the heavy death toll and after dispatching large slave labor details, the population dropped to 5,000. Then the western section was closed and the hospital occupied the northern half of the eastern section.

The day after arriving at Cabanatuan, I found Maj. Clarence White and talked of our separate experiences in the last days of Bataan. He was serious, and in a laconic, professional manner, agreed with my decisions, and seemed pleased with my good luck, particularly in avoiding the worst of the Death March. I felt more comfortable with Clarence at this time than at any time in the past.

After a few weeks in Cabanatuan, Dwight Hunkins suddenly popped into my mind. Nobody seemed to know if he was still alive. Using the headquarters roster, I finally located him in Ward 3 of the hospital. Drawn and skinny, his eyes had a vacant stare, and his voice was husky and weak. A ghastly contrast to his old self, he presented an unbelievable picture of a man beaten mentally and physically. We talked several times, the conversation invariably reverting back to the "I'm going to die" theme. Despite our depressing dialogue, I continued to see him. Hunkins brightened when he spoke of his wife, but generally he wanted to be alone. He complained of severe and almost continuous abdominal cramps, the residue of numerous bouts with dysentery. Reluctantly, he accepted the little medicine I had. I think he really wanted to die. He seemed to have had enough of this misery, a road which was just a little too long. The official records say Dwight died in 1944, but I believe he went long before that, just fading away. A wonderful soldier and friend. Now only two Whiffenpoof Boys remained.

John Wallace and Jim Brennan, my counterparts as surgeons in the 1st and 3rd Battalion, had survived in fairly good condition. These two were savvy men and good soldiers. To see them again, still thriving, gave me a tremendous boost. Company

140

Commanders Conrad and Pray were okay. Communications Officer Tooley was missing. Capt Sauer of "E" company was dead. Rumor had Beattie, of our medical detachment, in Mindanao.

At first I bunked with newly met line officers in an eight-man wooden barracks away from the hospital. My bed was a woolen blanket stretched between two bamboo poles suspended like a hammock. In a few weeks I was transferred to the west side hospital to join Col. Sullivan from California; Maj. Wendell Swanson from Denver; Maj. Mike Sult from Oregon; Capt. Bob Schoottin from What Cheer, Iowa; Maj. Clarence Strand and Lt. Black of the Navy--all jolly good medical and dental officers.

Until the reduction in prison population, the water supply was inadequate. With the addition of four more outlets, we had sufficient water for showers. The sprinkler heads consisted of perforated gallon tin cans. This replaced standing out in the rain. Once, some of us dug a hole two meters deep, big enough for two men to use as an outdoor bath tub. It would fill up at times during the rainy season, but the uncertainty of rain and lack of a drain, along with the resulting mud puddle stirred up after the first half dozen baths, made us abandon the project quicker than it took to dig the hole.

Real soap did not appear for months after capture. We produced our own soap from lard and ashes. The dark brown product, smelling strongly of rancid fat, was cut into irregular hunks. Before too long, we stopped making soap, since lard was more valuable for food than for cleanliness. Aromatic soap finally arrived later in captivity. Used sparingly, a bar lasted three or four months. The "romantic" odor stirred memories, but no excitement.

I did my own laundry now by holding it under the faucet and squeezing it out in my fist. I wondered what had happened to Rosita, my *lavandera* with the long fingernails.

The brown, dusty parched ground without a speck of grass or color was carved with deep arroyos that handled the runoff water and prevented us from "going down the drain" with the sudden deluges during the rainy season. Those ditches presented a hazard for the weak, staggering, half-blind inmates, who would sometimes topple into the ditch and fracture an arm or leg. It was particularly dangerous at night since we all had night blindness.

Guard towers manned by two soldiers with rifles and a machine gun were mounted at each corner and midpoint on each side of the fence. The odds clearly favored the victors, and left no sport for us in trying to escape.

The final deterrent was the grouping of all into ten men "shooting squads." The Jap's order called for each group to sit down in a circle and discuss the folly of escaping, and to get better acquainted with the other nine men who would be shot if you escaped. Every month my group readily agreed to stay put. One group of nine was executed after an attempt to escape, and luckily, another group of nine spent 30 days in solitary confinement instead of being shot.

One night in the early days of the camp three men were discovered dragging sacks of food back into the compound. This was before the three perimeter fences were built. Only one strand was in place at that time. The trio had just made it back inside the fence when apprehended. Two were U.S. Army officers, one a handsome first lieutenant, the second a stocky lieutenant colonel, the third a younger red-headed Navy lieutenant. After grabbing their precious cache of food, the guards, screaming and hollering, dragged them back outside the single wire fence, beat them with their rifle butts until blinded, and carted them off to the boarded jail cubicles.

Within the hour, the court convened for a night session, convicting them of a crime against the Emperor and the Imperial Japanese Army. By morning the sentence was pronounced: 72 hours of torture or immediate execution. All three opted for the torture, supposedly to be released if still alive. All three then labored with a shovel digging their own graves just outside the fence, where they could be easily seen by the entire camp. The officers were pilloried backwards to a pole in a crouched position with their hands tied behind them and a two-by-four tied behind their knees. Their weight slowly settled on the two by four cutting off circulation in their legs. The pain and the numbness of the legs became excruciating.

The colonel, probably 50, short, greying, and every inch a soldier, gave up in 24 hours and begged to be shot. He knelt at his own freshly dug grave, delirious and with a blindfold. The four Jap guards lined up five meters away. They pointed their guns at

142

him, and then shot him. Bloody spots appeared on his forehead, he tottered for a few seconds and then toppled forward into the newly dug grave.

The other somewhat younger Army officer was beaten beyond recognition. Blind and delirious, his moaning and crying broke the silence of the night. He asked to be shot. The execution came at noon, at close range but without a blindfold.

The third man, the Navy lieutenant, a gritty red-headed all-American type, toughed it out nearly to the third day. Beaten until an ear hung by a thread down to his shoulder and unrecognizable, but drained by the torture of self-amputation of his legs, he finally requested to be shot. He was a brave man. He gave it all he had. They killed him with a three-man execution squad as he knelt at his grave staring at them. I cursed them as the lieutenant crumpled and pitched forward. At least three men were not suffering, they were not growing old in a prison.

My ardent hope for the families of these good men, indelibilized by a hundred recalls, was to know of their valor. Their loved ones should wipe away their tears, tilt their chins upwards, and accept the thanks from us that remained. Their only crime was trying to help others. As the years slipped by, erasing much of the horror, this image remains all too clear. I vowed that if I survived, I would help everyone that I possibly could. Torture or revenge was never an ingredient in my plans.

A soldier I knew roamed the camp, begging to trade rice for a cigarette--first it was one spoonful for one cigarette, then my rice for one half of a cigarette," and, finally, "my mess kit for a puff," just before he became completely unhinged.

On another occasion a soldier was killed, shot through the neck by a sentry in the tower. The POW was a long ways inside the fence, picking okra from his garden when the guard opened up. The Japs dragged the dead soldier over the fence where he lay most of the day. "He too close to the fence," was the only explanation.

Among the captives were twin brothers. One was shot in an attempted escape after hanging up in the perimeter fence wire. The other twin wandered around the camp for several months with a hangdog expression, shouting, "You yellow bastards murdered my brother." One day, in broad daylight, despite warnings

143

and surveillance by his fellow prisoners, he ran towards the fence, yelling obscenities at the guards. He grabbed the barbed wire and tried to climb over it. They promptly shot him. So ended his torment, but in the end he must have compounded his family's grief.

One soldier I knew became depressed and discouraged about the whole mess. The turmoil, the helplessness, went on and on. He could not see the end of the tunnel. Too many deadlines had been reached. He finally was caught throwing his food on the ground. Despite pleading from his buddies, who could think of a better use for the food, he soon died of starvation.

Time of day was noted in the Navy fashion with a large metal triangle struck with an iron clacker. In true Navy tradition, the number of bells might vary from "personal error," but after a couple of attempts our timekeeper would yell, "All's well." The Japs echoed our bell system with their catchy national anthem "Kimigayo," bugled by a loudspeaker every night at 1700 hours.

Headquarters kept a home-made calendar and dutifully crossed off the days. The week was punctuated by Sunday church; otherwise one day was no different from any other.

The Japs made us line up before dawn and count off for daily roll call in Japanese, "tenko." The guards followed the counting closely and cracked the poor dumb linguist and chronologist with a "vitamin stick" if he failed his turn at ichi, ni, san, shi, go, roku, shi chi, ha chi, ku, ju, etc. One imaginative GI tried to teach his buddy how to count by association. "Just think of the expression 'Itch (her) knee and she go,'" he explained.

Once we counted one man too many. The Jap vowed the count would be reconciled by an execution if the error remained. The seriousness of "Iron Face," the Jap in charge of roll call, led us to believe he would really have killed an extra American. After three countoffs taking all morning without breakfast, the mistake was uncovered--counting the same man twice--at his barracks and at his work station. Tenko count was completed in Wards 4, 3, 2, 1 and 0 by counting feet and dividing by two since the men usually couldn't stand.

One "tenko" was short by two men. Despite repeated counts the total revealed two missing. The Japs became agitated, threatening reprisals. To me the count seemed accurate since escape was almost impossible. But where were the two men? Just at the final hour before the Nips did something rash, both were found: one in the straddle trench almost immersed, and the other, like a sick dog, clear under a barracks. Both were dead.

One prisoner, somewhat mentally deranged, managed to slip through the entire network of fences, long after they were considered impregnable. His escape, discovered at the pre-dawn roll call, precipitated a screaming fixed bayonet charge through the camp by the entire Jap garrison. Wild screams and accusations by the Jap commander continued for hours: "Why you let him escape? Velly velly bad for you."

All morning the guards circled the stockade, trampling through the cogon grass, poking vigorously into the small rice straw stacks. It was almost noon before a sentry in a tower spotted the naked American sprawled on top of a three-meter high rice straw stack. He had lost his "G" string in maneuvering through the fence. He was scratched and bleeding and appeared to be half dead. Making no response, he was dragged by the heels towards the gate. The guards, deciding abruptly to end the incident, shot him as he lay helpless on the ground. The young lad had suffered through his long ordeal of captivity to end up completely muddled in his mind. I'm sure his new world was an improvement on reality. How he navigated those fences defied explanation. The Japs didn't evoke the rule of shooting nine men for each escapee after our camp headquartoers explained that he was crazy and not trying to insult the Emperor.

I learned to count in Japanese and also a few expressions like "*Anata wa byoki desuka?* (Are you sick?). Forty years later I can still count in Japanese. It is amazing how a "vitamin stick" can improve your long-term memory.

One day, a prisoner who was working just outside the fence in the torrid tropical sun called to his buddy to throw him his canteen of water. When he tossed it over, the guard in the tower yelled a couple of times. The GI, not understanding, poured water out to explain the maneuver. With that the Jap shot him, the bullet traveling clear through from neck to groin. The poor devil implored, "My God, don't shoot me again." The Jap fired two more shots to kill him. The buddy scurried away, hid in his barracks, and was left unharmed. All day long the crumpled bloody form lay in the sun. After dark we were allowed to retrieve the body. This episode was explained by a Jap commander who said, "He try to escape, now we'll make you suffer."

The hospital, always overflowing, functioned exclusively as a triage activity so that daily the sickest were eliminated from the "general" work group and admitted to numbered wards. Then they were transferred through fourth, third, second, first and, finally, St. Peter's or "zero" ward, depending on their condition. A few became permanent guests, such as Dwight Gard from Oregon, who hovered at death's door for over a year and survived.

Each morning at sunup, after "tenko" and chow of *lugao* (rice gruel), we hurried to the wards for a live count. On several mornings men would be found lying at the entrance stairs to the ward, too weak to walk and rocked with excruciating abdominal cramps. They had crawled to a hospital barracks, the natural place to seek relief. They stared vacantly at the misery around them until death spared them further suffering.

The dead, stripped of all clothing, were piled in a cubicle at the end of the barracks, then picked up every day by a gallant burial detail. Rarely were the bodies held over another day because of failure to mount a gravedigger detail. How the detail was volunteered those three long years remained a mystery to me. The Japs with their vitamin sticks and beatings stayed clear of this group. Each detail consisted of 12 men, four digging for a ten-minute shift and eight resting.

Some tried to avoid the gravedigging detail; as one kid remarked, "To hell with your detail. I'm going to be dead in a few weeks, so I couldn't care less." That type of soldier probably crapped any place he wanted to. Fortunately, not many of that kind remained in camp. Although we often said, "The good guys die early--that's why there are so many eightballs," almost without exception, the men would help if able.

The daily procession of the dead moved slowly up the road around 0900 hours with the emaciated corpses laid on two bamboo pole hammocks carried by four gaunt pallbearers. Bony arms and legs dangled over the sides. Dogtags were placed in their mouths or tied on their big toes. The daily total evoked a response of resignation or, possibly, "Things are picking up." A mass grave, for the day's grim harvest, remained the only practical procedure. The bodies were slung from the litters into the freshly dug pit. During the rainy season, from May to October, the grave became a pond, so the bodies would float around, making it almost impossible to cover. At times more dirt was necessary the following day to cover an arm or leg. Dates and names of the dead were written in as small a print as possible on the back side of canned goods labels. No paper, including toilet paper, was ever provided. The ink was home-made from a mixture of charcoal and argyrol--an antiseptic of the time.

Zero ward had a floor of wood planking. It functioned best for the dysentery patients because it could be washed out. Those still alive, dressed in a G-string, were carried to a faucet, washed off, and laid out on the ground or mats to dry. The G-string was rinsed out. Then the floor in the ward, the ultimate in slime and filth, layered with bloody excreta and a million flies, was swept clean and washed by a bucket brigade. Despite our cleaning, the stench of death and rotting flesh permeated this area. The dying patients were skeletons, writhing, struggling, gasping and wracked with abdominal pains. Some joked, "I'll piss on your grave." They were transported back to the ward after the cleanup under the faucet, hopefully to struggle through another 24 hours.

I'll never forget seeing husky corpsmen, with a human scarecrow under each arm, carrying them back to the ward.

A couple of buddies lying side by side in zero ward argued all the time. "You stole my dungarees, give 'em back, you bastard," one would say, neither having enough strength to pull the pants off the other. One morning the ward surgeon found the previously naked soldier had stripped his pal and pulled the dungarees half-way over his emaciated body. Both men were dead.

Joe Wengronowitz of the 2nd Battalion, 31st Infantry, tells of waking up in his barracks and finding the soldiers on each side of him dead. He filled their two mess kits and his own in the chow line, ate all three rations, and then reported the deaths to his barracks leader. Later Joe volunteered for a detail to Lysa in southern Luzon where the Jap guards, "Donald Duck" and "Three Whiskers," took turns beating him. Yet the food was better than at Cabanatuan, so the gamble paid off. One time Joe said he got so thirsty he drank the water out of the radiator of their truck. In the tropics he didn't have to worry about antifreeze.

Beatings were a daily occurrence in the camp, on the farm

and often along the trail to the farm. Our soldiers never cried, moaned or begged. They just quietly turned their heads away and suffered. After the work details had returned, the Nips allowed us to go back out and drag in the fallen, injured, or dying who couldn't make it to camp.

"Bushido" (clemency) was never requested or offered, but the Japs recognized bravery. Even the guards acted as though they were going to be killed and behaved like they deserved it.

During our three years of captivity, the camp enjoyed few tidbits more delightful than when a Jap guard in a sentry tower decided to take a piss. His stream made contact with the bare wires of the flood light, closing the circuit. He toppled out of the tower, fell ten meters, landing deader than a doornail.

On one detail the Japs regularly ate out of the POWs' mess, always taking a bountiful portion. The American mess personnel, figuring that a little extra seasoning would be good for the Japs, once added castor beans to their portions. The Jap detail soon was sick and disabled with severe cathartic enteritis. As far as we knew, unfortunately, they recovered after a prolonged convalescence.

The one and only mess hall, the center of activity, served all the food but had no seating, so you traipsed back to your palm-plaited *bahay* to devour it. Twice daily about a half hour before chow time, the men shuffled down the paths to queue up. Most had a little stagger to their step.

The large open building, covered with a nipa roof, sheltered three open-fire boxes and cooling stands for the cauldrons. A huge oven, made from baked adobe clay bricks, hard as rock, reinforced with rice straw, was in constant use. That oven lasted for three years without maintenance. The tiered oven offered three compartments in front and two on the side. These latter ovens provided means of baking your own little concoction--*kwan*--without obstructing the main kitchen activity. A long hose provided water for cooking, washing, or diluting the soup to meet the troop strength.

The most ambitious of my culinary achievements in camp was a cake made from cassava or taro root, the origin of tapioca. To the flour ground with a home-made rock mortar and pestle were added brown sugar cakes. About the size of a pancake, they contained, by accident, a few stalks of rice straw, the residue swept up from the floor of some sugar central. The sugar cane melted into cakes was to us a dear luxury. These cakes were usually stolen from a calesa pony's daily diet.

After days of planning, grinding the flour and locating a metal pan for baking, the concoction was taken to the kitchen. Yeast, preheating, and temperature gauging of the oven were not available. I watched the progress of this masterpiece by frequently opening the iron oven door. It didn't raise much but began to boil in spouts like Mt. Mayon Volcano, which I thought was a favorable sign. After 15 minutes, the mess sergeant looked at the "mess" and said the oven had done all it could and suggested the cake be removed from his domain. Proudly carrying the pan back to the *bahay*, I announced to my *bahay* mates that a sampling was at hand. They were Lt. Jim Musselman from Nebraska, Denny Rees from Oregon and Charley Lewis from Oakland, California. All were contributors. We sat down to eat. After heavy sawing with my knife, each was served a square. We chewed and chewed and finally Charley broke out laughing, "I'm going to rest for a while." I almost cried. It was positively undigestible--fit for a steel-belted tire on a jalopy. After gazing at the cake minus four squares for three days, I finally threw it in the dump. Musselman suggested using it for half-soling my clogs. I retorted, "Smart ass."

Sago palm, *gabi*, soya and mongo beans substituted for rice occasionally. Our rice, because it was medium-milled or half-polished, contained very little of the outer coverings. These polishings, valuable for its Vitamin B content, piled up on the dirt floor of the mills.

Prompted by the medics, our rice detail asked permission to sack up the brown powdery flakes and feed it to the prisoners. The polishings, called *tiki-tiki*, were spooned into our *lugao* every morning for over a month when, for no reason, the Japs said, "No more." Typically, they couldn't figure out why we wanted the polishings, so they stopped it.

Commercially polished rice does not ship or store as well. Interestingly, most Orientals prefer highly polished rice even though it has less food value.

At times the rice, mixed with white rocks, often tainted with kerosene, reportedly swept off the floor, required three washings before using. It was cooked in huge cauldrons nestled in home-made brick fire boxes. The exact amount of rice was stirred into the measured boiling water and immediately removed from the fire and covered with gunny sacks for steaming. The cooks became very proficient in producing fluffy steamed rice. A charred layer of rice remained on the bottom of the brazier which was scraped off. It was eagerly sought by a hungry mob. If you begged, you might get a chunk to gnaw on.

The Jap guards, nicknamed according to their behavior, appearance and savagery, received handles of *Tiger, Wolf, Hatchet, King of Swat, Dumb-Shit, Donald Duck, Speedo* and even *Clark Gable.* One pictured himself as a linguist and was always coming out with pidgin English or asking for a translation. Once he came up to Sgt. Bill Delich, a real natural wit, inquiring, "What means yellow?"

Bill said, "It's a color," pointing to a banana.

"Me see," said the Jap, pleased with his expanding vocabulary. "What means *baston--bosta*?"

Bill studied for a moment and then came out with *bastard.*

"Hai, hai, okay. Call me yellow bastard. I know yellow. What mean bastard?"

Without hesitation, Bill explained, "Very good friend."

"Ah, so," smiled the little yellow bastard. "Good friend--me, yellow bastard. Ah so!"

Our barracks were rarely inspected by the Japs. That was fortunate since their post inspection critique usually meant more restrictions instead of improvements.

At times the Japs covered their mouths with a white cloth mask. I was never clear on whether this custom was to prevent halitosis, or as others advised, to prevent the spread of germs. The Japanese did a lot of hissing by inhaling through their teeth. We were told this was a polite gesture.

Protocol in the Jap army included camp followers, whom they homesteaded in Malinta Tunnel on Corregidor and in nearby Cabanatuan for the bi-weekly benefit of the Jap soldiers. As expected, the incidence of gonorrhea was high and consequently the Jap soldier was constantly looking for sulfa tablets to cure his clap. He soon discovered the American sulfa with a W imprinted on the tablet, cured the drip. As a result of this demand, the Americans began counterfeiting the magic cure, mixing rice flour, corn starch, and a sprinkling of mint-flavored Colgate tooth powder when available. The pills were stamped out with a hollow brass 30-06 jacket. For the ultimate authenticity, a W was imprinted with a hand-whittled letter on the tip of a carabao horn. The W stood for Winthrop, the pharmaceutical house which made the real thing. A slow bake hardened the beautiful gems, finishing them for the market. The business flourished for a long time, providing an income of extra food. Since this disease is self-limited anyway and boys will be boys, success and a profit were guaranteed. The way I figured, the benefits were mutual.

These Orientals harbored funny notions of Americans. Some thought that Americans had to kill either their mother or their father to be eligible for the Marines. One Marine supposedly admitted killing his mother just to reinforce the notion.

Consistent with the inscrutable Oriental mind, the Japs discouraged excessive children by decreasing the family food ration and punishing the husband with a 60-day jail sentence all because he was clumsy and got his wife pregnant. We heard of Filipino women in labor having their legs tied together by Japs as punishment (but not as a solution) to the population explosion or family planning.

Telling stories was a great pastime in our first year of captivity. Most tales were chiefly concerned with one's heroics in combat. Being a little short in that department, I changed the conversation to digging foxholes where I had no peer. It seemed to me everyone was sticking to the truth the first year, began to lie the second year, and by the third year it was impossible to distinguish between truth and fiction. Women were never a topic. There was speculation, too, like "When will we be freed?" during the first year, politics and religion during the second, and a grab bag toward the end.

Another pastime always good for a laugh was to figure out the time of day back home. The best answer was to subtract eight hours and add one day, that is, if you lived on the West Coast. For example: In Manila, Monday, 8 December, 0200 hours was Sunday, 7 December, 1800 hours in San Francisco, I think. Everybody always got mixed up on that.

B y fall of 1942, dysentery was still epidemic. Prisoners had contracted the disease from polluted water in the ditches, the carabao wallows, or from flies-food-fingers, the three Fs. With open latrines, sanitation was impossible. Agonizing abdominal cramps and retching would seize the victim and in a few days his strength would be gone and he would be, too. The sufferers could not make the trip to the latrine. Victims would lie down close to the latrine and die. The whole scene generated an overwhelming impression of disease and starvation. There was very little food and no medicine. Something had to be done.

Of all creations in the camp, nothing surpassed the septic tank engineered by Maj. Emmet C. Lentz, a professional medical soldier. The major was a Carlisle graduate, the West Point for medical officers, trained in military medicine. By the time his production came on line, it seemed the camp had been half dug up, first with the cemetery and then with old-fashioned straddle trenches. The trenches were inadequate, physically impractical, filthy with maggots and excreta scattered feet away due to user malposition. They overflowed during the rainy season. A desperate situation of survival confronted the whole camp. Stench, filth and flies were taking over.

He constructed a metal slide ten meters long from metal salvaged from a long-abandoned wrecked automobile resting in the far corner of the camp. Sheets pounded out of the fenders, sides of the body and the top, were molded into a trough. It was placed on an incline and covered with "the throne"--a wooden box with ten holes. At the upper end a 50-gallon drum cut in a sagittal section was fulcrummed on a rod so as to dump a load of water into the trough when it was sufficiently filled. A continuous water bucket detail provided for a flushing every ten minutes. Next came the septic tanks constructed of wood with a baffle board allowing the effluent to settle in the first compartment, overflowing into the middle compartment, and drain off into the third.

Its performance was so good that the effluent, a trickle of water, was clear, odorless, and wouldn't attract flies. This "ten holer" was the nearest to a man-made miracle I'd ever seen--the Taj Mahal of Cabanatuan.

It saved the camp, it made it livable. The sight of ten men sitting on the throne, high and dry, reminded me of the famous men's room at the San Luis Obispo Motel. It never ceased to amaze me--a thing of joy and beauty--a hand-made septic tank. Despite the attractiveness of the throne, the paucity of reading material precluded a prolonged perch.

In 1943, a think-tank of medical officers suggested installing one-meter-high standing bamboo pipes all over the compound to be utilized as relief tubes. Supposedly, this would discourage indiscriminate urination and improve our sanitation. The pipes, however, were not widely utilized in daytime and almost never at night. The idea dried up from lack of use.

Daily, I watched a poor soldier from St. Peter's Ward struggling from his bunk to the "throne" every hour or two. He was plagued with dysentery and getting weaker all the time. He soon began to fall short of his goal and was compelled to relieve himself before reaching his destination. Each day the trip became harder and shorter until one morning we found him stretched just outside his barracks. Death solved the problem of "easing" himself in places other than the throne. For him dying was difficult, but death was sublime finality.

Despite our improved sanitation, by 1943 the fly population became intolerable. At meals one had to continuously fan the hungry flies away while shoveling food in with the other. Even at that it was not uncommon to capture one with an open mouth. Medical headquarters, attacking the problem by a bold maneuver, suggested a bounty system--one Filipino cigarette for each 100 dead flies.

Filipino cigarettes, thin, dark and wrapped in newspaper presented no bargain in aromatics, but were adequate to stimulate an active campaign. Flies by the hundreds and thousands transported by haggard soldiers in cans, rags, cupped hands, boards, banana skins or papaya leaves, showed up at headquarters for the exchange. Incidentally, Maj. Maupin soon gave up counting, as he became proficient at estimating dead flies in batches of one hundred. Within ten to 14 days, the fly menace was controlled. Not exterminated, but greatly improved. The habit of fanning my plate was so idelibilized that even after going home, Mother would ask, "Ralph, why are you fanning? I don't allow flies in my house."

Another habit the languishing soldiers learned was the "Filipino squat," a position in which you sit on your haunches with your arms wrapped around your knees and your fanny touching the ground. Without furniture or a tummy, it was a natural position assumed for hours. On returning home, a hostess (Mrs. Jane Hughes of Shaker Heights, Ohio) suggested I give up the habit and use a chair instead of squatting in the middle of her living room.

Parameters of one's natural status were the rate of hair and nail growth, erections and wet dreams. The fingernails grooved transversely in periods of starvation, separated by smoother areas during times of better food supplies. Those nails resembled the rings on a tree stump depicting years of more rainfall. A haircut and scalp shave would last from two to three months depending on the diet. Erections and nocturnal ejaculations only occurred after receipt of extra foods.

In all fairness, the record should show that Japan, although not a signatory to the Geneva Convention, agreed to adhere to the provisions relating to prisoners of war, reserving the right to "make changes when necessary." The deal was arranged with the help of the Swiss government in February 1942. It's hard to believe a copy of this ever graced the desk of the Japs in the Philippines. They decided with the Death March to lash the whip. After confiscating his medicine, the Red Cross representative in Manila was thrown into jail. The Japs used the excuse that they were never signatories of the treaty, so they could make their own rules and regulations. A pretty weak alibi for torturing human beings. "We have a better system," they said.

Hunger and time on our hands produced gardens and fruit tree plantings. It was just another effort to survive or at least get rid of that incessant gnawing in the stomach. Of the two vegetables in this world I detest the most, both grew almost unattended in Luzon—eggplant and okra. I believe I could die of starvation with a smile on my face between piles of okra and eggplant. Although not bitter like quinine, the bland taste of okra with abundant seeds, mixed with the slime, leaves much to improve on. Both plants grew rapidly on the small plots of ground, three meters wide and ten meters long, which were alloted to each of us. A bountiful crop would be expected in a few weeks. Some prisoners, probably the majority, didn't fiddle with the farming, but being an Iowa farm boy and craving both food and activity, I tended a garden.

A honey bucket detail, two buckets filled with excreta which we called "benjo" or "night soil," were balanced on a bamboo pole, and carried daily from the camp to the farm three kms. away. At times, at bayonet point, human dung was spread by hand. Consequently the rule was, "If you could peel it, eat it."

In addition to okra and eggplant I planted a dozen or so papayas. Each tree produced six to ten fruit in about three months. Bananas produced fruit in six months. New plants sprouted at the base of the old trunk cut down after harvesting the fruit. Stealing of fruit never occurred to my knowledge. Probably the most essential foodstuff produced was soybean sprouts. Soybeans, covered with a burlap sack and moistened every hour, exposed to the tropical sun, would sprout an inch every day. The sprouts, pushing through the loose web, were harvested daily. Eating only a small amount for the daily salad was sufficient to prevent or cure scurvy since any rapidly sprouting plant contains abundant Vitamin C.

The British Navy struggled with that problem for centuries, carrying limes and then sprouting turnips aboard ship. We benefitted from their experience.

A Wall of Bilibid Prison near the spot where Pilar
passed food and medicine to the P.O.W.s

Aboard ship in Manila, 1940-41.
Pilar Campos as a reporter.

This rare photo shows the emaciated condition of those who survived the horrors
of a Japanese prison camp. Far right, Mr. F.V.J. Thornton.

15. STARVATION AND MALADIES

Defeat, starvation, pestilence, torture, neglect, disappointment, and hopelessness had reduced us to a powerless rabble presenting no problem of discipline or escape. Our doom had already been sealed. The hollow-bellied and dispirited GIs were trying to live under the equatorial sun in a desolate compound without even laughter.

Prison life for a medical man was a never-ending witness to the cumulative effects of starvation. The ration was always below starvation level. The extra foods we received from time to time made survival possible. Diseases, nearly extinct in normal times, were opportunistic here. The whole place was a pathological museum. Most doctors would never see such cases in their entire life. The medical activities were limited by lack of equipment, medicine and the health of those of us administering care. Everything happening in camp related to agony, cruelty, and dying. This was hardly a medical show. As a medical man, what could I do? Prison life was certainly not my destiny or my eternity, or was it? Something good must befall me if I was to survive.

Some men lost over 100 pounds during their captivity. My record was from 178 to approximately 120 pounds. Corpulence gave way to bare bones. Fat and the pot fronts were the first to go, not the mind. Interestingly, a self-avowed "alcoholic," at least in peacetime, was questioned repeatedly about his old drinking habits. He responded to the inquiry, "Have you given up drinking?" with "No, just postponed it."

By and large the condition of the men was horrible and shocking to me. Those walking around presented a picture of emaciation or a bloating beyond recognition. The paths of camp were usually empty except at messtime, since no one had the strength to waste. A few moped around searching for cigarette snipes. The searing paths fired by the tropical sun made sandals a must. To stumble and lie in the sun for just a few minutes would be tantamount to becoming a grease spot--if there was any fat left to render. The grimy scarecrows, their carcasses covered only by a

G-string, suffered silently in the unshaded barrenness of this primitive prison camp. The battling bastards of Bataan became a grave picture of hideous suffering and neglect, ravaged by a savage captor. It was nothing if not the most depressing scene I'd ever seen. Even the landscape of our camp seemed naked, as colorless as its inmates.

Medicines for all purposes were exhausted. No replacement of supplies were forthcoming from the Japs. Small amounts of quinine, both tablets and flaky powder, and sulfa showed up irregularly and mysteriously. After the war, over 50,000 quinine tablets were found on the shelves of Sternberg U.S. Army Hospital. How easy it would have been to save hundreds of lives lost to malaria, but someone would have had to convince our captors that that was important. Only the sickest patients in a life-threatening situation received treatment. Those with "cerebral" malaria, chills, fever, delirium, and even coma might receive three or four, five-grain tablets of quinine a day, for one or two days. If the poor devil had bloody diarrhea along with a chill and fever up to 105 or 106 degrees he would die in 24 hours. He was on his feet one day and gone the next. We had IV fluids to replace the fluid loss. Nobody could withstand that stress. Such was the course for hundreds and thousands of our boys. That was the acute way out.

Intravenous quinine, a desperate but essential measure for overwhelming malaria (celebral malaria) in a comatose patient, was never available as a sterile-packaged product. Consequently, quinine powder and crushed tablets were partially dissolved and suspended in boiled water and injected intravenously. The unsterile solution was used sparingly and only if the patient had been chilling and remained unconscious for several days. A febrile reaction occurred with the injection, followed by improvement and recovery in most cases. To the best of my knowledge, no one was killed with this unorthodox therapeutics procedure. At times a rubber Levine tube was threaded through the nose into the stomach and powdered quinine was fed to the comatose patient.

Our diarrhea medicine consisted of guava leaf tea as long as our few trees had leaves, corn starch, and charcoal made by the faithful crew from charred wood and coconut shells. An occasional dram of tincture of opium might be generously added. Its therapeutic value might be challenged but the patient was grateful to note the color change of the stools from a bloody mess to black. My pharmacy professor at the University of Iowa Medical School praised the adsorptive qualities and consequently the effectiveness of charcoal in intestinal infections. With this bias I dispensed this potion with just a little more enthusiasm than a placebo.

Nutritional edema, pellagra, ariboflavinosis, beriberi, peripheral neuritis, scurvy, xerophthalma and corneal ulceration had their onset in approximately that order between April and December 1942. This order was dependent on the storage capacity of each vitamin. The vitamins with the shortest storage capacity, water solube B and C, accounted for the early appearance of beriberi and scurvy. Long-storage, fat-soluble Vitamin A, D and E deficiencies appeared later.

Two types of beriberi were differentiated, wet and dry. With the former, the patient was bloated from head to foot, possibly grotesque and unrecognizable. He hobbled along, barely able to carry the extra 20-40 pounds of water weight. The dry type produced a peripheral neuritis of the legs. It was universal. My feet felt like they were going to sleep most of the time. It was characterized by the "Cabanatuan shuffle." The excruciatingly tender feet were gingerly placed with care with each high step, like walking on hot coals, the arms flinging in the air to lessen the impact. The feet burned with a prickly sensation day and night to further torment the poor souls. Unable to sleep, they would sit up, rub their feet and moan all night long. No pain medicine was available. At times the legs were dead and numb, but would wake up with an improved diet and vitamin supplement.

Optic nerve atrophy, severe and irreversible, caused blindness. Further eye involvement resulted from Vitamin A deficiency with night blindness, corneal ulceration, ophthalmia, spontaneous enucleation and loss of the eye. The grimmest picture in the camp was the poor soul with a bloody eyeball sloughing out of the socket. The palmar erythema of the hands, magenta-colored atrophic tongue, cracked corners of the mouth, huge purplish hemorrhages in the exposed surface, and blindness were further evidence of severe Vitamin B deficiency and pellagra.

Beriberi spots, a red, swollen, hot and painful subcutaneous lump with a predilection for the shins, usually resolved in 72 hours.

Tachycardia, enlarged heart, pericardial effusion, heart failure, and at times sudden death, suggested beriberi heart disease.

Hemorrhages into the eyes or muscles, nosebleeds, and spongy, bleeding gums were diagnostic of scurvy and lack of Vitamin C.

Dysentery, both acute and chronic, spread through the camp repeatedly. We had bacillary, amoebic and giardiasis. When a microscope was provided in 1943, a bacteriological diagnosis was possible. A scant supply of injectible emetine (a specific for amoebic infections) was used for liver abscesses or peritonitis. After one or two injections, the swollen liver would shrink, ending the treatment until the infection flared again. One patient who came to autopsy had an amoebic liver abscess, transphrenic spread into a lung abscess and an embolic septic brain abscess. Endameba histolytica was identified in all the abscesses.

Some men were disabled for many months by huge chronic pustular, foul-smelling leg ulcers or yaws. Skin antiseptics and bandages were not available and soap was in short supply. With nutrition so poor they just wouldn't heal. Cellulites of the scrotum was another indication of poor resistance and depleted healing potential.

Kidney stones were attributed to Vitamin A deficiency and negative calcium balance due to inactivity and dehydration.

Mental illness (who didn't have it?) was not managed since there was no treatment or compensation for the patient: The depressed or neurotic patient might stare at the ground for a day or two, and miss a few meals. Then, after being ignored by all, he would trudge off to the mess after a miraculous cure.

Unpredictable to an extreme, the Japanese guards exhibited an inordinate fear of people they thought were crazy. One day they spotted an American working on a road detail filling his mouth with rocks. The poor guy was mentally disorganized by heat and starvation. The guard asked what was wrong and was told the American was "crazy." The guard ordered the prisoner back to camp, relieving him from the work detail. The next day 24 POWs sat on the road stuffing rocks in their mouths. The glowering guard figured something was screwy so he beat up everybody, which cured the rock-eating tendency.

To my knowledge, there were only two suicide attempts among the prisoners. Both clumsily slashed their wrists. The wounds healed without complications. Depression leading to suicide usually resulted from concern about things that might happen. In our situation the daily suffering was sufficient without borrowing from tomorrow.

The "surgical suite," as described by Dr. Major M.C. Warren Wilson of Los Angeles, consisted of two rooms, one of which was the supply room where the chief of surgery slept, the other was a large room which had an operating wooden table and also an operating chair. There was one electrical operating light which was portable with a backup storage battry. There was also one sink, usually soap to scrub, but only cold water. Drapes were boiled but thre was no true sterilization.

Stealing, reported to POW headquarters a few times, at first carried a jail sentence which amounted to confinement in a barricaded nipa shack. On trips to the mess or straddler trench, the poachers was tethered by a rope, tied around one leg. An American guard traipsed along holding the other end. This amounted to nothing more than shame, which was in short supply anyway. The confinement kept a prisoner off the work details and a likely beating by the Japanese, so the net result was that our punishment did not fit the crime. This policy was abandoned. It was then suggested to the victim that he settle it with the thief himself. After a couple of thieves were beaten up and knifed severely, no further problem surfaced. Stealing, compounded by the lack of privacy and closeness of living, was intolerable. I knew of one poor soldier who vomited his food back into his mess kit, but it was stolen during the night.

The mess sergeants, tought and honest by necessity if not by nature, were also practical. One afternoon as I came to the kitchen just before chow, I heard someone shout, "Look, here comes a detail." Down the road marched 200 hungry and unexpected Americans, all ready for chow. The sergeant took one look and barked, "Turn the hose into the soup and let her run for two more minutes." This way the soup went around.

One of the mess sergeants received a gibbering monkey as a gift from his truck-driving pal. Tied with a ten-meter chain to a post of the mess hall, the pet monkey was allowed to run around the area and onto the roof. Bosco was the center of attention but also abuse. One soldier in particular maligned the poor animal constantly until one day the monkey, spotting his tormentor strolling up the path, sneaked along the roof, jumped on him and bit him on the neck. The monkey did a mysterious disappearing act after that. I wasn't invited to the wake.

One day the mess sergeant, worn down by arguments and stealing around the kitchen, stormed into headquarters demanding a "no rats will be cooked in the mess" policy. "One fellow is even raising them!" he hollered.

The truth of this matter escaped me, but there certainly were enough resident rats without trying to raise them. Garbage was almost non-existent, so the rats were struggling for food, too. Lt. Col. Jack Schwartz, our CO by then, agreed that the cooking of rats and other unorthodox food items had no priority and should not interfere with usual kitchen procedures. A desist order was distributed by word of mouth, but secretly the practice continued. If you could catch it, eat it. At one pre-dawn breakfast a mouse was ladled from the *lugao* into a mess kit before it was detected.

Another day I spotted a truly remarkable sight--four dressed rats evenly arranged on a metal platter, ready for the side oven of fire pit no. 4. My reaction was only disappointment at not being invited to their gourmet meal. Reputedly rat tasted like chicken. Another advantage of including rats on the *kwan* menu was not only to reduce their number but to stop the nibbling on your toes at night. Rats, finding the pickings slim, prowled the camp after dark. Scaling the posts of your bed, the rats would take a bite of your toes through the mosquito net. A sudden kick would end their foraging and send the rat flying against the wall.

No refrigeration, not even a cool well or a cave, was available. Consequently, meat was consumed on the day of slaughter. Fish, usually only the heads, could be kept briefly packed in salt in woven rattan casks.

Because the Japanese loved ducks and geese, both from an aesthetic and culinary standpoint, our guards quite naturally started a brood in the pond. The pond drained through the culvert across the road, traversing a fence into our area. The openings of the culvert were sealed off with a wire mesh. By some misadventure on our part the mesh was widened to goose size, allowing the little quacky morsels into our area.

The capture was painfully slow, painstaking, and dangerous. It required complete silence while using highly technical equipment. It was difficult but necessary to be out of sight during the entire heist. Also, complete riddance of the feathers was mandatory. A hook made from a pin, tied to a two-meter line on a short stick, baited with a kernel of corn, was flipped towards the culvert opening. The goose gulped down the kernel. Now, timing was vital. You waited until the kernel reached the voice box. With a sudden jerk, the goose was not only captured, but "gorked"--our word for quick strangulation. The goose was silent, never able to spread the alarm by uttering a squawk. By the time the Nips discovered our tricks, their flock of 40 was half gone. Mystified by the modus operandi, yet sure who the culprits were, the Japs ordered us to stop doing whatever it was we were doing.

Incidentally, the Japs one day issued three chickens and nine eggs for 500 prisoners. The following day a group of Jap officers inspected the camp. Capt. Mori, the camp commander, turned to Col. Beecher and said, "You had chicken and eggs yesterday. It's true, isn't it?" Beecher nodded sadly.

Maj. Clarence White came by my *bahay* one morning, which was not his custom.

"I want you to sit on a beriberi commission organized by the Japs," he said. "There'll be four Americans and three Japanese doctors meeting daily except Sunday at 0900 hours. Capt. Robert Lewis and Maj. Steve Sitter will be the other medical officers. The purpose is to observe and study beriberi in this camp. Tomorrow is the first meeting," he said in his usual no-nonsense manner.

"Yes, sir, I'll be there," I replied. "Thank you."

The following day, temporarily forgetting about it, I strolled into the room 15 minutes late. All six, including the three Japanese, were seated around a big wooden table, bare except for a teapot, cups and a small plate of the thinnest wafers ever produced by man. Clarence interrupted the session to chew me out about my tardiness. He chewed on me until I thought he'd never quit. I suppose the bawling out was to impress the Jap medical officers. The chairman introduced himself as Capt. Inada, professor of medicine at the University of Mukden, Manchuria. He talked firmly and slowly in good English, looking stiff and formal.

163

The captain was the neatest and cleanest-looking Jap I saw during the entire campaign.

"This war is just as unpleasant to me as it is to you," he said curtly. "There will be no political discussion allowed. Only scientific observations will be presented."

Capt. Inada served the thin wafers and tea only at the first session. That was almost the only good news or reward garnered from the month-long meetings. The captain learned something but we did not. No death statistics were allowed because it would clearly show neglect and indifference. The only other beneficiaries were 60 POWs who received thiamin chloride (Vitamin B1) by various routes--IV, intrathecally, and orally to determine the most efficacious route in reversing beriberi. In reality, the condition by that time had been present so long that it was almost irreversible, regardless of the mode of administration.

After the first meeting we strolled up the path and Clarence opened up again.

"I meant every word I said," he said. "Don't keep people waiting!"

That lesson has never been forgotten.

16. CABANATUAN, 1942-1943

Two thousand two hundred Americans, more than twice the number killed on the Death March, were buried at O'Donnell in April and May 1942; of these, 232 were from the 31st Regiment. More than 2,500 more died at Cabanatuan from June to October 1942. A total of 2,656 Americans were buried in the Cabanatuan cemetery. That compares with 27,000 prisoners, Filipino and American, who died at O'Donnell before the prison camp closed in August and September 1942. A total of 50,297 Filipino and American fighting men died in the defense of the Philippines. Why almost 25,000 Filipinos, native to the land, died so quickly in captivity remains somewhat of a mystery. Apparently, the Filipinos were no match for the disorganization, starvation, and disease dealt by prison life.

A diphtheria epidemic hit the camp about September 1942, after four months of captivity. At this time, with physical resistance at its lowest level, the opportunistic germ attacked. Even though everyone had been vaccinated with diphtheria toxoid, the immune defenses were inadequate and the horrible infections invaded hundreds of prisoners, attacking the throat, nose, eyes, penis, and peri-anal tissues. The typical lesion was a thick shaggy grey membrane adhering tightly to the mucus membrane. The commonest site was the throat, closing off the air passage. It was followed by a deadly paralysis. We had no treatment despite our pleas to the Japs to give us anti-toxin from our own supplies at Sternberg General Hospital. After nearly 130 deaths and innumerable cases of blindness and deafness, they gave us a miniscule supply of anti-toxin. It was enough to prevent deaths but not all of the complications. A shaggy membrane growing out of the mouth or covering an eye presented a ghastly unreal picture. The face and eyes of patients pleaded for help as they slowly strangled. The epidemic burned itself out in three months, just another example of the Japs ignoring our request for decent, humane treatment.

A hot sunny day set the stage appropriately about the 20th

165

of December 1942, around noon, when a huge unnatural shout went up. It was an American war whoop, a celebration like a touchdown cheer. People were running towards the main gate where a Jap detail incredulously was unloading Red Cross food packages into the arms of a prison crew. The distribution was 2.5 of the 9-pound, 10" X 12" X 4" packages per man. The joy was unlimited. The men milled around laughing and crying. Some sat down and pounded the ground to give thanks.

"They haven't forgotten us. Now we'll make it!" This marked the happiest day of the entire captivity.

It provoked a deep feeling of gratitude. The celebration went on for days. The morale soared and the death rate tumbled. The truly unbelievable had happened. Not "hundreds of planes and thousands of ships," but food--good old life-saving stuff--was placed in our hands. The smell of American tobacco permeated the camp. It was truly manna from heaven.

AMERICAN RED CROSS
Standard Package No. 8
for
PRISONER OF WAR
Food Contents

Evaporated Milk, irradiated: one 14 1/2-oz. can
Lunch Biscuit (hard tack): one 8-oz. package
Cheese: one 8-oz. package
Instant Cocoa: one 8-oz. tin
Sardines: one 15-oz. tin
Oleomargarine (Vitamin A): one 1-lb. tin
Corned Beef: one 12-oz. tin
Sweet Chocolate: two 5-oz. bars
Sugar, Granulated: one 2-oz. package
Powdered Orange Concentrate (Vitamin C): one 7-oz. package
Soup (dehydrated): one 5-oz. package
Prunes: one 16-oz. package
Instant Coffee: one 4-oz. tin
Cigarettes: two 20s
Smoking Tobacco: one 2 1/4-oz. package

166

Many of the packages had been rifled by the Japs, but, strangely, only the Old Gold cigarettes were removed. The guards looked amazed as we opened the packages and checked the contents. this one-time increase in the ration soon prevented almost all the deaths from starvation. Each of us hoarded his packages with varying discipline. My stockpile lasted for six months.

Some soldiers traded a can of butter or meat for a pack of American cigarettes. Smokers sometimes quipped, "I'm going to die anyway, and this is the greatest pleasure I can think of." After smoking a portion of the cigarette, it was snuffed out and stored. With the aid of a holder, three or four lightups were possible until the final butt was pulled out of the holder and saved in a tin. Three or four butts provided enough tobacco for a freshly rolled cigarette. Another technique was to spear the butt with a toothpick to get a couple more puffs without burning the fingers.

The equation was not as simple as "I'm going to die anyway." After all, one might survive with the help of butter and meat and then smoke up a storm. Incidentally, the odor of an American cigarette was soon detectable upwind 1,000 meters away. A Filipino type was easily differentiated from a Canadian, Camel, Lucky Strike, or the most common for us, Old Golds.

On one occasion, I traded a pack of Old Gold cigarettes for a can of butter. Afterwards, the transaction made me feel guilty, so much so I would never trade my smokes again.

The day's ration of 600 to 700 calories from the Japanese remained quite unchanged, however. The soup was ladled into your cup, but everything else was piled into your mess kit and generally mixed up. Nothing remained in your mess kit or the kitchen after a meal.

With the arrival of these packages, by mid-January 1943, the Grim Reaper counted less than double figures every day thereafter. The highest recorded daily death rate was recorded at O'Donnell 27 May 1942, when 77 Americans died. Our death toll decreased gradually from 50 to 15 per day during the period from June to December 1942. The daily average death rate in July was 30; August, 21; September, 14; October, 19; and November, 15. By that time, almost half the survivors of Bataan were dead. Death was part of our lives, but the Japanese reported none or inaccurate figures to the Red Cross.

One month after the first Red Cross distribution, on 18 January 1943, we celebrated the first day without a death. The camp buzzed with excitement--"No burial detail today! The pallbearers have the day off." By mid-1943, six months after the first Red Cross packages arrived, we celebrated our first week without a death. The macabre parade of corpses dangling on two pole stretchers dwindled. In a few months, only an occasional death occurred. The grim morning detail for the ward surgeon and corpsmen to search through the patients for dead ones was nearly past.

Even with the improved ration, however, tragedy struck one night when a lad, crazed with hunger, gorged himself on the pulp from the trunk of a papaya tree. The porous inside contained cellulose and fiber but not one calorie. The soldier craved the full feeling, the comfort of a big meal, so he satisfied himself with nothing more than tasteless pulp. Surgery, under local anesthetic without IVs and without adequate means of decompression of the intestinal obstruction, was unsuccessful, and he died.

Rummaging through the garbage dump was common practice. Our dump consisted of a hole in the ground, covered by a small lid. It became necessary to post a guard and padlock the cover to prevent pilfering. Little edible food made its way to the dump anyway. It was mostly the peelings, skins and spoiled food. One time uncooked sago swamp root peelings were discarded and found their way into the hands of two hungry men. The skin contains cyanide, a highly volatile and deadly poison which is quickly dissipated by heating. I always imagined sago peelings were similar to our water hemlock. The diagnosis and prognosis became apparent without their admission of eating the peelings. Death came quickly to those lads since we had no antidote.

On two occasions, Maj. Bennett from Florida slipped me food sent by Shriners in Japan. "Take it and don't ask questions." I did exactly that. Our thanks has never been delivered to them. At times the Jap guards might be involved in food smuggling, but this was risky. Several times Jap officers spotted the contraband in the seat cushions, hub caps, or a false bottom under the floor boards of an incoming truck. This incriminated the guards and the Americans as well, and called for beating up everybody, or a month's solitary confinement, and at times execution. One American driver who had helped the TB patients so much turned up missing. He was shot beside his truck when contraband food was discovered.

In September 1943, when life had stretched out to a long wait and the death rate was acceptable, we were dealt a blow out of the blue. It happened during the rainy season which kept everything wet with sudden downpours. Even if it had been available, rain gear served little purpose since you became wet with perspiration instead of rain. On this day, the shower was heralded with a bolt of lightning and a clap of thunder. Just as the deluge started, a runner burst through the door to report, "Lightning just struck a man over on the knoll and killed him. We tried to get his breath back." I looked at the heavens, wondering what lesson God was proposing.

Shoes (clogs, really) were whittled from wooden boards. Straps for the clogs, either leather or webbing, were difficult to come by. Your worn-out, mildewed shoes provided the best source. Two pairs of clogs lasted three years.

Beards were discretionary as were haircuts. But, because hair increased body hygiene problems by providing a homestead for cooties and lice, most of us were clean shaven on the top and on the chin. However, the tickling of flies strolling around a sunburned scalp was a nuisance. A 1918 general-issue mess kit knife was a premium, providing good-tempered steel for shaving.

Some place along the line I secured a Gem razor blade. It was sharpened for three years by rubbing it on the inside of a drinking glass. The barber, using this equipment, kept my chin and head bald. Depending on the food intake, my trips to the barber would vary from two to three months apart.

Good old Buster Conrad sported a dandy handlebar mustache for months which triggered every Jap guard to yank it or give him a blow with the vitamin stick. After a couple of deep bruises, administered for no reason, he gave up the mustache.

The GI khaki uniform slowly disintegrated. Both the arms and the legs had long since been cut off. By 1943 the prison dress code was almost identical to that of a nudist colony. The G-string was full dress. It consisted of a string belt tied around the waist and a crotch flap looped through the belt in front. Coded for modesty, a Jap issue, it was the only thing worth a damn the Japs gave us. Complete nudity was not practiced unless on an emergency run to the head. Jackets were not universally worn, and usually consisted of a collarless, sleeveless and buttonless vest made from discarded GI clothes. Mine was made from a discarded mattress cover. Several soldiers, starting from complete inexperience, became tailors. They salvaged cloth, unraveled thread, fashioned needles from wire or spark plugs, carved thimbles from carabao horns, extracted dye from logwood, and discarded nothing. They learned to patch and repatch skivvies. In return for their services, they could expect from nothing to a few cigarettes or a hearty handshake.

Night after night in the first months, a slinky figure came by our *bahay* and in a whispered voice gave us choice news bits, just off "the crystal set." To this day his identity and the source of the news was never openly admitted, probably the best kept secret in camp. After a while he stopped coming by our *bahay* since no one was interested. After months, and a few years went by, I wanted none of it. The news, Army broadcasts, was repetitious, not persuasive and smacked of overt propaganda. By now the remaining men were just sufficient to divide the ration, run the camp, tend the cemetery and keep the morning report up to date.

Scuttlebutt described a short wave radio hidden inside a canteen. It was the work of a mechanical genius. It consisted of a crystal, copper wire, a lead tube from a tooth paste container, and a single rubber tube fitting into an ear piece from a stethoscope. The construction, a miracle in itself, offered great consolation to many who indulged in wishful thinking. It wouldn't wash with me.

In 1943 our captors finally gave us our own microscope and fluoroscope from Sternberg General Hospital. The "mike" helped out, particularly in tuberculosis and dysentery diagnosis, but the surging unpredictable electrical current made the x-ray nearly useless. We didn't have any x-ray film anyway.

In June 1943, Col. North, God bless him, asked for volunteers to be the surgeon of the TB ward. The medical officers, about 30 of us, were all standing outside the Headquarters in our usual assembly area. As best I could see my hand was the only one in the air. The tuberculosis ward of about 40 patients became my responsibility and my love from 8 June 1943 to January 1945. It turned out to be a real challenge which I readily accepted. Supervision of the ward presented a daily routine with a modicum of professional activity. A personal mandate, which I never excused, dictated examining each bare chest twice a day with a stethoscope. No one was permitted to leave the ward until this was completed.

By mid-1943 the camp population was fairly stable, about 6,000, and everyone with a chronic cough and rales in their lungs had been screened for TB. The weak had died, and the disease hopefully was arrested in the remainder. The majority of the cases had a positive sputum confirmed with our newly acquired microscope. Our job consisted of isolation to prevent exposure and to stabilize the disease in the active cases. Consequently, in and out of the ward visiting was prohibited; no outside work details were demanded. Control of spitting and coughing was taught. No chemotherapy was available. Extra food was issued by the Japs to the workers but not to the sick. Supplemental food from the underground--fruit, sugar, canned milk or fish--although rarely available, might filter down to zero or the TB ward. Our policy was not necessarily to give it to the sickest, but to someone who might live because of the extra bit of food.

Our big medical deal on the ward was initiating and maintaining pneumothoracies (collapsing lungs) by injecting room air into the chest through a 20-gauge needle. Without anesthesia, other than vocal ("It won't hurt you at all"), we went to work. A puncture needle was threaded along the upper border of the rib, in order to miss the intercostal nerve and artery. The needle was pushed deep enough to lie between the two pleural surfaces in the space just peripheral to the lungs. The collapse was performed by injecting air into this space. The equipment consisted of two flasks, one with a two-hole rubber stopper which was empty and a second flask filled with water. Water ran from the elevated second flask into the first forcing air into the rubber tubing connected to the lung. In this way a measured amount of air was gently and slowly injected into the pleural space. In the circuit going to the lung was a glass Y-connection, one line leading to the lung and the other line to a monometer, a U-shaped glass tube filled with colored water mounted on a lined background. With a three-way petcock it was possible to open and close the air flow to the lung or measure the pressure in the pleural space. Measuring the pleural pressure was vital since the lung would not collapse unless the normal pressure was changed to positive. On the other hand, too much pressure might produce a tension pneumothorax, suffocating the patient.

We had tried collapsing the lung on both sides on several patients--one had died, two were uncomfortable with dyspnea from plural tension so most ended with a unilateral collapse.

The Rube Goldberg gadget functioned normally without cmplications for over two years, initiating 12 pneumothoracies and maintaining six for the entire duration. Refills necessitated a puncture every two to three weeks. No infections, emboli, ruptured lungs or aortas or life-threatening tensions were experienced.

Unfortunately, an x-ray, a *sine qua non* in this procedure, was not available. The needles and tubing washed in soap, boiled at the mess hall, were hung up to dry until the next session. As the tubing began to disintegrate with repeated boiling, this was discontinued.

One fateful morning, Sgt. Alva Vico, a severe advanced case of bilateral pulmonary, active tuberculosis, was scheduled for a refill. The tall, skinny scarecrow was lying on his right side on the bare wooden table in the small boarded cubicle which was our surgical suite.

Vico, the only soldier with sustained bilateral pneumothoracies at that time, volunteered, "I'm feeling pretty well, Captain; my temperature is about normal. I rarely cough, and I haven't seen any blood recently." I washed my hands and his chest, and began. Vico grunted as the needle was thrust without anesthetic through the eighth interspace in the posterior axillary line. I turned the petcock to measure the pressure in the pleural space. The monometer indicated--four with deep inspiration and 0 with expiration.

"You need air," I informed him. "When was the last fill?"

"Three weeks ago," he replied.

At that moment a huge grey bug, probably a beetle, crawled down the tubing to the glass Y junction where I first spotted it. I cleared my throat, sealed my lips and glared at Sgt. Carl Stuart, my corpsman, surgical assistant, and sterilization technician. Our eyes were glued on the bug in the main stem of the glass tube. It pondered its route at the crossroads. If it chose the left tube it was on its way to Vico's lung; the right led to the monometer and out of our way, at least momentarily. Its two long antennae probed the tube ahead moving slightly forward and backward, not committing itself.

"How are you feeling, Vico?" I inquired just to break the tension.

Unaware of the drama of the tubes, Vico said cheerfully, "Just fine, sir." His color must have been better than mine.

After an interminable time, replete with innumerable false starts, Mr. Beetle opted for the right or the monometer side and slithered up the rubber tubing out of sight. We finished the procedure hurriedly, removed the needle and carried Vico back to his bunk.

As Stuart returned, I let out my breath.

"You bastard, you," I blurted. "I told you to get the bugs out of the equipment."

We both laughed, but not for long as we began worrying about infection.

Vico never knew the difference, and was never told. He had no ill effects whatsoever. In the future it became standard procedure to give the tubing a few violent shakes followed by a sideways glance at Stuart before starting the procedure.

Stuart usually reassured us with, "No bugs in the equipment today, sir."

17. CABANATUAN, 1943-1944

Around 6,000 Americans died from the victor's neglect in the period from surrender through January 1943. But with the receipt of the Red Cross packages, the bamboo catafalques appeared less crowded. Even the most emaciated men improved in body and soul. The hospital census leveled off. Vacancies in Zero ward were reported. Maybe we all had a chance. There was real hope. I figured my chances were better than those we buried today. Starvation, always a problem, was manageable.

We settled down for the long struggle of survival. Almost all were proud, not cowing to torture or the threat of losing their lives. Malaria was on the decline since the anopheles mosquito was usually not resident at Cabanatuan. Dysentery was decreasing be-cause of natural immunity and improved sanitation. The diet was supplemented by our own gardens, smuggling, and rarely a com-missary. The biggest boost came from the Red Cross. The natural selection process in which the strong survive came on line.

Lt. Col. Jack Schwartz took over as CO of the hospital about mid-1943 from Lt. Col. William D. North, a rough, straight-shooting soldier medic. Bill's resignation came because of illness after two-plus years in command. Jack ran the hospital in a brilliant, quiet and efficient way. This skinny little bow-legged man was endowed with a soft-spoken leadership ability along with fairness and ingenuity. His natural smile, jagged nose, and soft eyes composed an engaging appearance. I judge his weight then at about 110 pounds on a 5' 6" frame.

Yet, one day, without provocation, the Jap squad appeared and grabbed Jack. Surrounding him with their bayonets, they marched him down the road. He looked so small and helpless. They locked him up in solitary confinement. I would have bet we would never see Jack alive again. He could not see out of his dark wooden cell, which was less than two meters long by one-half meter wide and boarded up to the nipa palm roof. Room did not permit him to straighten out his legs. Twice a day for ten minutes, he was allowed a ''head'' call.

Great secrecy and depression hung over hospital headquarters. Maj. Clint Maupin and Ed Wernitznig, Adjutant and Executive Officer, respectively, disclaimed any knowledge of a crime. Scuttlebutt circulated concerning smuggling of food and medicine as possible crimes. Interrogations continued for days and weeks with Jack, as far as we knew, admitting nothing. After a month, an eternity to us, we spotted him, a walking skeleton certainly not more than 100 pounds, staggering slowly down the road shading his eyes from the unaccustomed sunlight. He was brought to the hospital and examined for alleged abdominal pain. A diagnosis of acute appendicitis was made by Dr. Harold Bertram who urged that surgery be done immediately; to our surprise, the Japs agreed.

So, under local anesthetic, with a bright sunny day providing natural lighting, a relatively sterile field after scrubbing with soap and water but without antiseptic, a skin incision was made. An effort was made to sharpen the blade by stroking it on the inside of a drinking glass. Without any further exploration (using tablespoons for retractors), not opening the peritoneal cavity, the skin-deep wound was closed with thread sutures. Cat gut was not available. Buttons found at the last possible moment after a camp-wide search were used for tension sutures to prevent the knots from pulling through the skin. After surgery, Bertram explained to the Japs that the appendix was "very bad" and had been removed. They never requested to see the surgical specimen. Just in case they might ask, a small piece of the rectus muscle had been excised as an exhibit. Much to our amazement, he was allowed to return to his own quarters and the charges were dropped. I don't think they could ever have broken this guy.

We were not the only inventors in the makeshift hospital. The dentists, struggling without any of their usual tools, filled cavities with metal recovered from silver coins. A quarter or a 50-cent coin rubbed on a fine file produced a granular alloy which could be tapped into a cavity. Teeth from carabaos were modified and shaped to fill the gap of a missing tooth.

A real jolter was to crunch down on an undetected white rock while chewing your rice. You could hear it meters away. Everybody grabbed his own jaw in sympathy. Many good teeth were lost to grit. Cavities of the teeth, although of no consequence,

175

were few, presumably due to the low intake of refined sugars.

Besides the morning and evening rounds in my TB ward, my day was filled with playing chess and bridge, and reading the Bible. After going through it two and a half times, I was amazed at how bloody a book the Bible really is. Later, there was a wide variety of books from a Red Cross-supplied library. I read one a week. Outstanding among them was Galsworthy's *Forsythe Saga*.

Playing chess almost every afternoon honed my game immeasurably. On my return to my family, Mother said she played chess, so we set up a game. In five moves she was checkmated. She looked up from the table and stoutly declared, "Well, I'm the champ of the ladies club!" It was one of my life's most embarrassing moments.

Other diversions included the garden, with a rumor and bull session after the second meal. We studied astronomy lying on our backs until we could identify every star in the sky. The North Star and the Southern Cross were visible in the same sky. A sun dial was perfected after considerable trial and error and remained only a curiosity.

Pilar told me one time that the best way to learn Spanish was to have a dictionary with long black hair, but my present circumstances precluded that option. She had sent me a Spanish language book which I memorized. So, I attended a class in conversational Spanish taught by Señor Allen, an old Sunshiner and an American who had missed too many boats home. He was a kindly school teacher who had volunteered to come to the Philippines in 1905. Señor Allen was an excellent teacher with a good sense of humor that showed through the academia. One story which he stoutly insisted was true concerned the gecko, our ever-present lizard. Usually tucked in a corner of the ceiling, it preyed on mosquitoes and consequently was considered a household pet not to be harmed. Geckoes also inhabited palm and fruit trees. In the evening, they screamed a shrill two-syllable call which to some sounded like "F-- you!"

Señor Allen insisted that the tiny lizard caused a battle during the Spanish-American War in 1898. The Americano and Aguinaldo soldiers faced each other in positions near Manila. This particular night was marked with shouting and name-calling between

176

the trenches. The geckoes also opened up with their shrill name-calling. The Americans interpreted the taunt as "fuck you," and charged out of their trenches to stop the tirade.

Four of us--Wallace, Brennan, Musselman, my partner and I--opted to play a 1,000 rubber bridge contest. It lasted three months, came to the final day with a grand slam, doubled and redoubled, with our opponents the winner by less than 1,000 points. I never played much bridge after that.

About this time, spring 1943, details filtered in of the escape of ten Americans from the Davao Penal Colony in Mindanao. The reaction to the news was mixed. The prisoners that remained in that camp were punished by decreasing their food ration. They were running the course of life, too. They were an unwilling partner in the escape, using their own destiny as a gambit. Who was to say the escapees were heroes? My idea of bravery did not include a gamble with the lives of others.

A critical eye was always maintained on the mess crew or anybody else who exhibited significant corpulence. "Where in hell is he getting his food?" was the natural question. The crews rotated every month so as to present an acceptable profile. Favoritism in the kitchen was combatted by using measuring cups and changing the server frequently. Servers worked with their backside to the hungry line to prevent double dipping for a pal. Even a stirrer was utilized. He would constantly mix the ingredients in the huge cauldron so each hungry soul had an equal chance of receiving a small piece of meat. The fresh meat issue, almost always carabao, consisted of a side one or two times a week. At first that ration was divided among 8,500 men and then down to 5,000 men as our population dwindled.

Another factor determining the size of the ration seemed to be the progress of the war. On the receipt of the news of a victory somewhere, the Japs' belligerency would soon soar and our ration would go down. If the Yanks prevailed, we could expect more food.

The number of men turning out for the work detail determined the amount of rice issued. Each morning the medics decided whether your health was adequate to go out and work, although at first the Japs said, "Everybody works." Maj. Emil Reed, perpetual motion personified, from Dallas, Texas, was known as

177

"Death Rattle" since his avowed policy was you must have a terminal guttural ronchi before he would classify you as unfit for work. The system worked about as clumsily as anything the Japs suggested. It encouraged the sick to work and die, instead of resting and getting well.

With some consistency the Japs decided to give our chaplains half ration because "they just talk and no work." This generally might be true, but if you ever saw our red-headed, ruddy-faced chaplain, Bob Taylor, grapple with the Devil in a Sunday morning arena, you would give him a ration and a half.

The chaplains, for a short period, were responsible for distributing extra goodies. Canned milk, both evaporated and condensed, was available occasionally. The job was thankless and constantly criticized, so in the end the doctors decided who should receive it based on medical need and prognosis, i.e., those with a chance to recover.

A few blind prisoners tried to work but usually ended up receiving frequent beating. They couldn't see to bow, keep in the column or keep from wandering off limits. One man solved his problem with a sign "BLIND" hung around his neck. Finally the Japs quit beating him.

Although better off than most, the endlessness of this existence lay heavily on my hands. Thoughts of home, Mom and Dad, Dave, Betty and Ginny were securely locked up in my memory bank where they stayed for over three years. I tried not to dig them up. In fact, the sequestration was so absolute, I couldn't remember my home address after our recapture--120 K Avenue East, Oskaloosa, Iowa, or was it 192 East K Street, Oskaloosa?

This camp was like a never-ending road going on and curving around the mountain, through the valley, searching for home around the next bend but never finding it. Here I saw the wretched, smelled the dead, and heard the dying. One year, then two years, and more to come had been squandered in this hell hole. This was no sentence or it would have had an end. Death is more certain than the end of captivity. It ends the hopelessness of this life. Would freedom or death overtake us? I wondered.

Oh, God, there are those that need your help, I thought. How can you let this go on? Maybe I'd somehow survive, but a great portion of my life and an important part of me would be gone forever. It would never be returned. So many of my friends were gone and more would be going. Tomorrow would be the same. I ponder on a thousand things, never too far from life or death. I wait for this day to pass so it will shorten the waiting. Can it be without end? The agony of living out this God-awful captivity is as sure as tomorrow or the next typhoon. My destiny wanders aimlessly beyond my control. Please, oh God, strengthen my resolve.

Most of the time I presumed to contentment, apparently from a natural endowment. Some prisoners were constantly dejected, with a hangdog expression. Others who were just kind of out of it had fixed faces. Hope is a dreamer's opiate. Still others acted out an optimism; there were also those with a truly irrepressible happy dis-position like my good friend Charles Lewis. Charley was almost constantly laughing. Things usually went his way, like getting aboard a Jap truck and riding up the Death March road until a smart Jap kicked him off. He fooled some of the guards for a few miles.

In August 1942, Charley was assisting in moving Americans from Cabanatuan Camp No. 2 to Camp No. 1. Each load was counted (ichi, ni, san, shi, go, roku, etc.) and back Charley would go for another truckload. At the end the guard had counted one too many, but with Charley outside the gate the count was correct, so he wouldn't let Charley inside the compound. Charley demanded his "rights." After standing outside rattling the wire gate for an hour, the Jap duty officer came down and straightened things out, finally letting Charley inside to resume his suffering inside the camp.

One day the Japanese sent in one malnourished turkey--a mighty fine gesture but with little overall prospective benefit. A camp-wide raffle was held, and believe it or not our boy Charley won--one to 8,000 odds. Twelve men, including Charley and Col. Beecher, the Camp CO, were messing together. They decided to share their rice ration with the turkey hoping it would lay eggs. A 24-hour guard was mounted, but despite the "forced" feeding the turkey continued to lose weight and failed to produce eggs. No one confirmed the suspicion its name was "Tom." After one week's husbandry, they gave up and stewed the skinniest turkey in the Philippine archipelago.

Several chickens were fed with the hope of having a perpetual supply of eggs, but that wasn't successful either. Speculation pointed towards a psychological block, no playmates, poor variety of food and, in the final analysis, they didn't like the place any better than we did. Soon each new chicken graced the stew pot.

One small detail of Americans was assigned to policing the Japanese chicken coop. They fed the chickens and swept the droppings, but were not to gather the eggs. The GIs finally devised a scheme to savor the produce but avoid an overt crime. They poked a small hole in each end of the egg and sucked out the goodies. The empty egg was placed back in the nest for the Japs to gather later. The thievery continued for some time with the Nips blaming the empty shells on the lazy chickens. In true style, they cut the grain ration. Realizing no benefit in the quality of the eggs, the Jap guards decided to wipe out the brood. Another time when the chickens were molting, they put them on half rations as punishment.

A C.A.R.E. package from Australia arrived for me in early 1944 with a cheerio message, a brown knitted cardigan, socks and chocolate bars. How they got my name was a mystery. I never wore the cardigan. It always reminded me of the U.S. Embassy in Manila that sported fireplaces. It was as worthless as an empty hotel room on the morning after it was vacant.

One of the most difficult stories for me to tell concerns a major in the Quartermaster Corps and, believe it or not, a West Point graduate. At the end of the Death March at Camp O'Donnell, while the defeated army was being ground into oblivion, this major secured a few cans of condensed milk and held a class reunion for academy grads. I was told he was hated for it by everyone, including his classmates. Later, a friend of mine, a guy who didn't have to cheat, was on burial detail, and saw the major's body, a victim of the Great International Harvester. Remembering the selfish reunion, he removed the dog tag from around the officer's neck and switched it to the big toe of an enlisted man. In place of a single grave to which he was entitled as an officer, his body was pitched into a common grave along with enlisted men. In all fairness, my contact with West Pointers almost always revealed fine gentlemen and above-average officers.

Capt. Herb Ott, a soft-spoken, honest veterinarian, had the

180

weekly job of supervising our scant fresh meat supply. His butcher crew claimed everything from the slaughtered carabao including the tail, tongue, testicles, the hoofs and probably the squeal. For sure, the entire carcass, including intestines, teeth and even the horns were utilized. But not the hide, for without refrigeration, it rotted into a stinking mess before anything could be done. The horns were whittled into pieces of art, chessmen, cigarette holders, dominoes, awls, spindles, etc. The clotted blood was fried. After skinning, the tail was added to the soup cauldron. The hairy portion at the very end was fashioned into a kind of wand used as perpetual asswipe in lieu of toilet paper.

Although Herb denied any political affiliation, his butchering technique was labelled N.R.A.--neck, ribs and asshole. The carabao bones were boiled to extract the marrow. The hoofs were boiled until the crust separated, leaving the cartilaginous end of the bones which provided the ingredient for gelatin cobbler. The intestines were cleaned and cooked until crisp, then served as chitlings. At times an unborn calf was found, prepared and eaten without ceremony. The other organs were added to the soup, diluted with so much water that you were lucky to get a recognizable piece of meat once a month. The dirty brown, thin soup never had a fatty layer on the surface.

Over the years in captivity, my sleeping arrangement varied from a concrete slab at Bilibid to a mattress on springs in Cabanatuan. In between these extremes multiple innovations were tried--stretching a good Army wool blanket over a bamboo frame, it came apart; woven rattan or bamboo strips with a cogon grass pad or a rice straw tick, but it soon became a great hangout for all bugs resident in the Philippines. In the last year, 1944-45, most everyone slept on a mattress made available from deaths or vacated by men leaving camp on work details. Despite staining from diarrhea and soaking from typhoons, the mattresses, which originally had come from our own hospital, were salvageable.

Soon problems emerged from the newly acquired mattresses: bedbugs, lice, and ants. One night I stretched out and stuck my feet in a colony of vicious and voracious red ants. They had decided to vacate their hill for my mattress. I slept on the ground that night. The next day I placed the legs of my bed in water-filled cans to stop the ant migration. Alas, with the ants gone, there

181

was no one to eat the bedbug eggs, tipping the balance of nature. During the night I crushed them under my thumb. They were just as avaricious as ants.

American ingenuity was challenged and a mattress sterilization process was born. We made a double boiler stove by connecting two 55-gallon drums, one on top of the other. The mattress went in the upper chamber steam jacket, with the fire in the lower drum. Daily sunning of the mattress also helped.

One additional but rare critter was the scorpion. One "cool" evening, probably 75 degrees, after slipping on my home-made jacket, unworn for weeks, I felt a terrible stinging jab on the back of my neck, knocking me down. A big scorpion fell out of the collar. I thought for a minute a Japanese had bayoneted me.

Out of a clear blue sky one day, an emergency assembly was ordered. With all except hospital patients in formation, Capt. Mori, the Jap CO, announced that all "millionaires" would step forward and be identified. At first the men murmured in disbelief building to a general laughter. Nobody stepped out. The Japs abruptly halted the interrogation after a Bronx cheer went up from our ranks. They didn't like ridicule or losing face. I think they harbored the notion that about half of us were filthy rich.

On another occasion, they ordered a muster of all captives who were part or full-blooded Indian. At 1000 hours, about 50 men shuffled down the sub-baked path in their wooden clogs and assembled between the barracks. The Jap in charge requested that each Indian estimate the amount of Indian blood that he had. Next, to our amazement, three Japs started down the line raising an arm and sniffing the armpit of each man. I almost cracked up. What would these crazy people think of next? Each man was tested and scored as to the amount of underarm odor. The game ended with us still in the dark. Later, we learned the Japs had an idea that North American Indians as well as Japanese did not have an offensive axillary odor, but Caucasians did. The odor was thought to be related to the mixture of blood: the more Caucasian blood, the greater the odor. The whole affair turned out to be a little more scientific than it first appeared. We set up our own test, a blind survey, and to our surprise came to the conclusion there was a relationship. The explanation was due to the fact that Indians as well as Japanese do not have axillary hair or oil glands.

So ended the great research project.

We tried our hand at an old American custom--making home brew. Into a five-gallon narrow-necked glass demi-john, we emptied all the starch, including camotes, bananas, and skins of all types, burnt rice, papaya rinds, taro root, cane and sugar cakes, ginger root, etc. A rubber stopper tightly fitted into place with a single opening allowed gas to escape through a tube immersed in a second water-filled jug. Consequently, as the fermentation proceeded, the CO_2 escaped, but air could not re-enter, achieving the necessary anerobic conditions.

The still, located under the *bahay*, was loaded with yeast, and became active by the third day, evidenced by joyous bubbling. The intensity of gurgling was an accurate measure of the speed of the process. When to stop and bottle was critical. In a matter of hours, the pinkish sour-smelling mess might pass from wine to vinegar. After much discussion, the self-avowed vintner would announce, "It's time!"

Once, after much discussion at our *bahay*, I corked two bottles of this precious concoction, stuffed them under my vest and started for the other side of the camp to share with my pals.

My route passed the Jap guard house. I approached the guards, who were facing the compound with their rifles balanced across their knees. Not having a hat, I bowed from the waist in good form. If covered, a salute was sufficient; if the bow was not deep enough, it automatically brought a beating. I didn't want any snafu on this important mission. With the agitation of walking and bowing, the bottles popped their corks. The wine shot into the air in two streams, saturating my whole front. The Japs broke into hilarious laughter, apparently thinking I had pissed in my breeches. I wonder how they explained the dual streams. At least they didn't challenge me, thinking I had personal problems.

In truth, the stuff was lousy. In a wine-tasting contest from one to ten, it would have been awarded a zero, the booby prize. In other attempts, our product sometimes resembled vinegar; at other times a nauseating mess. Apparently, a wild yeast fermentation continued even after bottling. The alcohol content never was high enough to warm my ears or to stop fermentation. One's tolerance for booze was extremely low after drying out for years.

On most work details, the Jap used a rifle butt or the "vitamin stick" to speed up prisoners. "The load was just too heavy until 'the Wolf' swung the vitamin stick and then my feet sank two inches into the mud on the next heave," observed a POW. Beatings until bloody and even fractures, were a daily occurrence. Even more barbaric punishment was making two Americans slap each other. Unless the blows were real and damaging the exchange lasted for hours, so the best way was to knock your pal silly and get it over with.

The work details seldom involved favors but did offer chances to steal extra food. Pockets sewed inside your shorts or shirt provided a small hiding place for vegetables: onion, rambutan, kangkong, mongo beans. A dozen or so beans could be hidden in a seam so that in a couple of weeks you could make a cup of soup. Cunning and patience were helpful in this ordeal. Occasionally I would volunteer for the farm detail--more from boredom than the expectation of stealing food.

I heard of, but never saw, a canteen that had two compartments. The upper held water and the lower opened to hide small items. It was part of the smuggling technique developed by those moving in and out of the camp. Filling your unmodified canteen with corn or beans worked for a short while until the guards learned the trick of shaking it, disclosing the contraband contents, which resulted in one hell of a beating. The trick was to be able to pour water out of your canteen and still hide something.

During most of the year, scuttlebutt filtered into the camp continuously and daily. Truck drivers who were out of camp each day were the biggest transporters of hot items, both news and contraband.

"The British are advancing in Burma. The African campaign lights up again as tanks fire across the Libyan sand. Roosevelt declares his sincere concern for all Americans trapped in the Orient," were some of the headlines brought to us. They were so repetitive as to be unbelievable.

From the wood detail, which supplied our fuel for our mess, Cpl. Johnson brought me news of Pilar's imprisonment in old Fort Santiago dungeons. Although it occurred soon after my departure from Bilibid a year went by before word reached me at Cabanatuan. Built in 1565 by the Spanish, the dungeons bordered the banks of the Pasig River in Intramuros, the walled city of Manila. The cells represented the worst living conditions reserved at the time for major criminals. All cells were at water level, reached by grey stones leading down into small dark caverns and bare rooms. Each was designed architecturally to torture prisoners by rising water with each flood tide. The water depth varied with the tide and the elevation of each cell. It might be from one meter to neck deep. Some cells actually filled during times of high tide.

I froze as he related how Pilar was grabbed as she ran towards a column of trucks loaded with American POWs. Her arms loaded with food, her black hair streaming behind her, she dashed alongside the trucks. A Jap patrol soon appeared in answer to the noise. She was seen throwing them food.

"They're starving to death," she called to her friends. "Someone must feed them!"

She stood defiantly in front of the trucks until two Japs grabbed her and roughly dragged her away.

"Is she still there?" I inquired, realizing that place was almost as bad as starving to death!

"I really don't know. Many disappear mysteriously from that place," the corporal said. I never knew how long she was in that hell hole, but sometime later Pilar was turned loose. She had escaped the dungeon terror of Fort Santiago, but she was marked by the Kempei Tai as loyal to the Americans. Several months afterwards, the news reached me of an impending visit by Pilar with a group of other girls. It was incredible that she could manipulate a trip inside our prison. My anxiety resulted in the old stomach ache.

Pilar, Trophy Ocampo, Conchita Sunico, Chona Recto, Lulu Reyes, Benilda Castañeda and others, a small group of young, prominent Junior League type girls, formed the Volunteer Social Aid Committee, soon after December 1942. Their avowed purpose of helping poor Filipino people suffering from the war was extended to a clandestine mission of aiding American POWs. With talent and cunning, a singing and dancing program was put together. Pilar studied the Japanese language and cultivated acquaintance with some ranking Jap officers based in Manila. The VSAC then visited POW camps ostensibly to entertain the Jap garrison and in the process smuggle us food and medicines.

So, on 24 September 1943, a second message arrived. "Pilar will be visiting the camp tomorrow." With my stomach quivering and my heart palpitating, I positioned myself near the main camp road between two long palm-thatched barracks and waited. Sure enough by 1300 hours, they came. Eight pretty girls dressed in identical blue and white uniforms were huddled on a flat bed truck. As they drove past me, 30 meters away, Pilar spotted me, whirled and threw a baseball-size package. Unfortunately, her aim was poor. It struck the only tin roof nearby with a terrific bang, then tumbled to the ground. Moving quickly towards the package, I glimpsed a four-man Jap patrol trotting in my direction, so with an expert soccer maneuver, the package was flipped under the barracks. Reversing myself, I disappeared around the opposite end of the building as the grunting, bayonet-jabbing patrol charged around. They failed to discover the soccer player or the bundle. It contained badly needed medicines and vitamins, which we distributed throughout my TB and Zero wards.

After consulting with the engineers the day before, we came up with a plan for me to see Pilar and the show firsthand. Under the guise of repairing the PA system our camp electrician and I went to the stage where the girls were performing before the Jap audience. Carrying a pair of pliers and screwdriver, I moved alongside the elevated wooden stage as the girls sang. After tracing out the wires up to the microphone, I looked up and there was Pilar, singing not over two meters away. She was beautiful. She looked like a girl. She suddenly spotted me and bolted to the back of the stage. In my excitement I yanked at the wires and almost toppled the mike. The Jap guards, spying my behavior, came over indicating in Japanese, "What in hell are you doing?" I began to ease away with the music still in my ears. To my amazement the song changed in mid-air from a Japanese ballad to "I'll Be with You in Apple Blossom Time!" This produced a few heart throbs and tears as I trudged back to my barracks where I could plainly hear the score of "Over There, the Yanks Are Coming." She waved as the truck eased down the road. I was never to see her again.

I felt sorry for those fellows who had wives and children. So often those families were breaking up and the soldier had volunteered for foreign duty. The conversations over the years would imply a separation or impending divorce. But the thought of your little daughter or son gone from your life, maybe forever, was horribly traumatic. Hunkins, I know, agonized over the separation from his wife. Fortunately, I was spared that. My girl friends, many wonderful girls of long standing, presented no serious emotional involvement, except for Pilar. I was never really sure where I was going or what my intentions were. If John Haines and others had remained in the Orient and we had started a medical clinic, then Pilar would have fitted in. Americana would have been difficult to forego, but the professional possibilities in the Far East were unlimited. The decision, however, never presented itself.

One day the Japs, completely out of character, and without any explanation, lined us up and presented us with occupation paper money commensurate with our rank. Then I got in another line where ten pesos was extracted from the twenty they had given me. Although no formal explanation was ever presented, we conjectured that some Jap general read the Geneva Treaty of 1907 which provided that subsistence money should be paid POWs. The ten pesos we returned was to repay the Japs for our stinking chow. Anyway, there we stood with "bayonet" money and no place to spend it. The Japs recognized the potential market, so after a few days, they wheeled in a cart full of bananas to get the money back. The bananas lasted a few days and the co-prosperity scheme disappeared. It was a one-time show. Probably some Jap finance officer pocketed the occupation money. We had a good banana feed anyway.

Lt. Nogi, the Japanese medical officer in charge of all POW camps in the Philippines, visited Bilibid and Cabanatuan one or two times a month during 1942, 1943, and less frequently during 1944. He failed to show up the last six months of the camp.

Many things about him were peculiar. He was large-framed, 5'10" to 5'11", not fat, and lumbered along clumsily as though he had a physical disability of the hips, talked slowly, his voice inordinately soft for his habitus. His demeanor depicted either a lack of confidence or stupidity. He turned his back on blatant medical needs as well as the simple necessities of survival.

With diphtheria rampant, he wouldn't give us our own antitoxin from Sternberg Hospital until after over 100 men had died.

His actions never suggested a genuine medical or professional attitude. He may have been a professional soldier, but he never practiced medicine as we know it. Nogi never inquired about what he could do from a medical or humanitarian point of view. Although I was in the same room at one conference, we never addressed each other directly. Apparently, he spoke very little English. He stared blankly at the wall, said little, and seemed content to let us die.

During February 1945, in the last days of the fighting in the recapture of Manila, it was first reported that a former POW had spotted Nogi on the street. He was targeted by a survivor of his own neglect. The story circulated that when the POW notified soldiers of the 1st Cavalry Division, they mowed him down as he trudged along. Later this report was proven false. In reality, Nogi was tried by the War Crimes Commission and sentenced to 40 years in prison. At the time I preferred the earlier report. I never doubted his culpability.

During a routine afternoon chess game with my psychiatrist, Dr. Katz, we were interrupted one day by a self-appointed crier and comic. He stuck his head in the open door and jokingly declared, "MacArthur just rolled up in a tank."

With my eyes glued on the board, contemplating the next move of my bishop, I replied, "Tell MacArthur to wait." It had been just too damned long. Almost three years. Most everybody was dead. Nobody gave a damn. The chess game seemed about as important as fighting a war.

18. CABANATUAN, 1944

By 1944 prison camp life had stabilized, and the daily ration was down to a half pound of rice--a cupped handful--with dwindling extras of carabao meat, salted fish, whistle weed soup, coconut oil, sugar, and *camote* tops. Duck eggs, salt, canned fish, bananas, coconuts, *kalamansi*, and corned beef were occasionally available on the black market for at least five times the shelf price. Cost made little difference by then if it would fit into your stomach.

Another native food available to us that required a little conditioning was *balut*, a cooked unborn duck or chicken embryo still in the shell. The convenient way of eating it was to pierce each end and suck out the insides. Hopefully they were cooked before the feathers developed. Hardboiled duck eggs, dyed black or purple to preserve them, were smuggled in at times, but never as part of our ration. These were called "century eggs," and, as Filipinos said, "Very good, Joe."

An unpredictable and meager underground food source plus a little garden produce was barely enough to sustain life and control most vitamin-deficiency diseases. In December 1943 we received the second Red Cross food boxes, two per man, plus multiple vitamins for a daily distribution. The four of us in our *bahay* pooled the three cans of protein from each box. With a total of 24 cans, we opened one can every Sunday and split it four ways. Thus, the weekly "food orgy" guaranteed a minimal protein intake for six months. This occasion was touted as a banquet and cause for a great celebration.

One day, I watched a Jap infantry column, four abreast, march up the main road from Cabanatuan City, alternately jogging and double-timing, shouting the cadence. The searing noonday sun, the heavy field packs, and the pace presented an endurance contest. The column of about 30 men turned into the uphill camp road. Suddenly a soldier in the middle of the formation stumbled and fell, sprawling on the hot gravel road. Several soldiers jumped over him and one soldier paused to help him, but continued on after a loud bellowing from the Jap in charge. the soldier lay motionless for at least five minutes. His companion returned, kicked him a couple of times without any response, and then retired to the Jap quarters on the knoll. In another ten minutes, his buddy came down the road again, this time with a bucket of water which he dashed in his face. Failing to revive him, he threw the bucket, hitting the spreadeagled soldier on the head, and disgustedly retired up the road. In an hour, he came down the road again, turned his buddy over, who, registering no response, was dragged into the ditch where he remained until sundown. In the cool of the evening, the ailing Jap managed to stand up, swaying badly,and staggered up the road 200 meters to their quarters. I wondered, Who needed friends when you've got buddies like that?

Months later we witnessed a huge fire just at dusk on the knoll in the Jap security area. The fire burned for hours as sweaty men bare to the waist circled dancing and shouting. With a loud cheer a fallen comrade's body was heaved onto the blaze. By dawn, the fire was out, allowing the recovery of some ashes to be shipped back to the family. The whole affair seemed barbaric to me. Some of the antics were probably nurtured by a little saki or confiscated San Miguel beer. Strange people.

On another occasion, the Japs carried out a cremation of several foul-smelling decomposed bodies. The story had it that two of the soldiers were killed by an officer who was conducting a highly specialized class. In the class of 15 rigorously selected candidates, the officer detected an inferior student. In the process of punishing him, the soldier was killed with a blow to the head with a club. Then they were 14. The following day another intellectual misfit showed up, so he was bashed on the head. then they were 13. We never learned the final number of graduates, but were impressed by the difficulty of the course.

One day "Little Speedo," a guard at the farm, complained of the POWs crapping all over the place. "You go like cat, cover up, no?" The next day after the lecture, he stepped on a pile with his two-toed open shoes. That precipitated the liberal use of his vitamin stick on the whole detail.

Medical officer call came once or twice a week. Occasionally, a runner would come by the ward announcing a call at headquarters. If other than 1100 hours it was unusual, probably indicating urgency. The group stood outside the headquarters door while Maj. Clinton Maupin, the adjutant, a naturally friendly guy who didn't take himself too seriously, intoned some dumb Jap message and new regulations. Maj. Ed R. Wernitznig, the executive officer, blonde and serious, filled in but generally permitted the more palatable adjutant to handle the business. The Jap orders, usually based on an echo principle (rebounding from our complaints), resulted in further loss of privileges. The bottom line often stated, "Failure to obey would result in being shot severely," or "Shot to death severely." Our poor COs, Colonels Craig, North, and then finally Schwartz, returned several times from conferences with the Japs, bloody around the head. We other medical officers observed and said nothing.

Mail was distributed to us only three times in the three years of our imprisonment. The first time was 13 August 1943. I remember it well. Forty medical and dental officers assembled in front of the headquarters *bahay*. Not leaving this important business to the adjutant, Executive Officer Wernitznig called the names of the addressees. Wernitznig held the letter or card high, then presented the epistle like a sheepskin from a college president. At this first call, probably 20 pieces of mail were distributed. I held out no real hope for one, not that my family lacked the emotional intensity, but rather my training didn't allow for extravagant hopes.

"Hibbs," shouted Wernitznig, holding up a blue-bordered airmail letter. I grabbed it and, to hide my emotion, moved to the edge of the group. I gulped as I saw the name Mary Fran Riley, a great beer drinking pal from Des Moines, Iowa. She wrote, "I'm sure you won't receive this, but lying in bed thinking of the great times we used to have, the thought occurred I'll try anyway and send it to the Red Cross in Switzerland. I've nothing to lose. The Rileys think of you often and particularly Mary Fran. -- Love, M.F." Dated nine months earlier, it was transported on the *SS Gripsholm*. What a thrill! Life at the Kappa House and the University of Iowa flashed before my mind. The door opened. The Army Navy Club and the pre-war Philippines came back. Good old Mary Fran, a true-blue gal. The veneer of protection around that good life dropped away. Maybe we'll have it again. The mo-

191

ment was great, but obviously I couldn't allow too much indulgence. Stark reality of my "G" string, wooden clogs, and my hunger gut-ache soon aborted this dream.

Capt. Cyrus DeLong, a dental officer, grabbed his letter, tore it open, and began devouring it in front of the group. A sob. Then, "My God, Mother died," as he fainted away.

DeLong revived quickly, but still convulsing and shaking, he was escorted to the lonely seclusion of his own *bahay*, taking his grief with him. What a peculiar thing to write! Important news, yes, but the timing was unforgivable. His peace of mind overshadowed the necessity of bringing him up-to-date. To me, during the remaining years in captivity, he always seemed depressed. The worries of the camp were sufficient without borrowing from the homeland.

DeLong died at Takao, Formosa, after the second hell ship, *Enoura Maru*, was bombed and set ablaze while en route to Japan. They say he begged his buddies to kill him as he lay pinned under a big timber with the fire burning towards him.

Two other mail calls were held in October and December 1944, and, in the meantime, I was permitted to send three form postcards home. Some took over a year to arrive in Oskaloosa. All told, seven or eight letters were received, including one from every member of the family and three from Mary Fran. The majority came along in December 1944. The mail service seemed to improve with our military success.

Master Sgt. George Distell, having "neither chick nor child," sent one of three Red Cross form cards allowed during the three years imprisonment to Henry Ford and, sure enough, at the first mail call he received a letter in response, signed by the automaker's secretary, explaining, "Mr. Ford was delighted to hear from you," and "sincerely hoped for a speedy return to the U.S.A." The next two cards, to Jack Benny and Bob Hope, remained unanswered. George ended up in Medford, Oregon, after the war, the same place where I helped start a medical clinic in 1951. He was just the same, a rugged and seemingly indestructible little gentleman. His end came abruptly and mysteriously from a fall down some hotel stairs. He was always worthy of my admiration.

Sgt. Richard James "Jim" Costello, a professional Marine, was another fellow prisoner who ended up in Oregon after the war. Costello was one of Colonel (later General) Beecher's boys from the 4th Marine Regiment who came ashore just a few days ahead of the Jap invasion. Costello told me that by swimming the four km. from the shores of Bataan to Corregidor, he ended up on beach defense before the island fell. After the 26-day siege he was transferred to Cabanatuan, where he suffered through three years of starvation. Violently sick at times with malaria and dysentery, he held on, spending most of his time in Wards Nos. 1, 2, or 3. He finally went blind from beriberi. His vision was 5/200 in both eyes and his hearing loss was 75 percent.

Sgt. Costello had a buddy who continued to hassle him about his fancy pair of boots. He insisted Costello will the boots to him since he was going to outlive him. This made the sergeant mad so he began to "try harder." According to Jim, that is why he lived while his buddy died. He also insisted that by trading his cigarettes for tea, which kept his dysentery under control, he lived while others died. I never doubted his determination but questioned his therapeutics.

The greatest contribution that Jim gave to the camp was the "Cabanatuan flag." It simply consisted of a hank of cloth tied to a stick with a short string. This was the sergeant's solution to the toilet paper shortage. With each trip to the head, he used the cloth as a wipe, dashed it and down in a water-filled can and hung it out to dry on a nail until the next evacuation. Many followed suit, decorating the outside barracks walls with the "Cabanatuan flag" fluttering in the tropical breeze.

Despite near total blindness, he lectured on Caesar's wars from memory, describing the number of phalanxes of rock throwers, battering rams, flame throwers, ladders and scalers. He was always trying to fool our captors. One day he spotted a poor GI squatting beside the trail folding and unfolding bits of paper. Jim sat down beside him and soon picked up the paper trick. The Japs were told that both were crazy and they were excused from the work details.

He lived through the sinking of two "hell ships" on the 90-day trip to Japan. Liberated in Japan in August 1945, after nine years overseas duty, he finally made it home blind and deaf. At the time of liberation a picture was taken showing Jim peering into a garbage can outside a U.S. Red Cross canteen. He still couldn't believe there was enough food for everyone. On arriving home in Oregon, his luck began to run out, he became mentally disorganized, fighting the Japs to the last, dying at age 65 in Medford, Oregon.

Jim told me of another 4th Marine on beach defense who hid his trombone in a machinegun dugout. A bomb explosion near the bunker blew the horn into an overhead *ipil ipil* tree, where it remained silent for the duration.

I examined a soldier one day with his ring finger missing. He told me a Jap chopped it off to get a gold ring which was stuck on the finger. For most of us all jewelry disappeared after the first search.

At 1700 hours one scary day, without warning 50 or more men abruptly complained of inability to raise their heads and blurring vision. It was the damnedest sight, with dozens of men moving down the path on their way to the clinic with their heads hanging over to one side with both hands supporting them. "I can't hold my head up and I'm seeing double!" they moaned. "I've got limber neck."

"Oh, no!" exclaimed a medical officer as the entire medical staff groaned. "It must be encephalitis, sleeping sickness."

Prodromal symptoms of sleepiness, headache, fever and chills, nausea and vomiting, and stiffness of the neck were lacking. The offset was just as abrupt as the onset. Within two hours, all symptoms had dissipated and the affected were completely back to normal. We were quite relieved but mystified. Infectious encephalitis would hardly be that evanescent. Much to our amazement, immediately after supper the following day, the whole phenomenon reappeared and disappeared in about two hours. Evidence pointed towards a neuro-toxin in the food, since each paralysis had been temporary, post-prandial. probably from ingested material. Fish heads eaten the past two suppers were suspect.

Salted down in large rattan pots with their eyes staring at you, the poorly preserved mess was shipped to us without refrigeration. By the third day only a few were fed the heads and only those were paralyzed. The association was fixed. Our encephalitis epidemic was over. The veterinarians pointed out the similarity to limber necks in chickens.

The fish eyes made me uncomfortable. They stared at me and I stared back. Then I ate them to avoid being stared down. Unfortunately, one day I bit down on an eyeball. The loud crunch stirred my mess pals, Denny, Charley and Jim. "What did you hit?" one of them asked. Grimacing and holding my jaw, I answered, "Either a glass eye or a cataract." My tooth was chipped. I gladly gave up eyeballs in my diet after that.

"Imperial Rescript Day," the annual re-enlistment, was celebrated by all Japanese soldiers with recorded music, singing and shouting, reminiscent of our college "keggers." It was highlighted by bare-waisted soldiers stomping around a huge bonfire. The Japanese celebrated a universal birthday on 1 January with the same type of party. Because of the vigor and length of the parties, we surmised that they must have had much saki or San Miguel beer. During the 1944 rescript celebration, grisly heads from two recently beheaded Filipinos were paraded around the camp on long poles. This was one of the most barbaric things I had ever seen. Beheading was a frequent means of settling a problem since most of the Jap officers dangled a long one- or two-handled Samurai sword from their belt for just such a purpose.

The greatest camp entertainment for us was "the band." Cpl. Johnny Kratz, 59th Coast Artillery, leader, and his ten "Rice Balls," including Sgt. Pappy Harris, 59th CA on the organ; Cpl. Eddie Booth, Signal Corps, on the piano; Pvt. Chester McClure and Sgt. Melvin Rainherd on the guitar; Pat Kadolph on the drums; Martin Galos on the trumpet; Lt. Larry Porcher and Pat Salo, trumpet. They arranged and produced popular music for a show one night a week. The chief problem initially was to get permission from the Japs to assemble and enjoy ourselves. It was finally granted after two years of haggling. The band was excellent and their contribution to our morale was immeasurable. I never did learn where the instruments came from. All of the band members, save Marshall, were lost on a "hell ship" on its way to Japan. Several of us intended to recommend Johnny Kratz for a commission, but he never made it home.

Gynecomastia, enlargement of the breasts, appeared in early 1944 after two and a half years of prison life. About ten percent of all POWs were affected. The appearance did not closely coincide with the onset of any deficiency disease, nor was the condition limited to the severest cases of malnutrition.

The insidious onset was painless and involved both breasts which enlarged to the size and beauty of an adolescent girl. A small firm disk-shaped tumor, freely movable, non-tender, was palpable directly under the nipple. Maximum size in three months and regression in another three months, without residuals, was the rule. We were satisfied that the lesion was self-limited, requiring no treatment. The onset coincided with the second distribution of Red Cross food and sufficient vitamins to provide a capsule a day for almost two months of Vita-kaps, a multiple therapeutic vitamin. Almost all had gained ten to 20 pounds as the diet increased from 800 to 1,200 calories a day.

Could this be related?

Later studies revealed this phenomena, called "refeeding gynecomastia," was seen in males who have been on a severely restricted diet and then given a markedly improved balanced diet. This resulted in an increased production of a breast-stimulating hormone. By reason of the malnutrition the liver fails to burn up the excess hormone, further contributing to the increased blood hormone level. This also may account for a shift in the androgen "male"-estrogen "female" hormone balance.

About 0900 hours on a typical morning, no different than a thousand othrs, 21 September 1944, Charley, Jim, Denny and I were doing nothing, the same as we had some thousand other mornings. A faint, deep roar captured our attention, more so than usual. The origin of the sound was airplanes, different without any question from any we had listened to in the past three years. I dangled out the open window, scanning the sky, still not ready to push the "red alert" for an air raid.

"Funny sounding airplanes,"Denny observed as the noise became stronger and stronger. We kept looking up into that cloudless sky.

Soon the *bahay* was shuddering from the tremendous roar. Charley and Jim stuck their heads out the window. "My God, there's hundreds of them--they've got to be Americans," shouted optimistic Charley, his face red, his arms reaching wildly upward.

Wave after wave of the little black specks scurried to the west towards Clark Field. Everybody cheered and hugged each other, except me. I stared upward entranced by the formations. Too many disappointments over the years had hardened me to rumors and even the apparent. Maybe Mitsubishi had released a new bomber. In a few minutes heavy bombing thundered from the direction of Clark Field. These were not Japanese formations.

Suddenly a roar and blast over the camp whirled us around to see a dogfight less than 200 meters overhead. The trailing plane firing into the Zero was marked with a white star on the undersurface of the starboard wing and a dragon tail extending to the port wing. Later we learned it was an American Hellcat. He blasted the Japanese plane again and again until it blew up. Down went the Zero, crashing about 500 meters outside the camp. A huge roar went up from inside the camp. Goose bumps appeared. My whole body shook. I was finally convinced. Someone was on our side. In a few minutes, I heard screaming bayonet-wielding Japs charging through the camp. They herded everyone inside his *bahay*.

After this first American bombing, rumors circulated that the Japanese intended to execute all remaining POWs. Possibly because starvation had done such a good job on us or because of their preoccupation with digging foxholes, the executions never occurred.

I halfway believed the rumors, figuring the time would come when my ability to run and my physical capacity would be challenged. If the shooting and bayoneting started, my escape hatch was the ditch and creek under the fence at the duck pond. Crouched behind a *bahay* I studied this route for hours.

Later that day, Jap squads, looking dirty and frantic, came charging through the camp again, gesturing for everyone to get inside. I listened for the machinegunning to start. The orders were to stay inside during air raids and also not to cheer! We completely ignored them, dancing and waving on the hidden side of the barracks.

Dog fights high in the sky were frequent after that. The airfield close by made with POW labor was soon non-operational and the few Jap planes based there were blown up. A Jap convoy burned up on the Cabanatuan road as a result of one bombing run. The road traffic disappeared. The Japs scurried for cover. They cowered like rats. One cannot imagine the overwhelming

197

firepower of this Navy aircraft carrier task force. They would maneuver up to a target, strike with an overwhelming force of possibly a thousand planes, and destroy an entire war machine. The destruction lasted for three days. We heard it was Bull Halsey's boys.

From our vantage point, our fighters were superior in dogfights, a great improvement since the miserable days of Clark and Nichols Fields. Now the Hellcat outperformed the Zero in acrobatics and apparently in firepower! Our fighters tore into the Emperor's boys like a swarm of Italian honeybees.

About mid-September, suddenly at 1100 hours, three Navy planes roared overhead. They had pulled up from a strafing run over our POW-built airstrip three km. away. We all ran out of the barracks yelling and waving. The last plane pulled up and then dove again, laying a string of 50-caliber machinegun bullets right through the center of our camp. It was over in five seconds.

"Hurry, medic," came the frantic shout.

One slug had struck Pvt. Hall in the anterior surface of the thigh, rupturing the femoral artery. Soldiers nearby were trying desperately to stop the fountain of blood spurting into the air. He was in shock with a thready pulse by the time several of us arrived. A surgeon slapped on a tourniquet and stopped the arterial bleeding.

Although against camp policy, a blood transfusion was considered, but the idea was abandoned when an immediate amputation of his leg became necessary to control the venous bleeding. It was carried out without antibiotics, transfusions or sterile dressings. Fortunately we had a few cans of ether for the merciful anesthetic. A 50-caliber slug carries a tremendous impact, particularly if it strikes a bone. Hall survived this surgery without complications. He had just soap and water to cleanse the wound and a few clean bandages to cover it.

Generally our camp policy prohibited transfusions, since only a few could qualify as healthy donors and very often the very same donor became sick and needed his complete defenses a short time later.

We always wondered about that Navy pilot. Did he associate us with the airstrip? He obviously didn't recognize us as Yanks. Our emotions were mixed, yet most of us cheered for the pasting the Japs were now getting. I was gleeful after spotting a Nip soldier toiling, digging his foxhole.

The following day we made a red cross on a sheet and staked it out for clear identification. Within the hour Col. Schwartz was summoned to Jap headquarters, pushed around, slapped, and angrily ordered to remove it. I figured we weren't going to have to take too many more of these beatings. The poor soldier who was observed staking out the red cross was dragged to headquarters and also beaten up.

19. GRAND EXODUS

The bombings of September 1944 precipitated "the grand exodus" of the remaining prisoners. Three large groups, 2,000 each, were evacuated out of Cabanatuan in the next three months. Shipped by hot steaming rail cars to Manila, held at Bilibid prison and moved to the suffocating holds or prison ships, they were slated for transfer to Japan.

Included among the highest ranking were Col. Curtis Beecher and Lt. Col. Jack Schwartz. Hundreds of my best friends, officers and enlisted men, marched out the wood-framed barbed-wire front gate, never to be seen alive again. Each man carried his entire personal belongings, a small bundle tied in a handkerchief or towel and, surprisingly, an occasional musette bag. Wendel Swanson, Bob Schott, Clarence Strand, Mike Sult, and Sullivan--I can't remember his first name--all medical and dental officers and *bahay* mates at one time, and even Corporal Decker, waved as they turned up the road. Although this same uncertainty on separation and an unknown journey was old hat, most eyes were misty. I lingered at the gate until an officious Jap noncom shoved me with his rifle butt. We all realized the waiting was about over. The odds of survival favored moving out of this camp, going with the largest group. I wondered what was in store for us.

The first POWs to leave camp were billeted in Bilibid for a few days, boarded the *Oryoko Maru* on 13 December 1944, and embarked by dark from Pier No. 17 in Manila for Corregidor. During the night the identifying marks on the smoke stack were exchanged with one of the two accompanying Jap troop ships. The 1,619 POWs were jammed into the holds of this hell ship. The conditions were horrible in the steamy darkness; no water, men vomiting and evacuating on each other, some crazed so they had to be knocked unconscious, unable to lie down. Several suffocated and were trampled to death. This rivaled the Death March in inhumane treatment. the following day the doomed *Oryoko Maru* rounded Bataan Peninsula into the China Sea, where American dive bombers duly warned by a clandestine short wave radio launched an attack. The bombs nearly demolished the ship, which was beached in Subic Bay. Hundreds were killed and wounded outright. The rest swam about 300 meters to shore within a corridor set up by the Japs. Machinegun fire killed those who floated outside the markers. The wounded who were unable to swim were shot on the ship. The survivors were herded into Olongapo, where the wounded were laid out on a concrete tennis court in the unmerciful hot tropical sun. One water spigot, later sanctified with a memorial plaque, served the approximately 600 wounded and other survivors. No treatment was offered to the wounded. By the third day two new ships were readied--the *Brazil Maru* and the *Enoura Maru*. All POWs were ordered to march to the waiting ships. Those unable to walk were shot or beheaded. The column, battered from previous beating by rifle butts, limped by. Swany Swanson and "Governor" Strand, both from my *bahay* with shrapnel wounds in the legs and unable to walk, were shot in the head as they lay in the sun. I'll always remember Swany talking about a girlfriend named Heila Tweet and Strand's warm smile. I had heard both these men pray for their safe return.

I didn't know at the time, but later got the news that Bill Tooley and Decker had been on the *Oryoko Maru* and had drowned. My good friend Bill, the fourth of the Whiffenpoof Boys, was gone. That took care of all who were "off on a spree for all eternity," except for myself.

The *Brazil Maru* and the *Enoura Maru* sailed from Subic Bay and Lingayen Gulf with only 600 prisoners aboard. Both ships were bombed and sunk off Formosa. This time Clarence White lost his right foot, lay on the deck, bleeding without any treatment for three days, and died. Some 200 out of the 1,619 POWs finally reached Japan on 29 January 1945.

During the fall of 1944, over 4,000 servicemen were lost aboard ships sunk by U.S. planes and submarines. Our little group was dwindling fast, doomed to die by any means. I used to believe that survival was determined by guts, but now I realized that it was by pure luck.

In a few days news of the first sinking filtered back into the camp via the underground. Weird as the reports were, we had grown accustomed to accepting them as true. The exodus choice lost some of its attractiveness. There were no volunteers for the next outside details. I was lucky to be in the finals.

MacArthur had kept his promise and "returned" to the Philippines, landing on Leyte on 20 October 1944. Coincident with the Leyte landing was the second massive air strike by the U.S. carrier force. News of the operation had very little impact on us, since we were still busy feeding ourselves, wondering about our future and watching the Jap guards come and go.

One evening, just as the daylight was mopped away by the darkening purple haze in late October, a Zero thundered over the camp and crashed in flames 500 meters outside our camp. Later the Jap guards said he ran out of gas trying to find a safe landing strip.

The second exodus of October reduced the camp census to less than 2,000 men.

In the first days of December 1944, the third and final exodus occurred. The only ones to remain in camp were 500 of the sickest and most maimed patients, carefully selected by the Japs. Those that "could never fight again" included everyone in my TB ward. They were a sorry lot, many minus legs and arms.

Then all the medical officers, 35 in number, were lined up, and down the line came the Jap lieutenant pointing at each officer, "You go, you go, you stay."

He came to me, recognized me as the TB or "pest" doctor and ordered, "You stay." I looked at him in amazement, realizing this pipsqueak had just ordered my destiny. This order might be a death sentence, since we were still convinced the few remaining prisoners would soon be liquidated. Yet, killing a bunch of physical and mental derelicts would not help the Emperor's cause very much except for closing the camp with a zero census. Denny, Jim and Charley were all selected to stay, probably because they were busy in the wards. A total of ten medical officers remained.

The next day, everyone but the 500 plus ten medical officers marched out the front gate. Most trudged along resignedly, some relieved to clear this camp alive, while others were sad. We gathered at the gate, a no-no previously, to yell goodbye. One poor devil staggered and fell just outside the gate. The guards just looked on blankly, so, without thinking, I moved outside, grabbed a leg, and pulled him inside the gate. I hadn't looked to the guards for approval, but waited for the rifle butt to crunch my ribs. It didn't come. The column shuffled down the road out of sight, ultimately ending up on the Hell Ships. We ended up with 511 remaining in our final count. Some military records later said we were 513. That official total of 513 read like this: 486 Americans, three Dutch, 23 English, one Norwegian: soldiers, marines, sailors, merchant marines and civilians. Five hundred nine of us survived while almost all of the other columns died. At least we still had a chance. The waiting was almost over. After three-plus years here were the gaunt remnants of war and captivity--the dregs of humanity. I never have reconciled those two counts.

The grim news of a massacre in Palawan Island on 14 December 1944 filtered in by bits and pieces. This isolated island off the southern Philippines in the Sulu Sea was the site of a small prison camp. By late December the horrible event was confirmed. This reinforced our fears that our camp would be liquidated.

At noon, following two raids by American planes, the Japanese ordered the entire garrison at Puerto Princesa on Palawan, about 150 Americans, British and Dutch, into three two-meter deep trenches holding 50 men each. Gasoline was poured into one end and lit. As the burning, living torches scrambled out, they were met with murderous automatic weapon fire. Only a handful, six or eight, escaped by jumping off a 20-meter cliff into thick brush, hiding until dark and then swimming across the bay where friendly natives whisked them away to a guerrilla camp. In a few days a U.S. seaplane picked up the only two survivors they could find. Such was the fate of this small group.

After Col. Schwartz departed, Col. Duckworth, the ranking officer, was designated the Camp Commander. He sent for me one morning. I reported in two minutes.

"You'll serve as adjutant," he stated.

"I'll be delighted," I answered.

The Japanese camp command was breaking down. Their troop numbers were decreasing. The sentry towers were manned at all times but fewer guards filled the pill boxes on the corners. Even the Jap COs, unidentified by name, changed frequently at this time.

Meetings with the Japs were irregular and only at their request. Duckworth, stooped badly, probably no more than 5'8"

203

tall by this time, he and I would shuffle with a limp across the bare compound to the Jap headquarters. The three years had taken their toll on him. Although he obviously was in poor health, he presented the picture of a hungry Boston Bulldog. His haughty nose and his body struggled to provide a home for a determined man. The padlocked wire gate was opened by a sentry, and the colonel was led into the wooden boarded office, bare except for a desk, devoid of any papers, with two chairs facing each other across the deak. We stood and bowed at the entrance of the Japs, usually an interpreter and the commanding officer, possibly a lieutenant. The conversation was usually a monologue in Japanese, mixed at times with English, with the interpreter filling in. It was not very precise nor important.

"You must stay in the camp, work hard, give us no trouble, or you will be severely killed," they said.

The customary harangue of bitterness and bellicose threatening was still present but in smaller quantities. Duckworth and I said nothing unless asked.

It was 5 January 1945, with heavy cannonading clearly heard to the northwest in the direction of Lingayen Gulf, 100 km. away. We later learned it was our pre-invasion Naval bombardment of the beaches. The deep rolling thunder continued all morning. About noon the Jap commandant ordered Col. Duckworth and me to appear "on the double."

The colonel's double was only a shuffle, so I lingered at his left side as a sentry pointed us to the headquarters building. The severity of the small bare room was striking. A dirty, smelly guard motioned for us to stand in front of a bare table. The unshaven, furtive-eyed and nervous commandant, who was new to us, with an equally fidgety interpreter moved in quickly and sat down. The lieutenant, squirming and ill at ease, began speaking in blustery outbursts.

"We leaving in two days. No guards left. You must stay in camp. Here new boundary. If anybody leaves, we kill everyone severely," he barked, hissed through his teeth and not waiting for his blank-looking interpreter.

"How about food?" Duckworth asked in a steady, commanding voice.

After a few minutes of discussion the interpreter, sweating by this time, responded in a low voice, "We leave one week's supply here," pointing through an open window toward the warehouse.

"We kill badly if you no obey," insisted the Jap commander. He seemed very anxious that we understood that point. The meeting was devoid of the usual harangue about Americans not learning the Japanese language or other crap.

About this time a low-flying American strafer roared overhead. The heavy thunder of naval gunfire increased, rattling the old building. The Japs looked very uncomfortable with surprised glances at each other. I was doing handsprings inside.

Let the little pusillanimous pups crawl, I thought.

"What is the tactical situation?" I inquired twice, before the suddenly gone-deaf interpreter grasped it.

The image of this moment, printed in my mind forever, embodied feelings; the worst of the past and the best for the future as our military might rattled the very timbers of the building. The Jap commander consulted with the interpreter, then stood up struggling with his emotions. With his back to us, he gazed through horn-rimmed glasses across the cogon grass and deserted rice paddies in the direction of Lingayen Gulf and the thunderous shellfire. He was resigning himself to die in a foreign land. Why we were not included, I'll never know. He focused on the corner of the room looking the part of a father trying to talk to his son about girls.

After a long pause which I thoroughly enjoyed, he answered in a barely audible whisper, "Velly obscure, velly obscure," never looking at us. So was his future, I mused as we trudged back to our headquarters.

"Let's have officer call at 1300 hours," the Duck directed grimly. "I want everyone to be fully informed, ordered to stay put, no escapes or shenanigans. Keep a low profile and avoid any excuse for these wild bastards to start shooting at us."

All this and a new boundary was explained to the eight other medical officers who hurried off to their wards with the exciting news.

The American garrison, 511 beaten, starved, sick, the halt and the blind, received the news placidly. Too much had happened. It had been too long for anyone to be bullied now.

Was there yet to be another disappointment, I wondered.

205

Two days later at dusk on 7 January 1945, the Jap guards climbed down from the towers, spilled out of the pillboxes, assembled on the knoll at their headquarters, and to our amazement, lowered the Rising Sun flag. They marched down the road without song or cadence, heading towards Cabu, a town east of Cabanatuan City. Unknown to us, we still had 23 days to wait.

Horizon in scope, my desire was to be free from hunger and immediacy of death. I longed to be free beyond the fences, with the barricades melted away, the sentry towers collapsed and the perimeter wires gone. In my mind I would stroll in the cogon grass fields, cross the rice paddies, go up the bare foothills into the sky-ward etchings of the purple Nueva Ecija mountains, and walk and walk towards the mauve sky splashed by the setting sun. I would reach the indelible border of the horizons. Nightly for three years the panorama of this dream returned, yet it stopped before reaching into the inner secrets of home--Nancy, Bert, Mary Fran, Billie Jane, Mother. I spent a lifetime in that prison, although life did not end with it. I had an undying and unswerving belief in our ultimate victory. Time, although running out, moved inexorably onward. I must wait, crying for the tortured living and praying for the dead. Patience, I said to myself, patience, you must wait just a little bit longer. Our war was winding down.

Later that night, four of us sneaked through the gate, and finding no Japs, proceeded to inventory the warehouses. Suddenly we heard a noise and spotted several crouched figures. With our night blindness, recognition was impossible until a soldier whispered, "Hula, hula, hola, hola." Thank God, they were American POW soldiers foraging for themselves. I could hardly discipline them since our hand was stuck in the same cookie jar.

"The pickings are pretty good," whispered one soldier.

After finding some cases of condensed milk, we decided to lug them back and get the hell out of Jap territory. There was a great time in the old camp the next day with the distribution of a milk ration, cream on the *lugao*--manna from heaven! The richness of the milk nauseated me, requiring three swallows to keep it down once. With the Japs gone our fresh meat and vegetable ration stopped, but we substituted canned fish and fruits found in the warehouse.

During the first three days after the Japs left, we were entirely unguarded. About that time, Sgt. Gavin of Iowa came by saying, "I've got a deal too good to pass up."

"What's that, Sergeant?" I inquired.

"There are three carabaos in the corral behind the Jap headquarters. One of them belongs to us," he said. "What do you think?"

"I don't want to give them any excuse for liquidating us," I replied hesitantly, thinking out loud. "I'll be by later and let you know." I thought, Why take the chance? I had no intentions of meeting a brave and quickly forgotten death at this late hour; on the other hand, fresh meat would sure help the men.

About 1600 hours that same day, I found Gavin and said very quietly and firmly, "Go ahead right now, quickly with a dozen men and get the job done. Bring everything back. There's no Japs in the compound at this time to my knowledge.

Armed with a maul and knives, they moved rapidly through the gate and disappeared behind the Jap Headquarters. Believe it or not, in just a few minutes a squad of Japs came marching up the road and disappeared into their barracks, apparently fixing to bed down for the night. My heart stopped. There was no way out. Our boys were trapped. Soon Sgt. Gavin and his butchers came swinging by carrying the entire butchered carabao, bowed to the Japs and proceeded jauntily to the mess, just like it was a daily routine. They were never challenged by the bewildered Nips. Can you imagine a whole animal for 511 people? The soup even had fat floating on top of it. Neither Col. Duckworth nor the Japs knew the truth of this escapade. The guards left the next day, none the wiser.

Within a day or two Filipinos moving along the road, not spying any Japs, tossed fruit--*kaimito, kalamansi*, bananas, papayas, and jackfruit over the fence. It was a rare treat, but our freedom from guards didn't last long. Transient Japs moved in and out of the area, and in a few days had taken up guard positions in the corner pill boxes and sentry towers. At night Jap infantrymen, sometimes tanks and armored vehicles, would stop and then move on before dawn.

One evening, about mid-January, three tanks lumbered into the camp and after some shouting and confusion, a dirty, raunchy-looking Jap second lieutenant, burst into our area looking for help. He spoke no English, wanted a doctor, and soon produced an unconscious Jap soldier. The clinical picture--a bloody head--indicated a skull injury and possible fracture. Surgeon Jim Musselman and I examined him and indicated by sign language that he needed further examination. Handling him like a sack of rice, two of his buddies carried him to Jim's surgical barracks where he was placed on a bare wooden table. His uniform was filthy, soiled from inside and out. He smelled to high heaven. Long black whiskers suggested a week's neglect. He was young, probably no more than 18 years old. Poor kid, a long ways from home, I thought.

Musselman found a long spinal needle while I tried repeatedly to impress on the officer the gravity of the injury.

"He will die," I declared, presenting my best characterization of a terminal situation.

The Jap officer gave me the impression we'd better save him or else. The youthful disheveled officer was dead serious.

With only a candle for light, Jim thrust the needle into the spinal canal. Gross bright red blood shot out, confirming the diagnosis of a hemorrhage from a skull fracture. So I stuck the needle back into the spinal sac. This finding encouraged my charades with a strong performance of "not much hope, very bad, keep quiet." The tank officer, obviously not very good at charades, started to pick up the wounded man when I stepped between them. I wondered what the outcome would be as he glared at me.

"No more riding on tank!" I shouted. "Must not move!"

The standoff lasted a moment until he slowly turned around, and seeing none of his soldiers, slipped away in the dark. The night seemed longer and darker than usual. Both Jim and I tended to the lad all night long. Jim lay on the hard wooden floor nearby while I leaned against the thatched wall. I checked the soldier's pulse every 20 or 30 minutes. It began to slow gradually at first and then more rapidly, finally sinking to 40 per minute. His breathing was waxing and waning--both were ominous signs indicating increased intracranial pressures. Occasionally the tank officer would appear out of the dark grunting and pointing toward the wounded lad.

"No good-o," I hissed, shaking my head.

208

The Jap did not acknowledge any understanding, but indicated the soldier had fallen off a tank while dozing the day before. Although he was the enemy, the thought never entered my mind to do anything but to try to save the young soldier's life. I didn't need to resurrect the Hippocrates' oath to get direction, to give him medical care or just figuratively turn our back and do nothing. Before dawn the officer abruptly reappeared at the ward. Jim and I nursed the bashed-headed soldier through the night. His coma was deepening.

Despite violent remonstration on my part, two of his buddies picked him up, hoisted him onto the tank, and tied him loosely around the head and feet. The rope was looped over the turret, and off they went, bouncing down the road. It was a queer sight indeed, a human with his head all bandaged up, tied on the outside of a war machine. Our best estimate was that he wouldn't last half a kilometer. We both felt sorry for the lad, knowing our therapeutic acumen had been wasted.

Almost every day we had to argue with the intransigent cadre of Japs to get our daily ration of a half pound of rice per man. They knew nothing of past arrangements. We tried unsuccessfully, bullying them with big fat lies regarding issuing other foods, but generally they left us alone since we didn't present any threat to them. With our stolen food the ration was much improved anyway. One time four bayonet-thrusting Nips charged around the area. They looked like an execution squad to me, but after a great commotion, we figured out they were looking for a guerrilla. The affair was a complete mystery to us. A guerrilla would be crazy to venture inside our camp. Stray rifle shots echoed in the distance as the guerrillas became more active.

We were entirely defenseless. Any wild undisciplined Jap outfit could wipe us out for kicks or for the Emperor. No plans, instructions or intrigue were offered to our troops in case of an emergency. Our options were zilch. We waited with grim smiles on our faces.

Tension mounted in the camp. We could hear friendly artillery in the distance.

20. RECAPTURE

Denny, Charley, Jim and I waited cautiously. Our patients steeled themselves for anything. If fired upon, my personal "War Plan Pink No. 57" would go into effect immediately. This simply called for my crawling down the ditch leading to the duck pond, swimming 50 feet to yonder shore and catching a "ferry" to somewhere. Hopefully, my weapon would be a butcher knife borrowed temporarily from the mess.

Artillery fire from the west echoed closer as January wore on. We had no idea what was going on. We were in a news blackout. Without our men moving in and out of the camp, our communication with the outside world was lost. The clandestine radio had disappeared. Filipinos outside the fence spoke of landings at Lingayen Gulf, 100 km. away. We guessed the Yanks were advancing.

About one hour before darkness blanketed the camp on the evening of 30 January, six Jap light tanks along with two platoons, about 70 foot soldiers, slipped into the area. This had been the pattern the past few nights. Unbeknownst to us, 300 additional Jap soldiers were bivouacked 5 km. to the west at Cabu.

The tanks hid in the warehouses while two soldiers climbed each of the sentry towers and half a dozen or so sat in the corner pill boxes behind staggered sandbags. Open only in front, they faced our compound with their rifles pointing towards us. Just before dark, a huge black plane, not over 200 meters up, swooped over the camp, soon followed by another. An occasional distant rifle shot echoed--most unusual.

"Funny plane," Charley Lewis observed, his head cocked toward the disappearing aircraft.

We later learned it was a P-61 "Black Widow" fighter with infrared equipment, piloted by Lt. Ken Schrieber of the 547th night fighter group. They were snooping for Jap troops or tanks. Even more importantly, the planes were a diversionary tactic to distract the guards. Something was up. I moved along the barracks down the path towards the main Jap guard house. The guard was changing. I could barely see eight or ten men taking seats behind the barriers, quiet and solemn. I watched for awhile and then strolled back up the bare path and, with dark coming nearer, sat on the headquarters steps with my three good pals. "Something funny is going on around here," said Denny.

Suddenly, at exactly 1945 hours, small arms fire exploded at the south gate and in a few seconds rapid automatic fire erupted at the main guard house where I had just been five minutes before. In a few seconds firing commenced all around the perimeter.

"My God, they're finally going to kill us," shouted Charley as he jumped up looking for an escape route, or something. About that time shots rang out to the east and in the evening glow we saw both Jap sentries topple over the railing of the towers. That looked a little more promising.

"It must be a guerrilla raid," I said.

Within ten seconds the attacking forces, who turned out to be Rangers, had silenced the main guard house. The Japanese, sitting on their haunches, were cut in two with automatic weapon fire. The shooting around the perimeter fence diminished in a couple of minutes; after that, only an occasional slug whistled overhead. Suddenly a blast, followed by a fiery streak, then another and another, sailed over us. Up to this time we were crouching, but then all four of us dove into a deep drainage ditch.

"What in hell was that?" shouted Denny from the bottom of an arroyo.

"That was some Roman candle. It must be someone's Fourth of July," I quipped.

In truth the weapon flaming from both ends and the Roman candle were our first look at a bazooka. Half of the Jap tanks were destroyed in fiery explosions from the rocket launcher.

Several more flaming meteors sailed over our heads, followed by explosions and fires in the Jap headquarters area. The remaining three Jap tanks were blown up. A Jap truck loaded with troops just moving out, silhouetted by leaping flames, disappeared in a beautiful, tremendous explosion.

Yelling began in the wards down below.

"We're Yanks," came the call. "You're free. All Americans

211

head for the main gate!"

It was reported later one very proper Englishman among us said, "I'm not an American, but I'm going, too."

About five minutes after the first shots, up the path came three big, tough, green fatigue-clad Americans with their tommy guns blazing from their hips, raking the Jap buildings across the road. Another Ranger had a grenade in one hand and a knife in the other. I jumped out of the ditch and grabbed the nearest, making sure to sidestep his gun and knife.

"What in hell is going on?" I shouted.

"We're the Rangers; you're free!" he bellowed. "Careful, men, don't kill any of the prisoners," he yelled over his shoulder.

"Who are the Rangers?" I pleaded. "Are you guerrillas? Where did you come from?"

The Ranger turned to me and yelled, "Listen, you get the hell our of here. We're Gen. Krueger's boys!"

I pleaded, "My men can't even walk."

"The rest of the prisoners have been carried out. You're the last damned one--now get going!"

He picked me up with one hand and turned me downhill. Then he gave me a "ten-foot kick" squarely in the ass.

I picked myself up, stumbled to my *bahay*, and threw my first aid pack over my shoulder. All it contained was a cigarette holder made from the brass jacket of a 30-06 shell fitted into a whittled horn mouth piece, a picture of Pilar, letters from home and an armband with Japanese characters worn by our POW officer of the day. My chess set made from carabao horn was overlooked in the mad rush. I ran through the nearest barracks. It was empty. I hurried back to my *bahay* and then down the path to Col. Duckworth's hut--both were empty. I went on to my TB ward, stuck my head in the doorway and yelled, "Come on, let's go; you're free!" My calls were unanswered. The ward was vacant, giving me an odd feeling. My God, I thought, how did they do it?

As I stumbled down to the main road a soldier yelled at me, "Hurry, a Jap column is approaching our road block. You're the last man."

Over my shoulder I could see orange flames from enemy rifles dotting the knoll. I could hear a withering counter fire from dozens of advancing Rangers. Yellowish flames streaking from rockets launched by bazookas leaped from alongside the camp road. It was a magnificent show with the Jap headquarters all aflame amidst a deafening roar from our boys.

The fighting in the stockade was nearly over. All the 224 Japs were killed and the six Jap tanks destroyed. I didn't know of our own casualties but certainly the POWs seemed to be safely out. The red streak and explosion of a Very pistol lit up the camp.

Gen. Krueger, I thought, who the hell is he? This is a hair-brained scheme. Five hundred cripples, 20-30 kms. behind the Jap lines. Well, anyway, this is it; MacArthur needn't wait much longer for us.

I stumbled over a body; turning him over, I recognized a dead Jap. He needed a shave. Two Jap mortars exploded nearby just as I passed in front of the main Jap guardhouse where I could dimly see the bodies of the same men I had observed earlier, now slumped in their seats. I hurriedly crossed the main road and stumbled onto a trail along the rice paddy dikes.

Earlier we heard gunfire raking the rear gate pillbox. Later the team was identified as Ranger Cpl. Roy Sweezy from Michigan and his three buddies. Their automatic fire silenced the guns of six Japs still sitting inside. Roy's mission completed, he crouched and scurried along the east perimeter fence towards the main road and then a stray slug tore into his chest.

"It was crossfire from my buddies," he protested. "My God, help me," and he was dead. It was all over in just a few minutes.

Distant firing broke out behind us first from the east in the direction of Cabu and then down the road to the west towards Cabanatuan City. Capt. Eduardo Joson commanded the road block five km. to the west and Capt. Pajata commanded the road block five km. to the east. Both had 150-200 Filipino guerrillas lying in ambush ready to spring the trap. The Filipinos had set up their guns and bazookas after sneaking all day through the tall grass. Within ten minutes a hell of a fight with rapid fire rifles, machineguns and mortars blew up to the east. The Jap column, reacting to the firing at the POW camp, trotted into the jaws of a V-shaped road block and blown-out bridge, flanked by 30-foot bluffs. Wave after wave of the Emperor's finest trotted to the end of the destroyed bridge to be cut down by a murderous fire until the pile of bodies was neck-deep. Filipino guerrillas led by Capt. Pajata, a Filipino guerrilla, slaughtered nearly 400 Japs before they ran out of Kamikaze kids. They also hit eight Jap tanks circling in a palm tree grove. The tanks were destroyed with bazooka fire before they could get untracked and effectively fire back.

It was many years later that this brave Filipino officer, Capt. Pajata, was recognized. A few days before he died in 1976 his request for American citizenship was finally granted.

I turned back toward camp once more to see flames leaping skyward, fueled by the Jap tanks. Flames from our captors' headquarters building lit the water tower on the knoll. I would not be listening to "Kimigayo" anymore. For the first time I was finally convinced that I was honest-to-God going to make it. Thank God for the safety of our little group. Guerrillas and civilians appearing out of the darkness guided me down the narrow trail.

"*Mabuhay!* You need help, Joe?" many inquired.

"No, I'm OK," I responded, stumbling along.

In a few minutes we caught up with our column--a few walking alone, others being assisted, some piggybacked on the shoulders of big tough Rangers and Alamo Scouts. Soon two-wheel carabao carts bedded with rice straw were picking up our men. Empty carts trailed behind loading the stragglers, and the sickest men who were still walking.

I came alongside a fleshless, burnt-out limping Bataan soldier using a stick, who bragged, "I'll make it, Captain." He soon fell and we loaded him into a cart on a bed of straw. I saw two green-clade Rangers take off their shoes and put them on barefooted prisoners who were trying to walk. They tucked our men under their arms like babies. Shaking their heads in disbelief, tears filled their eyes at the tragic sight of these emaciated Americans so far down the starvation trail.

"How could another human treat you like this?" they inquired incredulously.

A call for a medic came from the rear. Hurrying back I found Musselman huddled over a quiet, pale Capt. Jim Fisher--the only medical officer with the American attacking force. A piece of shrapnel had penetrated his belly just as he came through the main gate near the end of the fighting. Probably the same rounds that landed as I jumped across the main road. A Ranger medic provided supplies, and with a flashlight penetrating the darkness,

Jim started an IV of saline and gave him a syringette of morphine in the arm. His condition was poor to guarded, the shock was deepening. He needed help *now*. His pulse was over 100 and thready. A jagged, bloody mid-abdominal shrapnel wound about six cm. long, the worst possible injury to happen in this inaccessible location, was outlined as the beam of light played back and forth. It was a desperate sitution requiring immediate hospitalization, which was impossible. Fisher groaned and bit his lip. His breathing was jerky, and ended with a grunt. A litter team hurriedly transported him to a barrio, Blagkare, near Platero, three km. away where Jim planned to set up for surgery.

"Radio for help and medic evacuation. Get more lanterns and candles--anything for light. We need blood now, O-positive volunteers, right now!" Jim growled, his voice rising. "Ralph, you go on with the men; I'm going to stay and attempt surgery. Dr. Layug is here." I took off without argument.

Dr. Carlos Layug, "Platero Rose" they called him, was a tough Filipino guerrilla doctor dedicated to our cause. The Japs had a price on his head. We learned later that he had been treating guerrilla forces all over Luzon for three years.

The two worst obstacles on the escape march towards friendly lines were the Pampanga River and the scary crossing of the Rizal Highway.

After a few kilometers, our main column waded the warm, knee-deep waters of the Pampanga River. Suddenly a hail of bullets peppered the water. It was soon quieted by the rear guard Rangers. This was the end of enemy firing and the pursuit. We were safely over the first obstacle.

I trudged along the line and stumbled on a slouched hulk leaning against the dike of a deep rice paddy. I didn't recognize Col. Duckworth in the darkness until he spoke. He was holding his left arm.

"How are you doing, Colonel? Here, let me help you," I volunteered, pulling on his arm.

"Ouch," he muttered. "I fell and broke my goddamn arm. Help me out of here, but don't pull on that arm. Let's get going."

The bones grated as he moved, but he refused anything for pain. I managed to make a sling with handkerchiefs and my precious socks. Later this human bulldog, one tough cookie, was helped into a cart where he rode the rest of the night.

The column inched cross country, along the dikes, through the barrios, and the groves of trees. People lined the trail offering bananas, mangoes and rice balls. The children would run up and touch us.

"Thank you, Joe. God bless you, Joe," they would murmur.

One bashful, yet brave girl, gave me a sampaguita, the Philippine national flower. Dropping her head she whispered, "You are free; we are friends. You're OK now, Joe," and moved into the shadows.

Two of my TB patients, Erickson and Johnson, were sinking fast. Despite being carried from their beds and nursed with care in the carts, they were not making it. We mixed a canteen full of sugared tea. "Make them drink three ounces every half hour, you hear?" Hovering over them, I broke a candy bar in two and stuffed pieces into their mouths, but they didn't pretend to chew them. They just looked kind of bewildered, their heads tossing with each gasp. Time and strength were running out. Their supply of life was dwindling. "Oh, God, not *now*," I sobbed.

It was midnight as we approached Rizal Highway, the main north-south road in Central Luzon. Japanese military traffic, including tanks, was heavy, running all blacked out. We crouched in the ditch and edged towards the road. We could hear the approaching trucks and tanks hurrying northward. Small groups of the carabao-pulled carts lumbered across. They had to wait at times to let a dozen or more Jap trucks roar by. Then three or four carts would go, leaving the groves of durian and mangosteen trees bordering the road. After a long hour of hide-and-go-seek, believe it or not, the entire column had crossed undetected.

I found a Ranger company commander, Capt. Robert Prince, sweaty and dirty, resting against a coconut tree with his long rifle balanced across his knees.

"Two of our POWs, my old TB patients, are dying. One is semi-comatose, barely responding, and both need medical support *now*," I blurted. "We need something more than we've got here if we're going to save them."

"We've got radio contact with the First Cavalry and a station hospital at Guimba," he said. "They're sending a plane for a medic supply drop and evac as soon as they can see, and an armored column is pushing this way. Hold out until dawn if you can. Keep 'em going, Doc--it'll be just a few hours.''

Prince stood up slowly, shuddered, then with lowered head, continued in a husky voice, "We can't let anyone die *now*, not after what they've been through.''

I went back and moistened Cpl. Johnson's lips with coconut juice as the cart jounced along. His cadaverous head nodded a silent thanks.

"Oh, God, please spare these men," I prayed silently.

Abouy 0200 hours, on the morning of the 31st, retracing my steps towards Platero, I found Musselman and Dr. Layug hovering over Capt. Fisher in a hut dimly lit by candles. Jim had an intravenous of saline running and had established a vein-to-vein transfusion from a Ranger to the captain. The flow was slow and clotted so quickly that the transfusion failed. With some local anesthesia, moving the candles and peering into the abdomen with the aid of a flashlight, Jim had performed a laparotomy and stopped most of the bleeding except in one place--the hole in the liver. Long retractors, surgical lights, mattress sutures and blood by the gallon were desperately needed but there wasn't going to be any and Jim knew it.

"A plane will be here at dawn," I told them. "A rice paddy has been marked with sheets for a landing strip."

Jim never looked up as he hovered over the sinking captain, listening to his belly. Jim shook his head indicating uncertainty and doubt. Capt. Fisher, a highly skilled man, a medic, the only wounded officer, lay dying in the most primitive conditions on a wooden table in a candle-lit nipa hut. In any other place or set of conditions, with a minimum of medical support, he could have been saved.

Fisher, weak and pale, breathing hard, turned to me and smiled, "How am I doing, Doc?" he asked in the twilight of consciousness.

"OK, they'll be picking you up shortly," I responded, turning away sharply to hide my real answer.

Later Jim and I walked outside in the lush pre-dawn air scented with odors from tropical blossoms.

"They'd better hurry," Jim said looking skyward. "He needs a massive transfusion now. I got the spurters tied off but the liver was badly torn. I couldn't see well enough to find all the perforations in the bowel. God, how we need help, *now*!"

"You can't do anything more," I said, trying to encourage him. "The Japs will never catch up with us now. At least we're free, Jim."

But Jim then said, "Yup, but this man isn't. Have you seen Charley and Denny?" He cleared his throat, changing the subject.

"Yeah, they're OK, up at the head of the column helping out," I replied.

A tiny grey-haired Filipina lady came out of the darkness holding bananas, a cooked chicken wrapped in banana leaves, in her outstretched hands. "You eat, Joe," she said. "I pray for you many years." I could see tears glistening on her wrinkled face. She crossed herself and moved away.

The iridescent streaks in the eastern horizon heralded the false dawn. A small plane, probably an 0-4 utility craft, circled the torch-marked field. Soon in the hazy light the plane bounced to a safe landing. I turned and ran to the barrio to help Jim load the patient. Jim stepped slowly out of the hut at my approach.

"He must have died just as the wheels of the plane touched the ground," Jim said in a subdued voice. "He's gone, he's gone forever. With just a little help he could have been saved."

Yet another man had paid the price for our freedom.

In a broken voice, Jim muttered, "His buddies suggested we bury him on that palm grove knoll."

A memorial was later erected in that tiny native barrio near Platero to a very brave soldier--the son of Dorothy Canfield Fisher. We later learned that Dr. Fisher had delivered a Filipno baby the day before, bringing life into this world one day and giving his the next. He had volunteered for this mission. Father Hugh Kennedy, a POW who stayed behind with the Alamo Scouts, conducted funeral services, in this place so far from Jim Fisher's native land. Father Hugh and three Scouts, surrounded by a circle of little brown people who were all crying, lowered the body into a grave freshly dug by the Filipinos.

"He was a good Joe," they said.

"Oh, God," intoned the priest, "accept this brave soldier into your heavenly home."

The Filipinos erected a little cross, captioned: DOCTOR FISHER MEMORIAL." The last I knew it was still tended by the natives.

By dawn the bamboo wireless was alerting Filipinos far and wide. The head of our POW column arrived in Matoana and went on to Kahoy where more carts joined it, making a total of 51. Coming out of the barrios, emerging from the bamboo thickets, tumbling out of the stilted huts behind the dikes, lumbering across the dry paddies, appearing out of the shadows of mango groves, more and more carts lengthened the column, pulled by the Filipinos' most precious possession, the carabao.

Fifteen more carts appeared in Balancari. The Americans, so cruelly confined, pawns the Japs were planning to use, were slowly but surely slipping away. The column, over 70 two-wheelers, stretched over two kilometers. Every step separated us farther from our tormentors.

It was after daylight as I hurried to join the lead carts.

"Erickson just died, Captain," blurted Sgt. Gavin. "He would not eat. His breathing became more irregular and then stopped."

I heard them yelling, "Welcome back, Joe." But Erickson did not make it.

We were almost free, but, oh, Lord, at what a price! Erickson had struggled through three years of hell without victory. His dues were finally paid up. But only on his final day.

"Now we are 510," I said resignedly to myself.

Someone yelled, "Air raid!" A faint roar was heard as three planes dove straight at us. I stood up, entranced as they screamed over our heads. One plane banked straight skyward, a star glistening on the wing--American planes--those are our boys, as a tremendous roar echoed across the rice paddies. More planes waggled their wings as they patrolled the skies over us. The thrill of being a Yankee! Hundreds of planes had arrived just like they promised in 1942, but, oh my God, they were so late!

The trail lined with Filipinos was soon surrounded by U.S. tanks, armored cars and troop carriers, ambulances and a Red Cross van with food. All were filled with wildly cheering Americans. I was never certain which vehicle was the first to reach us, but I think the Red Cross van beat the tanks.

"Captain, we need you. Johnson is not doing well," reported

Sgt. Carl Stuart to me.

I hurried over to the straw-filled cart where Johnson lay breathing his last. I climbed in, cuddling his head on my lap, and begged, "Oh, God, don't take him now. Not another one!" I could see medics running towards us with IVs, but it was too late. He died there; one more to lay on the macabre escutcheon of a savage enemy. We cried openly.

"He knew he was free," Stuart sobbed. "He said so last night. 'Those are Yanks, aren't they?' He was in the twilight of consciousness. 'I can go now. I'm free at last.' Those were his last words."

This day, his tomorrow, saw the end of his struggle for freedom.

"And now we are 509," I muttered.

In reality, only 508 of us marched out of camp. Edward Rose, a stone-deaf Englishman, had failed to hear the shouting, shooting and instructions to leave, so did not clear the camp until the next dawn. He awoke to find the place deserted, so he leisurely ambled down the road and fortunately was spotted by Alamo Scouts who were still patrolling the area. They snatched him off the enemy-controlled road into the safety of guerrilla land.

We were anxious to evacuate the sickest immediately, so several of the ambulance corpsmen attached to the First Cavalry medical unit and our medicos hurriedly sorted through our group of shrunken, wrinkled, cadaverous skeletons with inordinate big heads and eyes. IVs were started on others not responding well. Hip bones stuck out. Spindly feet and legs, with bruised purple discoloration showed large chronic putrid ulcers.

"You should have seen me before January when the guards left and the chow picked up," said one POW to a husky Ranger who was scrutinizing him. The contrast between our rescuers and our motley crew belied their common American origin.

Big healthy American GIs, even nurses with curvaceous figures, Red Cross dames with full lips, reporters, radiomen, surrounded us, everyone pressing in to assist us. With the swift rescue, many were stunned and bewildered. The tattered shirts, G-strings, repatched shorts and wooden clogs or bare feet were part of our pitiful appearance. Most of our men huddled like hound dogs in the shade. No men ever tried more valiantly to regain their pride which the Japs had destroyed, and to control their emotions. They smiled weakly as the nurses tried to talk with them.

"We're alive because of luck and the will to live," I responded to the most frequently asked question, "How could you stand it?"

As naval officer Alan McCracken wrote some years later, an important ingredient in survival was to keep your sense of humor. He remembered two POW soldiers waiting in chow line.

"What are you going to have for breakfast?" asked one.

"Oh, I think I'll have hotcakes," the other replied.

The first one responded, "Not me, there's no more maple syrup."

McCracken wrote that you "live one day at a time; never give up; and be thankful you made it through this day." He admits his "funeral parlor" experience made him easy to feed, but it was difficult to graduate from this school alive.

"To get the most out of life, take big bites but chew slowly," he advised.

The 1st Cavalry had moved up kitchens far beyond their line to greet us with a breakfast of bacon and eggs, grapefruit, biscuits, butter, jam, coffee and milk. I finally swallowed most of it, but it turned out to be a choleric portion as well. It came up before I could recapture it for future consumption.

"Do you want some more?" asked a pretty thing shaped like a girl.

"Where I came from, they put you in the guardhouse if you ask for more," a prisoner replied.

Several of the men, acting from habit, carefully snuffed out their cigarettes and placed the butts behind their ears. One POW bent over to clutch a recently discarded butt before realizing he didn't have to hoard tobacco anymore.

My heart stopped at the first sight of an American flag fluttering from the turret of a tank. What a sight, blurred through my teary eyes. My chin came up. This produced an exhilaration I hadn't experienced in three years. I was free; proud to be an American!

It's a grand old flag--the stars and stripes. Can you imagine going for three years without seeing Old Glory? In the last hours of fighting in Bataan the 31st Infantry regimental flags were hidden in the dark recesses of Malinta Tunnel on Corregidor. The Japs never found them. Here, with the flag flying again, I felt like "the man without a country," who had just been nationalized.

By noon all of our men had been transported by ambulance to the 92nd Evacuation Hospital at Guimba, about 60 km. from Cabanatuan.

The Rangers stretched out on the hard sun-baked adobe clay for a siesta, their first sleep in over 24 hours. A tall Ranger in dirty, sweaty fatigues, packing an M-1 rifle and grenades attached to his waist belt, ambled up and blurted, "You Capt. Hibbs?"

"Yes, sir," I responded.

"I'm sorry, sir. I'm Sgt. Richardson, and I'm the guy that gave you a boot down the trail last night. I'm sorry, but you didn't seem to be moving in the right direction."

"Yeah, you're right, Sergeant. I needed a little booster. Someone to light the fuse," I said with a grin.

"Sorry, sir," he said, ashamedly putting his arm around my shoulders. "I just wanted to be sure you didn't get hurt."

I gulped. "You and I both. I just couldn't see how you were going to move 500 cripples. You're a fine soldier. You got the job done."

Col. Duckworth and I responded on CBS, NBC, British and Australian radio and to numerous reporters. Supposedly we were heroes since dead soldiers give poor interviews. There never was any doubt in my mind about that label. It belonged to those in graves in the jungle, to those buried on the Death March, or at prison camps, not lucky bums like us.

Lt. Melville Schmidt, the rugged and tireless platoon leader of the U.S. 6th Rangers, suggested that I ride with him to the evacuation hospital. This was my first motor vehicle ride in almost three years. On the way, soldiers stopped to wave, tanks wiggled their guns, even bulldozers swung their blades in recognition. What an army! The equipment was staggering, their morale was overwhelming. As we motored along, Lt. Schmidt related the details of the raid and our recapture.

About two weeks before the attack, in mid-January, intelligence reported the location of our POW camp near Cabanatuan.

Immediately plans were developed at 6th Army Headquarters to rescue us because scuttlebutt reinforced the suspicion the Japs would exterminate the whole camp. Col. Henry Mucci, CO of the 6th Ranger Infantry Batallion, attached to Gen. Krueger's 6th Army, was selected as overall leader.

Lt. John Dove and Lt. William Nellist, both volunteers from California, led two companies of Alamo Scouts. Capt. Robert Prince of Seattle and Lt. Frank Murphy, along with 107 picked Rangers, all volunteers, were to lead the assault. Maj. Robert Lapham of Davenport, Iowa, had 286 armed guerrillas in the vicinity nearby. He was a handsome dedicated soldier who had outwitted the Nips in a hit-and-run show for three years.

Two days before the attack, ten Alamo Scouts advanced on foot about 40 km. inside the Jap lines. They melted into the countryside, sneaking through the cogon grass and along the dikes of nearby rice paddies to within 200 yards of our camp. They lay quietly for hours, noting the movement of the guards. Others, dressed as Filipinos, lounged in chairs at nearby native shacks, spying on the whole camp activity, watching the Jap tanks and troops moving in and out.

The information from the Filipino guerrillas, abundant but contradictory, placed a division of Jap troops at Cabu, 10 km. to the east; 1,000 troops at Cabanatuan City, 12 km. to the west; and 12 tanks and 300 Jap soldiers in the camp headquarters. The guerrillas reported most of this force was expected to move north. A worried Col. Mucci wisely delayed the attack. He could not afford to attack without more accurate reports. Within the next 24 hours, the Alamo Scouts and a Filipino messenger, Lt. Tombo, painstakingly scouted our camp. Tombo was a tireless guerrilla, who slithered about the countryside like a rice cobra. They accurately established the number and position of the Japanese. The six tanks, the location of the tank shed, the manned sentry towers, the guardhouses, and our POW barracks were pinpointed.

The overall plan called for the use of two Filipino guerrilla forces to establish blocks commanded by Capt. Pajata and Capt. Eduardo Joson, a handsome pug-nosed native of Nueve Ecija province who later was elected its governor. Instructions were to hold the roadblocks until two Very flares were seen fired from the camp. The first indicated the camp was completely evacuated and the second would be an order to withdraw their forces to the South drawing the Japs away from our scheduled northern route of escape.

By noon of the 30th of January, the main Ranger force of 107 men was hiding on a hill 700 meters away. They split up and began crawling across fairly flat and open rice paddies towards the pill boxes and the front and rear gates. The 400 X 600-meter stockade, shrunken in the past three weeks, was completely surrounded by American troops. Everyone was nearing position by 1930 hours. Lt. Murphy waited calmly another 15 minutes for good measure to be sure his forces were in position.

It was dusk, 1945 hours, when Murphy's men began the assault by opening fire on the guards at the rear gate. Lt. O'Connell's men swept the west boundary with automatic weapon fire, then assaulted the main gate and opened fire on the Jap tanks and trucks in the corrugated tin building. Lt. Schmidt's platoon raked the east boundary. Sgt. Millican's squad attacked the Jap detachment sitting in the heavily defended northwest pill box. Simultaneously two Americans stepped around the corner of each dugout with their automatic weapons blazing, cutting the guards in two. We saw the sentries topple out of the towers, the tanks go up in flames, the Jap officer's and enlisted men's barracks raked by fire until all resistance was silenced.

One of the toughest jobs was to cross the main road, blow off the lock and open the main gate right in the face of the strongest bunkers. Sgt. Theodore Richardson, a tall lanky Texan, rushed forward. When the butt of his submachine gun hit the lock, the clip fell out. He pulled out his pistol, which was shot out of his hand by a Jap sentry. He calmly retrieved the pistol, shot the Jap, and opened the gate to begin the evacuation. Fortunately, the telephone lines had been cut before the attack precluding any call for help by the Japs.

After 20 minutes of pandemonium, every Jap was dead or dying. At 2015 hours, Capt. Prince fired the first Very pistol flare signalling the evacuation was complete. When our column had gone two km. from the stockade, the second red flare was fired to signal the guerrilla forces to withdraw.

Gen. MacArthur's official communique on recapture day:

"Five hundred and thirteen prisoners were freed by a force of 121 Rangers and 286 Filipino guerrillas. Two of the prisoners died from attacks in the course of the rescue. The Japanese guard of 73 men and 150 other Japanese soldiers were killed in the camp. In the action at the camp proper, two Rangers were killed and two wounded. Our total losses were 27 killed and two wounded. Jap losses were at least 532 dead and 12 tanks destroyed. Col. Mucci asked every man to take an oath to die fighting rather than let harm come to them. He was awarded the Distinguished Service Cross and every officer the Silver Star and every enlisted man the Bronze Star. Nothing in this entire campaign has given me so much personal satisfaction."

Signed: Gen. MacArthur

Lt. Schmidt and I arrived at the evacuation hospital in Guimba by mid-afternoon. Assigned to the second floor of the old wooden army barracks, I found myself next to Col. Duckworth. He was sleeping. Pale and drawn, managing his usual siesta, his broken left arm still supported in the sling made from my precious socks. The Japs hadn't worried him, but his pasty face worried me.

At dusk on 2 February, there were heavy footsteps on the boardwalk outside and an officer stepped inside and yelled, "Attention!" Both Col. Duckworth and I sat up on our cots and peered at the tall advancing figure.

"Carry on," he barked.

It was Gen. Douglas MacArthur paying a visit to his "old Corps." He finally spotted Col. Duckworth in the dusk. Duck and I, as well as the others in the room, remained seated. The General sat next to me on my cot facing the colonel. His shaky voice was low, vibrant and emotional. The craggy nose and his handsome face were barely discernible in the fading light. He cried as the colonel solemnly related the Japanese atrocities--the beatings, the tortures and slaughter of the general's soldiers. MacArthur asked specifically for word of senior officers. Most had died on Bataan, Corregidor, on the Death March, in prison camp, or disappeared on the Hell Ships.

"Nearly everyone is gone, General--probably 9,000 out of the original garrison of 12,000," Col. Duckworth reported.

"Oh, my God, no!" MacArthur said, his voice cracking.

225

The great man covered his face with his hands and sobbed. "I was afraid this would happen." His body shook. The tears fell without any attempt to wipe or hide them. He put his arm across my shoulders as I stirred uncomfortably.

"I'm sorry it took so long," he said in a deep husky whisper that was barely audible.

He talked with Duckworth for over an hour. I sat quietly, my head down, saying nothing. It turned dark. MacArthur's staff strolled impatiently outside but never interrupted. Finally the General rose, stretched himself, then shook hands with each man on his cot, greeting many of the frail POWs after asking their name. With a compassionate, tear-stained face, he told them to eat and get well.

"God bless you. Good to see you," he said.

"As of this day, I have ordered every man to be promoted. I'm sorry I didn't make it sooner," MacArthur added after his tour of the ward. He turned back and muttered, "It's been a tough road and all too long, but, oh my God, so many of my old soldiers are gone."

Then was my opportunity to remind the General of my oft-repeated expression, "Tell MacArthur to wait." It had been too long. Most everybody was dead. But years later I was glad the situation was not smudged by a flippant remark.

MacArthur then stood motionless in the dark, quietly struggling with his emotions. He must have been reflecting in disbelief on the miserable image of his old corps. He slowly moved towards the door. He walked outside where a staff officer informed him that a civilian wanted to speak to him.

"Sir," the man said, "what about the people in Santo Tomas?" This was the civilian internee camp at the old University of Sto. Tomas in Manila.

The general gazed towards the fast fading red of the sunset and then back to the civilian with his answer.

"You know, I don't give a damn about the civilians in Sto. Tomas. The only people I'm interested in are my old soldiers, the missing, and those sick and dying in this hospital," he said, pointing back towards us.

He abruptly turned on his heel and moved with a long determined stride down the ramp. He didn't make friends with that man, but the message was vividly clear to me. MacArthur was a precise, dedicated, and brilliant military man, but not a politician.

One of our men, Capt. Dennis King of Austin, Texas, approached the general's staff requesting permission to lead a combat team against the Japs on Corregidor. They took his name and assured him the general would approve if possible. In February 1945 MacArthur declared:

> Bataan with Corregidor made possible all that has happened since. History will record it as one of the decisive battles of the world; our triumphs of today belong equally to that dead army. The Bataan garrison was destroyed due to its dreadful handicap but no army more thoroughly accomplished its mission. Let no man henceforth speak of it other than as a magnificent victory.

Later I wondered whether the general's visit was a guilt trip. He had left the battling bastards of Bataan three years earlier. But that departure was not of his own making. A direct order from President Roosevelt was necessary to remove him from the battle in 1942. Beneath his pompous and grand style was a sensitive, caring man. His grief could not have been more genuine. The natural leader exuded brute confidence, determination personified. On my return home, people asked, "What do you think of MacArthur?" The answer was a simple, "He cared."

What he saw and heard that night had a tremendous impact on the general. The unsoldierly cruelties to the military and civilians alike fired MacArthur to pursue the war crimes trials to the ultimate. In the war crimes trial of Gen. Masaharu Homma in 1946, MacArthur said:

> There can be no greater, more heinous or dangerous crime than the mass destruction under guise of military authority or military necessity, of helpless men incapable of further contribution to war effort.

Both Generals Homma and Yamashita paid the price with their lives. Homma was executed by a firing squad on 3 April

227

1946, and Gen. Tomoyuki Yamashita was later sentenced to hang. Lt. Col. Shigeji Mori of Cabanatuan and Yoshio Tsuneyoshi of Camp O'Donnell were both sentenced to hard labor for life.

After 72 hours in the 92nd Evacuation Hospital at Guimba, the healthiest of us moved onto the shores of Lingayen Gulf to an R&R camp. Charley, Jim, Denny and I were billeted in a cute little sin shack on the beach. Slowly the tension was leaving.

"You'll be going home soon," was the official buncombe. I put on my watch and even washed my teeth with toothpaste. Brand new uniforms and shoes were issued--but the "universal size" was just too big.

In a couple of days a Sixth Army G-2 officer invited me to take a day's ride over to the old prison camp. After an enjoyable two-hour ride we arrived to find the whole place ransacked, dug up, with mattresses torn open, floors uprooted, apparently by our intelligence troops and Filipino civilians looking for records and non-existent caches of valuables. I didn't have the heart or strength to start digging. The intelligence officer assured me the hospital rolls and death records buried in jars had already been retrieved. The camp scene was depressing and only tended to open wounds so recently dressed by our liberators.

Our dream of seeing our country and friends again was nearing reality.

21. DEATH OF PILAR

Rumors filtered in from the 7th to the 10th of February 1945, describing vicious fighting in Manila between the advancing Americans and the Jap Marines. The battle centered in south Manila in the four to six blocks between Dewey Blvd. and Taft Avenue paralleling Manila Bay leading to Intramuros, the walled city. The battle for Intramuros, the home base of our 31st Infantry Regiment, was the battle for Manila. As American troops entered the Philippine capital, the Japs retreated, laying waste the city behind them. The Japs dug themselves in, on every street, in every house, behind every wall. Pilar's home at 1462 Taft Avenue lay directly in the path. American artillerymen, their guns pounding day and night, reduced the great walls of the city to rubble as our doughboys pushed steadily to smash the last remnants of Japanese resistance.

An estimated 100,000 Filipino civilians died in the battle. Most of the deaths came from artillery fire from both sides. Jap troops, particularly the Marines, added to the carnage by murdering, raping, burning and bayonetting the hapless Filipinos caught within the lines.

On the 12th of February, two Filipinos came into our camp inquiring for me. They were about 40 years old, skinny, barefooted and dressed in native breech shorts and broad-brimmed planter's hats. Dangling behind were their bolo knives. They were directed to my shack, where they apologetically asked for me.

"I'm Major Hibbs, you want me?" I responded from the doorway.

"Sir, we have bad news," one said. "Pilar has been killed," he finally added, speaking softly and slowly in good English. We all froze and then he continued, "Friends sent us here after hearing of your release. They wanted you to know. The Japs shot her in the belly through the door as they smashed into her home. She was bayonetted and died."

"Oh, my God, no!" I said, slumping on the steps. Is there no

229

end to the slaughter? Everyone is gone--George, Bill, Dwight, Joe, Howard, and now Pilar. Please, not her.

"Do you know what happened?" I finally mumbled through misty eyes.

The two Filipinos, loyal friends of the Campos family, squatted on the ground and with many pauses and with great difficulty related the tragedy.

When the fighting concentrated down Taft Avenue, Pilar took over 100 people into her home. The Japanese Marines were wantonly killing the occupants of the homes along Dewey Blvd. and Taft Avenue as they retreated. The Campos' mansion, across from De La Salle College, provided ample space and hopeful security for the neighborhood people, but they found themselves in no man's land directly between the two forces slugging it out at pointblank range. A protecting stone wall with iron grill and gate led to an inner locked gate to the front entrance. The noise of exploding shells, tanks firing, buildings collapsing, fires out of control and crazed soldiers threatened beyond the walls. The rampaging Jap Marines stormed the outer gates, shot the house attendants and pounded on the front door. Pilar opened it, leaving the chain latched. She stood alone and ordered them both in English and in Japanese to get their commanding officer. The Japs, wild, bayonets fixed, made no effort to obey her. As Pilar shouted, her hands raised to stop them, they shot through the door, the bullet hitting her in the belly. They rushed the door, broke it down. They dragged her out to the front lawn. Then as she knelt, a Marine lunged at her with a bayonet. The blade at full length twisted and sliced upward. Blood gushed from her chest. She fell quietly and lay bleeding, mortally wounded. She moaned quietly as she lapsed into coma.

Pilar clung to life for three days.

Firing with automatic weapons, the Japs killed the helpless civilians lined up facing the walls. Pilar's mother crumpled to the floor in her own home, killed by murderous machinegun fire. A fire fueled by gasoline completed the massacre. Several Filipinos survived by climbing out the second-story windows and hanging onto the edge of the roof.

Pilar's father, Pedro, as an international banker and president of the Bank of the Philippines, was one of the first Filipino businessmen the Japs contacted. After harassment and threats he had a heart attack and died in January 1942. She had spared me this sad news.

Pilar's brother, Tony, had been dragged away by a Kempei Tai a few nights earlier, supposedly on charges of treason. Friends later conjectured he was mistaken for Tom Ocampo, a much sought-after guerrilla. Nevertheless, he was strung up by his feet to a marble column at the Spanish Club and let die with his head hanging down. Three days passed before Tony quit breathing.

The story unfolded that earlier Jap intelligence officers had searched the Campos' home and found a shortwave radio and a U.S. Army footlocker with Lt. Ralph Hibbs, U.S.A. stenciled on the lid. The house was marked, and so were the occupants, as "enemies of the Emperor." I remembered Pilar had gone to my apartment and whisked away that damned old locker.

The fighting in Manila had raged on from house to house. Smoke swirled in the streets as bombs and shells rocked the neighborhood. Friends, including Dr. Ramon Campos, an uncle, and Lulu, a cousin, a few blocks away, had news of the carnage, but couldn't get to Pilar's house because of the fires and intense fighting. Three days went by, Pilar's soulful eyes searched for help, her slender hands reached and begged for water. The hot unmerciful tropical sun parched her lips. The bleeding from the bayonet thrust had stopped. Her blouse was crusted with dried blood. Then her life stopped forever; she died, all by herself, on the third day.

The Americans of the Sixth Army moved in to survey the piles of grotesque figures and summarily declared individual burials were impossible. According to Lulu, the advancing American forces were kind, firm and businesslike. Huge bulldozers dug graves for mass burials. Pilar along with her dear mother, and a hundred other loyal Filipinos were pushed into a single grave in the front garden of her once beautiful home. There were no headstones.

One Filipino messenger stopped talking, and then he looked at the bay through the *alibangbang* trees. He seemed to be searching the endless waters of the China Sea for succor. Although horrible and almost unbelievable, I knew it was true, tested by so many previous experiences.

231

"Are there any of her friends left?" I asked after several minutes pause, tears running down our faces. "How about Trophy, Chona, Conchita, and the rest of Pilar's gang?"

"I don't know. OK maybe. We know of no bad news about them," he said, his voice barely audible.

"*Muchas gracias* for coming all this way through enemy lines to tell me. You're brave and loyal men," I said, putting my arms around them. "I don't have any money but I can get you some food for your return trip."

"Not necessary, Joe. Me houseboy for Señor Pedro all my life. This I do," the little man protested. "Pilar good to me. She my friend, too."

"Goodbye, Joe. *Mabuhay*," they both muttered and slowly retreated down the bougainvillea-lined path. One turned and bowed, "Sorry, Joe." I was demolished.

Was it possible for war to extract one more pound of flesh? My hope and plans were to go to Manila and talk to Pilar before going Stateside, to home and loved ones. At least to get a feeling and make some decisions before shipping out.

Now Pilar was gone.

Her brave heart was stopped forever. My sufferings and sacrifice paled in the reality of this patriot's devotion. She volunteered, stepped forward, stood tall, and died helping others. I sat stunned until the sun sank into the South China Sea. A never-to-be-filled void was born in my life. I was denied ever seeing her alive again, and now she lay at rest forever in a mass grave.

Pilar was Americanized at Marygrove College in the States. She was born with a fierce loyalty. Her courage came naturally. As she told her friends who pleaded with her repeatedly to lie low, especialy after being thrown into the dungeon of Fort Santiago, "The Americans are dying of starvation. If I don't feed them, who will?" she cried over and over. Her unselfishness was as perennial as the flowers. She died a soldier's death with bravery as her only weapon. Guilt overcame me. I was the one in uniform. The end should have been mine, not hers. Somewhere our love was buried--but not my memories.

On a bronze tablet in the Marygrove Chapel are the words, "*Requiescat in Pace*" and beneath it among the Duggans, Brennans, Murphys, Ryans and Sullivans is Pilar Campos, a little girl from far-away Manila. Graduates who died for their country.

My mind went back to Pilar's origin in the rural country of these beautiful islands where she was endowed with a broad base of understanding, and love for the common *tao*, unfettered by wealth or other biases. Her family was strong and her education purposeful. She was a patriot of both countries, a friend of her president, and also of the peasants. Standing 5'4", tall for her race, she was beautiful both inside and out. Dedication was her life, a natural gift. She had done all that she could. In the end she asked only for water. The race was over. She was only 28.

Although the president of her country would have come to her funeral, there wasn't one and she lies in an unmarked grave known only to God and to her friends and all those who I believe would like to have known her.

As a classmate, Helen Elward of Monroe, Michigan, said, "She seemed to learn our western ways early, but yet held on to her eastern traditions. As is evident from the last days of her life, Pilar always had a special place in her heart for her close friends --the Americans."

Now the die was cast. The price was paid. War does this. It takes your loved ones but fortunately not your freedom if your country has brave soldiers. I must go home now, alone and heavy-hearted. The war was over for me.

I remembered her in the moonlight at Pagsanjan Falls; as the first Filipino woman guest at the Army Navy Club; standing at attention facing the American flag at retreat at old Ft. McKinley; standing in the street blocking Jap trucks, arms loaded with food for American POWs; singing "I'll Be with You in Apple Blossom Time" and then "The Yanks Are Coming" on the stage in Cabanatuan, facing the Japanese guards; standing in flood tide water in the dungeons of Fort Santiago; riding by on her bike; and crawling to the walls of Bilibid to hand me medicines and money. She stood alone in the doorway of her own home defending it against the enemy. She gave her life for *the* cause. Freedom was her goal, belief her destiny. And for those of us remaining, we thank God for this beautiful woman.

22. JOURNEY'S END

The next day a telegram from my sister, Virginia, helped establish my relevancy to home and friends. The wire read:

All's well here. Thrilled with news of your release. Most of your old girlfriends are married. Love, Ginny.

"Some are killed also," I grimly added to myself.

Bewildered by the realities of freedom, elimination of hunger and fear, I appreciated a new lease on life, a good feeling inside. Even though my step was lighter and the inner doom was fading, I couldn't do handsprings with the ever present awareness of the terrible price paid for the defense of the Philippines. With overwhelming gratitude for my safe recapture and realizing an end to all of this, I spent the next few days wandering along the sandy beach waiting to start our long trip home.

The peaceful setting provided a comfortable *bahay*, plenty of food, and friendly natives. The Sixth Army staff officers came over to talk out of curiosity but also to bolster our depleted morale. Unlimited cigarettes, food, living space, and the American flag did wonders.

On 15 February, rather abruptly we were told to be ready in one hour to fly out to Leyte a few hundred kilometers south, the same place where on 20 October 1944, MacArthur had returned to the Philippines. The short trip was made in a DC-3 and included flying over the smoking ruins of Manila and my last goodbye to Pilar. We stole a peek at Corregidor, which was at that time still in Jap hands. Bataan came into view as we winged our way across Manila Bay. It was goodbye to a gruesome four years.

Our stay in Leyte was short and sweet and included contact with girls--American nurses. I talked to several but Charley Lewis not only talked but missed the sailing of our troop ship the next day. The incident had some humor but not to Charley's folks, who later were at dockside to meet us in San Francisco. They were not placated by my explanation. "Charley missed the boat and will be along on the next one."

Finally, to satisfy their crying, I blurted, "He got mixed up with a nurse and missed the boat."

"That sounds more like our boy," rejoined Mr. Lewis, displaying the happy nature that Charley inherited. Duckworth had been airlifted to the States, sparing him the long boat trip.

In five days we made Hollandia, New Guinea, after an uneventful and unescorted passage through the beautiful, lush, white sandy islands of the southern archipelago. With nothing to do but catch up on conversation and eat six times a day, discipline was necessary to prevent a dietary orgy at every meal. I was determined not to gorge myself on potatoes and gravy and bloat like a poisoned pup. Great difficulty was encountered at first to prevent barfing a meal because my digestive system was not accustomed to the rich foods. The old liver just groaned and couldn't handle it. No liquor was available, fortunately.

We had a lot of catching up to do, particularly in politics, morals, medicine and just trivia.

Penicillin was a complete surprise to us. "It will cure pneumonia, clap, and even blood poisoning," the doctors declared. A new miraculous navigational aid had been discovered by the Allies tabbed as radar. The world was shiny and new again after a completely isolated existence. I was a Rip Van Winkle, 100 years removed.

The two-day stop in Hollandia, a natural harbor, surrounded by verdant tropical hillsides reminiscent of Olongapo, presented more celebration, food and encouragement from brass to Red Cross workers. And now for home on the 20,000-ton troop ship, the *General A.E. Anderson*. Blacked out, she ran fast and unescorted, cruising a zigzag course. She sported a single 6" gun mounted on the fantail. Gunnery practice was announced one day. A green marker floating 600-800 meters away was the target. After a dozen shots, none closer than a football field, the captain called a halt to the miserable and hilarious demonstration. Fortunately, no need for marksmanship arose on the 20-day trip to San Francisco.

Numerous inquiries from intelligence personnel aboard and cables from Stateside sought information regarding possible court martials or other irregularities. After a hurried, impromptu conference of the few officers in our group, a clean bill of health was declared for everyone. In our wildest imagination, no crime existed to be punishable after this experience--even stealing, wrecking my last ambulance, or insubordination. One soldier lost his arm in a stolen wrecked vehicle while AWOL, but no charges were pressed as all disabilities were judged to be in the "line of duty."

A representative from the finance section came by to inform us regarding our back pay and compensation for lost personal belongings. Included in my list was a sterling cocktail shaker but I didn't have the heart to include my gruesome neckties.

On 12 March, at 1100 hours, we approached San Francisco in a fog. The Golden Gate bridge was not visible when the captain came on the horn: "Ahead is the Golden Gate bridge. This is the end of an awfully long journey for many of you. I thank God for the safe passage of the most precious cargo of my entire life."

I looked east towards home. Within a minute the sun broke through illuminating our first look at American soil--the Golden Gate bridge and the headlands on either side. Aircraft and balloons filled the sky. The bay was crowded with escorting boats, their whistles tooting a welcome. All San Francisco had turned out to the "greatest homecoming" in "Bagdad by the Bay's" history. I leaned against the rail on the quarterdeck wondering, "What God hath wrought--the torture of four years and now this?" The band was playing a piece called "God Bless America" as I slowly descended on the ramp, knelt and kissed the soil of my homeland. A huge roar went up.

I heard someone calling my name and turned to find a little old lady. Mrs. Bertha Wells from Redwood City put her arms around me. "I saw your name among the rescued list so I wrote your mother, who said she couldn't come, so I volunteered," she said. "Here's her letter." We both cried.

"My son was missing in action a few months ago so I was happy to welcome you. Here's a package, just some cookies. He used to like them," she continued.

A pretty Navy WAVE came alongside, gave me a kiss and thrust a folded note into my hand. On it was written her telephone number and address in Tulare, California.

"Give me a call if you don't have friends." A few months later I did call her. She was a darling gal. But by then she had a boyfriend.

I called Mother and Dad that night.

"I'm sorry to have caused you so much trouble. You won't have to wait much longer. I'll be home in a couple of days." After a long pause, I said, "Pilar won't be coming . . ." my voice broke. "The Japs killed her."

Despite the crushing crowd, the noise of the harbor, the roar of the overhead planes, dirigibles, the band, the people screaming greetings, we were quickly shepherded aboard buses and whisked off to Letterman General Hospital. Supposedly we were "quarantined in protective custody" for 24 hours, but no sooner had I got to my room when an orderly handed me a note from Mary Fran Riley, the author of the first letter I received in Cabanatuan.

"I'll meet you at 8 p.m. tonight at the front door," the note said.

I was there and so were Mary Fran and her husband. We talked until 0200 hours in the morning about the crowd in Des Moines, the University of Iowa, and I even inquired about the rumor that a "wave of immorality" was sweeping the country.

"Is it over yet?" I inquired.

I said goodbye, still clutching my half-filled glass with my first drink, a far cry from my med-school capacity for "Iowa Champagne," spiked near-beer. My alcoholic tolerance was zilch.

Next morning at a mess table I requested the waitress to bring me fresh cow's milk until ordered to stop. This was one of the most missed foods since leaving the States. After consuming 12 half pints of the beautiful ice cold white stuff, I looked up at the waitress expecting plaudits, but she remarked, "That's nothing, last week a GI drank 18 bottles!"

Tests of all descriptions, including a stool examination, interviews with finance officers, intelligence experts and even a psychiatrist, filled the next days. Incidentally, the doctor reported the stool specimen was so contaminated it climbed out of the lab jar and got away. A later capture revealed endameba histolytica and giardia lambia, both causes of dysentery, acute or chronic.

About this time the ward surgeon entered the room with outstretched hands, saying, "Howdy, Ralph, haven't seen you in a long time."

I brightened, trying to recognize him, but struck out.

"Remember the good old days at Presbyterian Hospital in Chicago?" he asked anxiously trying to establish a mutual ball park. "I wonder what our good friends Lynwood and Afton are doing."

He waited for my response but for the life of me I couldn't come up with a visual image. I drew a complete blank.

"Who?" I mumbled embarrassedly.

He looked at the door for an escape route and although he examined me several times, he was content to leave my mental disorganization alone.

After a few days the coating on my memory bank peeled off, exposing correct names and addresses. Lynwood Smith, one of my closest friends and often my hunting partner, came out all shiny and clear. I even corrected my home address. It was simply a case of preserving sanity by isolating the sensitivities of ante bellum life from the unnatural life of war and prison. Fortunately for me, although not realized until challenged, I had sufficient discipline to give me peace of mind in both worlds.

On 13 March, the mayor of San Francisco helped with the homecoming, throwing a party for all of us at the Palace Hotel. He ordered the band to play "The Star Spangled Banner" and "Don't Fence Me In." He gave us a key to the city, too.

The airplane trip from San Francisco to Iowa took 24 hours. Fog prevented landing in Des Moines, so we finally touched down in Davenport. Via train, the Rock Islands' Rocket took me to Grinnell, where reporters met me and drove me to Oskaloosa. I'll always remember when we cleared the last hill and could see through the cold mist a few scattered lights ahead.

Oskaloosa, my hometown. My country. My home. My loved ones. My freedom.

The reporter quoted me: "It's been oh so long," although I don't remember saying it.

It had been a long journey, almost 15,000 miles, and a long time, almost four years, since leaving the U.S. I sailed 6 June 1941 and returned 24 March 1945. Of the 12,000 Americans comprising the Filipino garrison, 8,000-9,000 had died in the three and a half nightmarish years.

History was written in blood by the "Battling Bastards of Bataan." The Death March was paid for by 1,000 tortured lives. The remainder paid a price as high as 77 deaths in a single day. The whole scene was so foreign to us that we couldn't comprehend it at times. The suicidal charges of the Jap soldier, bombing the hospital, needless and unwarranted executions. Even more of a crime was the torture before the unmerciful killings, the parading of a gristly head after beheading, the ignoring of human suffering even by professionals, and the mass killings and the murder of innocent people. Pilar was gone and so were thousands of other friends of our country.

Our mission was accomplished but at a price even dearer to the Filipino nation than to the United States. We would do well to remember the supreme sacrifice of the Philippines in that conflict. Nearly one million Filipino lives were stilled by this war. We had great soldiers, but there were others just as brave who wore sandals and had dark skin.

There should be no cheering on our return, I thought, but a sober reflection on those heroes that lie in unmarked graves in the cane brakes. The price of freedom comes high--not only in lives but in suffering and those who mourn their passing. Who yearns to be Gold Star mother? For myself, I did not hire to fight or want to be a hero.

On my return home, I tried not to remember Bataan, and I'm sure Bataan's jungles don't remember me. It left marks unique to that period, never simulated by events in the rest of my life. I had managed to live three lives separately--one before the war, another on Bataan, and the last in prison camp, a gift from Pilar.

The oriental experience incited a gamut of emotions. The absurdity and disgust of war; the panic of danger; the frenzy of combat; the agony of defeat; the despair of captivity; the hopelessness of endlessness; the sadness of losing friends; the apathy of starvation; the callousness of gross deaths; the defiance of bulliness; the repulsiveness of torture; the bitterness of indifference (neglect); the repugnance of cruelty; the fire of revenge; the complacency of forgiveness; the disgust of killing; the delirium of love; and the elation of victory. All were encountered in varying mixtures and regularity, as the combat and captivity moved inex-

239

exorably onward for almost four years. The end product remains unknown but it obviously and profoundly changed me. I hoped that Stateside society would accept me.

After our first return trip to the Philippines in May 1967 to celebrate the 25th anniversary of the Fall of Bataan and Corregidor, the idea of requesting an award for Pilar was born. Comments by the military, so many friends, and even a column in the *Manila Herald* by Maximo V. Soliven praised this young woman, even 25 years after she was gone. The recommendation for the award was finally forwarded to the Department of Defense around 1975. In 1980 the posthumous award, Certificate of Appreciation, the highest peacetime civilian award for a foreigner, was issued.

Three years went by in which time the Army, including the U.S. Embassy, failed to find the nearest of kin. She had a cousin, Lulu Abreu, the daughter of the late Dr. Ramon Campos, Pedro's brother. A final letter arrived from the Army saying they were discontinuing the search. I decided to go out and get the job done.

In May 1983, on my second return, after 15 minutes and three telephone calls, I was talking to Lulu Abreu on the phone from the Mandarin Hotel in Manila. On 13 May 1983, at JUS-MAG (Joint U.S. Military Assistance Group) in Manila, the official posthumous presentation was made by Gen. Charles Getz to Lulu Abreu. The citation reads:

The President of the United States of America, authorized by Act of Congress, has awarded the Certificate of Appreciation to PILAR CAMPOS for her heroic contributions in behalf of American Prisoners of War at Bilibid Prison in Manila and Cabanatuan, Camp #2, the Philippines, during the period of May 1942 to January 1945. At considerable risk to her own life, Miss Campos sneaked past the prison guards to smuggle in food, medicine, vitamins and money with which to buy food. These supplies were used to treat the sickest among the Prisoners of War interned here. Her help saved dozens, possibly hundreds of American lives and prevented blindness and permanent disability among the prisoners. Pilar Campos was a leader of an organization of Filipino women dedicated to assisting United States forces. As a result of this unfaltering loyalty, when the Japanese Marines took Manila in the Battle of Manila in February 1945, they seized Miss Campos' home. She was shot in the belly through the door and dragged out onto the lawn and bayoneted, where she died. The extreme bravery and heroic dedication to the American cause demonstrated by Pilar Campos exemplify the highest traditions of the United States Army and reflect credit upon Miss Campos and the citizens of the Philippines.

And so, after 40 years, her bravery was recognized.

Her grave is filled with an eternal spirit, restless for right to emerge and compassionate where wrong is suffered. Her life which touched so many lives lives on forever.

Oh, Pilar, for your dedication, we love you.

EPILOGUE

The purpose of writing this book was two-fold: first and foremost was my guilt that Pilar's death lay directly at my doorstep, and my attempt to assuage this feeling. Secondly, I ardently hope that my wife, Jeanne, who died on 17 August 1986 without ever reading it in its final form, and Jill, Jack, Steve and Jennifer, our children, would understand their ornery, knot-headed old Dad a little better. I hope they respect my definition of patriotism and appreciate my survival through jungle warfare and a "lifetime" of captivity.

And to Jeanne, who responded many times to the query, "What's Ralph doing?" with another query, "Ralph who?" my undying love. Fortunately for her, she was the little girl next door until 31 March 1946, when we married. She was spared the agony of waiting through my captivity. She always understood I left part of my soul in the Philippines, but not all of my love.

I hope the *sine qua non* of the children's inheritance will be a way of life. My overriding desire was to present the funny side of the irrepressible American GI. Besides myself, two things lived on--my patriotism and my sense of humor. I never was nor did I aspire to be a hero.

There never was a time during the four years of active writing that my enthusiasm waned. Many times I would go to my den in the morning to write and look up with my seat tired to discover it was dark. During office hours and while interviewing patients an old incident would pop into my mind. It was duly recorded as a little note and stuck on a spindle. The patient assumed this represented important medical data being recorded about his own malady.

My deep gratitude to Beverly Sandblast, my first typist, who struggled through gallons of print eraser, typewriter ribbons and four manuscripts. My sincere appreciation to Robertson Collins of Jacksonville, Oregon, who convinced me to give up my old-fashioned modus operandi for his word processor. And to Nancy Laurent, who finally transferred these scribblings to floppy disks, providing me a reprieve from scissors, clippings and scotch tape. And thanks to Tam Moore of Medford, Oregon, my friend and neighbor, who deserves credit for whatever literary excellence this book may achieve. My indebtedness to Jay Mullen, the catalyst without whose prodding this book would never have been started or finished.

I apologize to whoever has been erred against or slighted, and particularly the unpraised men of my detachment who have gone unnamed. Accuracy, although pursued, has been compromised by passing years and a fertile imagination. Pilar was intended to be the central character with Decker, Beattie, Buster, Bill, Denny, Charley, Jim, Dwight, Jack and Mary Fran in supporting roles. I hope the book confirms these intentions. The moral is to avoid peninsular campaigns--one may end up in salt water or in prison. As you can see, I always wanted to participate in the postmortem of our last battle.

Buster Conrad is retired in Daleville, Alabama, after 30 years of service in the U.S. Army. Dr. Charley Lewis is retired in Piedmont, California, after many years of practice in obstetrics and gynecology in Oakland. Dr. M. M. "Jim" Musselman, who chaired the Department of Surgery at the University of Nebraska, is retired and lives in Omaha. Mary Fran Riley Lawler lives in Des Moines, Iowa. Dr. George Campbell made it home and died in 1984. Denny and Dwight are dead. Warren Wilson died in 1987. Col. Duckworth died in Atlanta soon after returning to the States. Gen. Jack Schwartz, Col. Ed Wernitznig, and Clint Maupin of hospital headquarters, are dead. It was difficult to learn the whereabouts of Sgt. Beattie or Cpl. Decker. They both had their dues paid up for life in my book. Reports indicated Cpl. Decker was lost on the Hell Ships, but that Sgt. Beattie returned to the States.

The following are some of my friends awarded citations during the Bataan campaign:

Sgt. Irving Beattie, Distinguished Service Cross. The finest medical corpsman I've ever known. He was part of our medical detachment of the 2nd Battalion, 31st Infantry Regiment. Not only fearless and dependable, he was always available, the volunteer type. By his nature, in our first experience in

243

combat, he moved into the firing zone leading the evacuation of the wounded. Despite enemy fire, with casualties everywhere, he worked oblivious to his own personal safety. On several occasions during the fighting at Abucay Hacienda, Beattie almost singlehandedly dragged wounded soldiers back to a point where a litter team could reach them. This required him to stand up in the face of intense fire since it was impossible to move the wounded in a crawl. As the volunteer detachment barber, he received our thanks but not this citation. The last time I saw him was on 6 April 1942.

Capt. Jim Brennan of Waterloo, Iowa, 1st Battalion Surgeon, was awarded the Silver Star on 17 January 1942, the first day of fighting at Abucay, for saving Capt. Tom Bell's life.

Capt. Denny Rees received a Bronze Star and Purple Heart for his outstanding work on the frontlines, particularly in the last battle at Mt. Samat. He was the only medical officer I've ever seen who was on duty with an arm in a sling. He returned to the front with a fracture.

Capt. Charles Lewis of Oakland, California, received a Silver Star for bravery under fire for attending to two wounded officers during an artillery barrage. He also was awarded a Bronze Star, according to Charley for his "happy disposition" in prison camp. This I might say is not an accurate appraisal of his contribution. His happy personality was exceeded only by his performance.

A scar remains which is offset by a feeling of gratitude for survival, a philosophy and a desire to help my fellowmen. Enjoy life; it's the only one you're gonna have. A little bitterness remains and a sorrow for the Japanese people. The Jap officers were punished summarily and I think this was just. War crimes must not go unpunished. On the other hand, I refused to go to Tokyo to testify before the War Crimes Commission. The war was over, the killing should stop. After all, our Navy flyboys strafed survivors of sunken ships which turned out to be unrecognized Americans. By definition, war is hell.

The scar was indelibilized by combat and the nearness of death, separated in captivity by a missed meal or the whim of a blundering guard. Years have softened the scar so now I "ain't really mad" at anybody. Without a second thought we invited a Japanese college student, Nobu Hayashi, to spend a year in our home. We never discussed politics or the war and, in fact, his grandfather was the first Christian minister in Tokyo.

The majority of the survivors have suffered mentally and physically since liberation. At least I learned to be an easy keeper and belong to the "K.P." (clean plate) Club. On several occasions after my return to the States, I would unconsciously reach across the table to help myself to leftover food on another plate. Even to this day I don't like to see food wasted.

Friends reported to me that Mother left a banquet for her during the war after being informed the food was from the blackmarket. She could hardly accept that with four children in the service. She was elected "Mother of the Year" in 1944 by our little town.

There are those of our group whose whole lives have been tragic, constantly fighting for stability and emotional organization. Some have been plagued with depressions, nightmares and tension crisis. Others have endured a delayed stress syndrome. Most had permanent physical disabilities.

I published a report of the beriberi study in our prison camp in the *Annals of Internal Medicine* in August 1946. In 1947 the observations on gynecomastia were published in the *American Journal of Medical Sciences*, the first known report of "Refeeding Gynecomastia" in medical literature.

Some of the men who lived through Bataan rose to the top. Gen. Harold Johnson became U.S. Army Chief of Staff. My Air Force acquaintances, Sam Maddux and Rosey O'Donnell, became general officers. Jack Schwartz received his second star as Commanding General of Letterman General Hospital in San Francisco. He invited me to play golf at the Presidio with him and former President Ike Eisenhower. Unfortunately, a waitress refilled Ike's cup with scalding coffee the night before, burning his mouth. Ike cancelled golf for the day. What a thrill that would have been. Instead, Jack and I had to wallop the Sixth Army Surgeon and a San Quentin prison psychiatrist. Jack earned my deepest respect and friendship during those long, tough years in Cabanatuan. I had not been on his hospital team during the fighting, but in camp he took me "into the fraternity." In 1972, the new theater at the Presidio was dedicated as Schwartz Memorial Theater. He is probably one of the greatest little men I've ever known.

These experiences added another dimension to my life, particularly in dealing with adversity. I learned "things get tougher," "to back up and take another run at it," or "remember you're passing this way only once," that "other people are having trouble," and "to live with confidence and patience."

Pilar never told me about her friendships with Filipino cadets at West Point and Annapolis whom she visited while in school at Marygrove in Detroit. Nor did she mention the close friendship with Governor Frank Murphy, who later became High Commissioner of the Philippines and Justice of the U.S. Supreme Court. The following is a copy of a letter from Justice Murphy to Rita Blanchard, Pilar's old roommate at Marygrove College:

20 March 1945
Dear Mrs. Blanchard:

The news I received about Pilar is sad beyond words if correct and I understand that it is. For her loyalty in helping the Americans, Pilar was executed and before execution, she was terribly mistreated. Pilar was such a lovely little girl—staunch of spirit, high in ambition and a good character. All there is to do now is to pray for her.

Sincerely,
Frank Murphy

She apparently was "one of the first family" of Michigan. It was 40 years later, thanks to a great bunch of people, Pilar's old friends from college that this part of her life surfaced. Sister Anthony Mary Fox, Sister M. Timothy Kelley, Margie Guerin Moody, Rita Blanchard and Peggy Schmoll, the latter three classmates and close friends, have been most helpful in sharing precious memories and hoarded pictures of Pilar Campos.

They dug up pictures and negatives taken in 1937 and 1938; articles in the *High Tower* written by Pilar in 1938 and even a letter dated 3 November 1939 from 1462 Taft Avenue, Manila, after she returned home. All of these plus a wealth of memories from other wonderful people were shared with me. Pilar left a legacy of friends and lasting memorabilia wherever she stopped. Even General MacArthur spoke of her bravery after he returned to Manila. She only passed this way once but always shared her kindness. As my sweetheart for only four months before the war, and then separated for over three years by a wall or barbed wire fence, Pilar might have been presented differently in the book and filled a different role in my life. My talents as a writer and a lover leave much to be desired. Because of these deficiencies, the citation and the book were both unduly delayed. The Japs ended the romance on 8 February 1945.

Friends have told me of the treatment of Pilar when she was mortally wounded, but I see her--standing tall at the door of her home--her only weapon courage, her only defense beauty and her life. Nothing more adds to the truth of her passing.

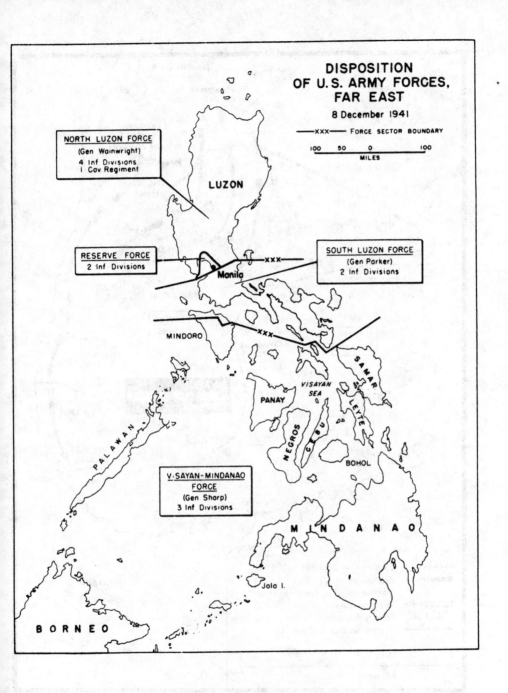

DISPOSITION OF U.S. ARMY FORCES, FAR EAST
8 December 1941

———XXX——— FORCE SECTOR BOUNDARY

100   50   0   100
MILES

NORTH LUZON FORCE
(Gen Wainwright)
4 Inf Divisions
1 Cav Regiment

LUZON

RESERVE FORCE
2 Inf Divisions

Manila

SOUTH LUZON FORCE
(Gen Parker)
2 Inf Divisions

MINDORO

SAMAR

VISAYAN SEA

PANAY

LEYTE

NEGROS

CEBU

BOHOL

PALAWAN

VISAYAN-MINDANAO FORCE
(Gen Sharp)
3 Inf Divisions

MINDANAO

Jolo I.

BORNEO

Map of the Philippines

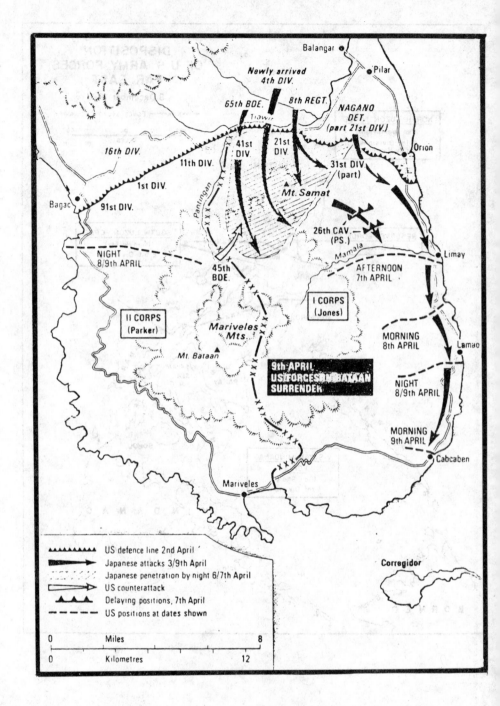

Battle of Bataan

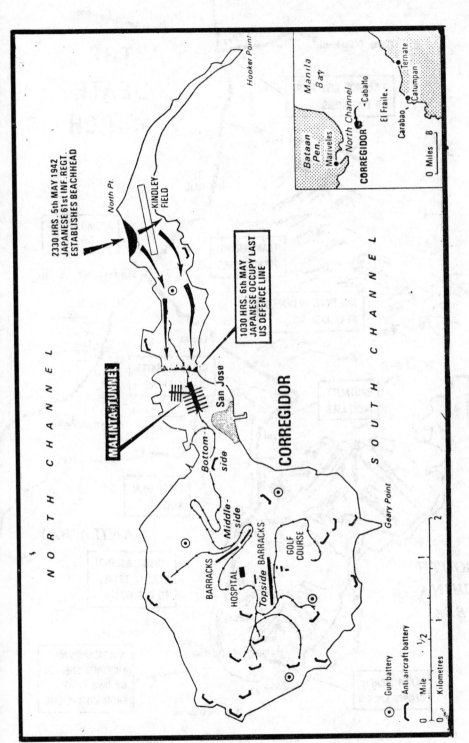

Map of Corregidor

THE DEATH MARCH

Cabanatuen

Camp O'Donnell

Capas

FILIPINOS GIVE FOOD TO PRISONERS

Clark Field

BY RAIL

AQUINO MEETS HIS FATHER

TRANSFER TO FREIGHT CARS

San Fernando

AMERICAN BEHEADED NEAR RICE MILL

Lubao

BLUEMEL SAVES GEN. STEVENS

Manila

BRUTALITY INCREASES

Orani

FIRST MEAL SERVED

Balanga

MANILA BAY

SOUTH CHINA SEA

ON FOOT

PRISONERS SHOT, BEATEN, TRYING TO GET WATER

Limay

HOSPITALS 1 + 2 +

Cabcaben

AMERICANS AND FILIPINOS SHELLED BY OWN GUNS FROM CORREGIDOR

DEATH MARCH BEGINS APRIL 9

Mariveles

CORREGIDOR

N

252

0   10   20

MILES

BIBLIOGRAPHY

A. Books

Johnson, Forrest Bryant. *Hour of Redemption*. New York: Manor Books, 1978.

Knox, Donald. *Death March*. New York and London: Harcourt Brace Jovanovich, 1981.

Lee, Clark and Richard Henschel. *MacArthur*. New York: Henry Holt, Inc., 1952.

Manchester, William. *American Caesar*. New York: Dell Publishing Co., Inc., 1978.

Morton, Louis. *The Fall of the Philippines: The War in the Pacific; U.S. Army in World War II*. Military History. Department of the Army, 1953:

Sprector, Ronald H. *Eagles against the Sun*. New York: Macmillian Free Press, 1985.

Toland, John. *Rising Sun*. New York: Bantam Books, 1971.

Weinstein, Alfred A. *Barbed-Wire Surgeon*. New York: Macmillan Co., 1961.

B. Selected Articles

Bluemel, Brig. Gen. Clifford. 31st Division (PA), Report of Operations.

Brown, Dr. David, "Sunset at O'Donnell," J.A.M.A. Vol. 199, 30 January 1967.

Call Bulletin. San Francisco, California. 1 February 1945.

Cleveland Free Press. Cleveland, Ohio. 14 April 1942.

Conrad, Eugene. Operations of the 31st Infantry. Defense of Bataan, 1946.

Des Moines Tribune. Des Moines, Iowa. 2 February 1945.

Hibbs, Ralph E., M.D., "Beriberi in Japanese Prison Camps," *Annals of Internal Medicine*. August 1946.

Hibbs, Ralph E., M.D., "Gynecomastia Associated with Vitamin

Deficiency Disease," *American Journal of Medical Sciences*. February 1947.

McCraken, Alan, "A POW's Philosophy." *Quan*. Vol. 38, August 1983.

Mydans, Carl. *Life*. February 1945.

Oskaloosa Herald. Oskaloosa, Iowa. 1 February 1945.

San Francisco Chronicle. California. 13 March 1945.

Manila Times. Manila, Philippines. December 1945.

Wengronowitz, Joseph, 2nd Bn 31st Inf. Bn., "I Came Back Alive." *Quan*, Vol. 35. 5 March 1981.

Zich, Arthur, "A Nation of Islands." *Signature*, Vol. 15. 9 September 1980.

LIST OF GIRAFFE BOOKS

GIRAFFE books are available in major bookstores in the Metro Manila area; for inquiries, call 928-92-69, or write to Gloria F. Rodriguez: # 7 Visayas Avenue, 1128 Quezon City, Philippines.

Typesetting by GIRAFFE BOOKS
using 11 pts and 14 pts Southern
for text and titles, respectively.

GIRAFFE BOOKS
are published exclusively by
Gloria F. Rodriguez